LONDON HIGH

Herbert Wright

LONDON HIGH

Herbert Wright

F

FRANCES LINCOLN LIMITED

PUBLISHERS

Frances Lincoln Ltd
4 Torriano Mews
Torriano Avenue
London NW5 2RZ
www.franceslincoln.com

London High

A catalogue record for this book is available from
the British Library.

ISBN 10: 0 7112 2695 4
ISBN 13: 978-0-7112-2695-1

Printed in China

9 8 7 6 5 4 3 2 1

Captions for prelim images:
(Endpapers) Trellick Tower Grid & 25 Bank Street
p4/5 The City Cluster from Tower Bridge, 2005
p6 Euston Tower
p11 10 Upper Bank Street

Contents

Preface 1.
by Terry Brown

On April 16 1992, less than a week after the building had been hit by an IRA bomb, I was surprised to find myself clambering over twisted concrete slabs and smashed stonework in the wreckage of the Baltic Exchange in the City of London. My practice had been working on proposals for a radical adaptation of this Grade II* listed building, but the terrorist bomb now meant that there was a more pressing task: to ensure continuity for the Baltic's business.

It was to be some time later that I would be locked in intense discussions with Peter Rees, the City planning officer, about a new groundscraper designed to replace the badly damaged Baltic, but still incorporating the restored trading hall and the old pedimented classical façade facing St Mary Axe. The discussion seemed to turn on an acceptable height limit for our proposals – ironically, in retrospect. On one occasion Peter quipped that he always looked for the hair crack in the architect's presentation model that was the giveaway clue to the floors that might be sacrificial and could be bargained over. The discussion was about whether a ten or a twelve-storey building was acceptable, and Rees made us opt for the lower alternative. We subsequently secured two sequential planning permissions for this complex project, trying to build up the floor space to create a viable scheme. It didn't work, and in due course English Heritage relented and allowed that the Baltic did not have to be restored, provided that an international competition be staged to choose the architect for the new building.

The forty storey 'erotic gherkin' that was eventually built on the Baltic site is of course now a world-renowned and seminal building, but my story serves to illustrate a basic fact about high-rise buildings in general: we judge them by a completely different set of criteria to those applied to the general mass of townscape. Two fundamentals probably distinguish a tower. First, it is significantly higher than the general townscape it inhabits; secondly, it has a generally vertical proportion, viz. its height is significantly greater than its width. When a building flips over into the high-rise category, actual height becomes much less significant than verticality, slimness, silhouette and those elusive qualities architects dream of: elegance, lightness and transparency. A high-rise building also enters a rather exclusive and very public realm, where strategic-views legislation protects the skyline of world heritage sites such as Westminster Palace and St Paul's Cathedral, and where appeals are fought over environmental and aesthetic issues. Today it can cost the applicant well over a million pounds to secure a planning consent for a high-rise office building in the centre of London. Star architects become as crucial to this process as do the *galacticos* of Manchester United and Chelsea to club profile and match results.

Historically, it was principally the discovery of the tensile properties of, first, iron, and then steel that unleashed the full potential to build vertically. At the forefront of the industrial revolution, Britain witnessed the pioneering work, and the new technology that was literally forged in such seminal structures as the iron bridge at Coalbrookdale and, later, the Crystal Palace of London's Great Exhibition of 1851. But somehow the United States stole a march on the UK in the late nineteenth century, and the spearhead of development shifted to Chicago and New York, where, around the turn of the twentieth century, the riveted steel frame and the invention of the electric elevator together allowed apartment and office buildings to push skyward.

While the iconic high-rises that later inspired London architects were often the dream schemes of Mies van der Rohe and Antonio Sant Elia rather than the built reality of Manhattan, it was probably through the cinema that most of us in Britain gained

Canary Wharf towers (left to right: HSBC, One Canada Square, Citigroup, Berkeley Tower)

our earliest experience of high-rise buildings. Thus, by the time the first real modern towers appeared in London, the genre was not only well established in the States, but had bounced across the Atlantic into Europe, with German, Italian and French architects citing the American precedent, and drawing, if not always building, pared-down, refined or romanticised versions of the American skyscraper.

This book is about what happened to the genre when it eventually took root in our capital. Because it limits its territory to London and its scope to the high-rise, it can offer an insight hitherto not available to the general reader. Quite apart from its practical value as a comprehensive, attractively illustrated and well-researched guide to almost everything that rises above the general background rooftops of London, this book brings a particular intelligence and sensibility to the genre that cross cultural boundaries. I personally have been criticized on more than one occasion for a populist approach to design, but it remains clear to me that buildings and architecture inhabit many different cultural realms. The recent popularity of design- and building-based reality and lifestyle TV programmes together with the proliferation of building-spotter websites demonstrate a popular appreciation of architecture. This response is a live cultural force, so it is right that popular values should figure in any true appreciation, history or compendium of buildings, alongside the refined and cerebral musings of the gurus, high priests and international stars of architecture.

Architecture, then, is a popular art as well as having a highbrow side. Like music, it's actually this way round. That is, more pop architecture is produced than, for want of a better word, serious, but often not designed by trained architects, who can be a bit precious because of this. Popular music embraces the kitsch and the sentimental as well as the truly poetic. What is so attractive to me about Herbert Wright's approach to buildings is that it combines the exhilarating edge and freedom of the untutored voice with the

wealth of understanding that comes from in-depth personal research, which I would guess ranges far beyond the usual architectural journals. It is good for us to hear this. For Herbert, I believe, there is none of the malice or envy that can haunt other architectural raconteurs who might just have liked to have designed (and seen built) the odd building themselves. Instead, an unbridled enthusiasm for and enjoyment of buildings, their creators and their history shines through and carries us along towards new insights. There is, after all, a flash side even to Sir Norman Foster, which just may contribute to the unprecedentedly popular success of the Gherkin.

I was still at school when *Architectural Review* was first eulogizing the *Vickers Tower*, at Millbank, and Castrol House, on Marylebone Road, while berating the Shell Building. The practice I would eventually join, Gollins Melvin and Ward, was started in 1949 by three young architects who, like many others during the post-war years, built their reputation on public works, mostly in the education sector, and it was this experience that informed the lean elegance of their early office buildings, including Castrol House. By the time I joined the practice, the Commercial Union building was completed, setting a course for the practice with a smooth North American style which would later become the realm of those great American high-rise specialists themselves.

London was not a natural for high-rise. The London clay is challenging to the engineering of heavily loaded foundations, and the guardians of an ancient city would soon campaign against the impact of tall buildings on the London skyline. In the thirty years or so that I have been practising in London, at least one major revolution in architecture took place. In the wake of challenges to the first (mainly social housing) high-rise buildings as an oversimplified and inadequate approach to the practical, social and cultural needs of people, Post-Modernism emerged, with its historical references and its yearning for cultural depth and complexity. The contextual approach of Post-Modernism mostly dictated lower buildings, but the few London high-rises that were built in this period rejected the minimalism of the first wave, and adopted what many have considered fancy dress, taking their cue once again from North America. It was, however all too difficult to get right and somehow never achieved the necessary authenticity.

The powerful resurgence of a new, more sophisticated, modernism in London was probably because, in some minds, it had never gone away. To start with, through the pop art and consumerist dreams of a group of young London architects formulated in a magazine called *Archigram*, and then in the highly crafted high-tech architecture that was its just-about-practical built reality. This new genre was, in true British style, tested abroad before being allowed to flourish here in its high-rise manifestation. The next generation of high-rise buildings will dwarf those that went before, as can be clearly seen in models at the New London Architecture Centre and the Corporation of London's City Marketing Suite. This is now a mature and confident idiom!

The new high-rise is also the tip of the iceberg that is the London property industry. The story of the commercial high-rise is not just about architecture. It is about ambition and money as well. Some of the highest-profile projects are promoted by property mavericks such as Gerald Ronson and Irvine Sellar; others by great investment and development companies such as British Land, Land Securities and Hammersons. The strange concoction of kudos, ambition for wealth and celebrity, sober business-speak and solid investment credibility that ferments among developers and agents, and investment funds to produce a high-rise building today are, of course, fertile ground for enquiry, drama and journalism. The ultimate questions as to who will occupy the buildings, and whether they will ever get built, can only be answered as the closely guarded episodes of the brave speculation unfold.

The whole of this fascinating and culturally complex story may be read in the high-rise buildings built in London over a relatively short period, and this book is both an invaluable introduction to the subject and a companion for anyone fascinated by the genre and its background.

Though there have been attempts to weld it into a single entity, London has always been more than one city. The London County Council, the Greater London Council and, more recently, the Greater London Authority under the auspices of Mayor Ken Livingstone have sought a unified vision for the capital as a whole. The reality is an amalgam of 35 London Boroughs, with the twin cities of London and Westminster at its geographical and cultural heart and a ring of characterful but interlocked individual towns and villages around. In the present climate, the GLA has identified a need for continuing growth within this area, pushing out to the east, northeast and the south. It has also opined on the subject of sustainability and the intensification of use on land already built on at least once in the past. This new pressure to increased density has led to a new enthusiasm for high-rise, with probably more proposals for tall commercial and apartment buildings in the pipeline for London than ever before. The subject of high-rise as an appropriate urban form will likely be discussed ever more intensely over the coming months and years, in thousands of planning consultations and countless planning committees and appeals.

The achievements and mistakes of the past are at least a part of what we should take into account when looking towards the future. Buildings exist in their most pristine form in the imagination, and are sold to us with hyperrealist computer-generated photo-representations. The building will then be with us for fifteen to a hundred years, during which time it will age and take on a patina. It is instructive to look at the reality, to experience a building as a part of day-to-day life. *London High* will, I hope, encourage more to enjoy this experience and in the process develop their own critical faculties. It will certainly set the reader and site visitor off with some interesting and valuable insights.

Wright has ferreted out the origins of high-rise in London a little over eighty years ago, but building true skyscrapers only really got going here in the last fifty. An historical perspective can distil and magnify the critical wisdom of an era, but, on the other hand, as buildings begin to be re-examined from a new cultural perspective, remote from the babble of the arbiters of taste of their time, their value and significance can and do change. Maybe Wright, with his unprejudiced view, can help us also to enjoy what we don't necessarily admire *and* admire what we don't necessarily enjoy! That would be not only a good starting-point for a pluralist culture, but also an excellent springboard for a rich and diverse urbanism.

54 Lombard Street (architect in charge Terry Brown, GMW)

Preface 2.
By Conor McNicholas

As I write this I am 75 metres up in the air. I'm sat in my office at the legendary rock magazine *New Musical Express*, which is high on the 25th floor of the achingly Seventies King's Reach Tower on London's South Bank. The view is incredible. I take the opportunity to scan it whenever I'm spending long hours on the phone to managers and other record industry types. As I look, beyond the Tate Modern and across the river I can see London's financial district, home to the dapper *Tower 42* and futuristic *30 St Mary Axe* (the Gherkin). Further down the river, looming out of the winter afternoon mist is the distant copse of Canary Wharf skyscrapers, broody and self-absorbed at the far end of the city. At street level is the empty plot of One Blackfriars Road, still awaiting a decision on a magnificent seventy-storey tower from Beetham.

London, once particularly known for the absence of tall buildings breaking its skyline, is suddenly embracing height as it reaches for a new future. The stolid eight- or ten-storey buildings of Government departments and corporate headquarters are now being embellished by a new generation of skyscrapers and (potentially) super-scrapers. Though not a skyscraper itself, the London Eye observation wheel has done more than any other structure in recent history to make Londoners think about their city in the third dimension, rather than just a solid extension of their *A–Z*. This is an exciting time.

London has flirted with tall buildings in the past, but it has been an on-off affair. Skyscrapers have mostly come to be associated with the failed social experiments and questionable building quality of the late Sixties and Seventies. That London has now begun to properly fall in love with tall buildings, seduced by the possibilities of modern architecture and materials, is a wonderful thing.

I love skyscrapers. Rather, I love good skyscrapers – buildings that are aware of and comfortable with their own drama. A building that reaches for the sky shouldn't just be functional. It has an obligation, as one of the most dramatic symbols of mankind's progress, to reach skyward with some sense of panache. Skyscrapers are rock 'n' roll architecture, the rockstars of our city skylines, the ones who can't keep quiet, the ones who love the attention.

Because they've been so rare, London skyscrapers have more character than most. A New York skyscraper, even if it reaches up twenty storeys, will always be one of a mass, but towers in London stand alone. Whether glittering city office blocks or East End residential towers, they are local landmarks that have come to represent and inevitably define the character of their neighbourhoods. These stars of the London skyline can be as brash as John Lydon, as dandy as Ziggy Stardust, or as magnificently haggard as Keith Richards. These towers are oversized, overblown and increasingly over here.

Herb and I discovered a mutual fascination with tall buildings by random after a few gins and tonics at a post-gig afterparty. He talked of his skyscraper project. Months later the result is this fabulous book. This is a compendium of urban stories featuring some of the city's most famous larger-than-life characters, the first book of its kind to celebrate London's rocky love affair with the sky. This is London's debut skyscraper album.

Dusk, Hyde Park

Author's Preface

As a child, I used to sneak into the Penta Hotel (now the *Holiday Inn, Kensington*) and climb the fire escape stairs by the Cromwell Road. When I was high above the traffic noise and the surrounding Victorian terraces, I would stare, awestruck, across London to the east. London above the rooflines has always been exciting, at least as far back as the time when the original, mediaeval St Paul's Cathedral, burnt down in the Great Fire of 1666, was one of the world's tallest structures at 149m high. But I was looking out across the time of Richard Seifert, whose skyscraper designs, to many people's dismay, were popping up all over London. The emerging City cluster behind the new St Paul's in the distance was like a glimpse into another world: a thrilling, futuristic citadel of power, defined by skyscrapers. I imagined a time when London would be awash with skyscrapers, like New York.

Luckily this did not happen. London remains one of the world's most diverse environments, with zones of urban fabric clearly preserving many periods from the past. Threatening any part of this haphazard legacy with redevelopment is quite rightly challenged or blocked by conservation legislation. At the same time, the global splash that *30 St Mary Axe* (the Gherkin) made has put London firmly on the world's skyscraper stage, and these are heady days of exciting new proposed towers. The internet is buzzing with London skyscraper enthusiasts. But what is increasingly clear is that skyscrapers are part of London's heritage as well as its future. The tower blocks and glass boxes of the sixties and seventies tell us important things about London's socio-economic history as well as about architecture of the times, and they often have colourful characters behind them as well. This book will hopefully make people look up and re-assess skyscrapers, old or new. Every one has a story to tell. The tragic loss of Seifert's *Drapers' Garden* is a warning that we shouldn't junk our old towers just for commercial gain – we may be painting over an Old Master just to re-use the canvas.

This book covers the whole history of London's skyscrapers, including plans now on the table in 2006. There are over 300 London skyscrapers over 50m high, and lots more planned. It's impossible to cover them all, but well over 100 tell their stories here. It's impossible to be up-to-date in a book format, but I have tried to be as little out-of-date as possible. To help cross-referencing, any skyscraper with an individual write-up elsewhere has its name in italics. If skyscrapers interest you, you may find a closer look opens the door to enjoying other architecture as well. If architecture is your thing, you may find its evolution in high-rise fascinating stuff. If you love London, this may extend your passion to its skyline. If you care for the planet, you may learn that skyscrapers play a vital role in a sustainable future. But whatever your motivation, get out and enjoy the feast of skyscrapers just a tube ride away!

Herbert Wright, May 2006

Drapers Garden demolition underway, July 2006

Chapter 1:
Classical Jazz

When *One Canada Square*, the pyramid-topped tower at Canary Wharf, became London's tallest building in 1990, its American architect Cesar Pelli boasted that 'this is the first skyscraper in England'. What a cheek! England, and London in particular, has an amazing and long skyscraper history, covering at least most of the twentieth century. There's even a case to be made that London's skyscraper story begins as long ago as the eighteenth century. . .

Horace Walpole, a politician sometimes credited with starting the Gothic Revival in architecture, as well as creating the gothic novel, settled in Strawberry Hill in 1747. From this idyllic patch by the Thames, he noticed that a very tall construction was climbing above the trees in 1762. Aghast, Walpole declared that 'in a fortnight you will be able to see it in Yorkshire!'. And what a bizarre building it was, too. The Pagoda was a finger of stacked roofs, each of varnished iron, decorated with eighty enamelled dragons (which were later flogged, probably to cover George IV's debts), rising from a patch of trees in Kew. The architect was William Chambers, who had been commissioned in 1757 to lay out Kew Gardens. The Pagoda seems to have come straight from China, and indeed Chambers had been a globetrotter in his youth, traveling to India and China with the Swedish East India Company. His greatest work is Somerset House, by Waterloo Bridge.

Was the Pagoda London's first skyscraper? What is a skyscraper anyway? It's now generally agreed that a skyscraper should be a building of stacked, enclosed floors where people can work or live. How high a building needs to be to qualify as a skyscraper is arbitrary, but in this book, with a few exceptions, I've settled on fifty metres, which is about sixteen floors of social housing or twelve floors of a modern office building. The Pagoda is certainly tall, rising just 32cm short of 50m, although to be visible from Yorkshire it would have needed to be 4km high! It has just ten floors, so calling it a skyscraper is a bit of a stretch. In any case, Kew in 1762 was over a century away from being engulfed by London, the edge of which was then still seven kilometres away, so we must look again for London's first skyscraper. . .

The two most critical urban conditions for skyscrapers are prosperity and lack of space. At the height of the British Empire in the nineteenth century, London was the world's leading city, packed solid with people and commerce. Building upwards was inevitable. Victorian development dwarfed almost everything from before – railway viaducts swept high above the modest dwellings behind the giant new railway termini, grand offices were squeezed into the dense urban fabric of the City and West End, and new terraces, stacked with elegant high-ceilinged flats, spread west from around Hyde Park. All this was a leap in scale over the older city and must have felt bewildering to many Victorians. Furthermore, the skyline of Wren and Hawksmoor was being redefined by great new churches, as well as institutions, hotels and public landmarks such as Sir George Gilbert Scott's Midland Hotel over St Pancras Station (1865) and Horace Jones' Tower Bridge (1886–94). The Houses of Parliament, by Charles Barry, finished in 1859, are book-ended by the most famous Victorian towers of all: St Stephen's Clocktower (popularly known as Big Ben) rises 96m, and Victoria Tower, 102m. And yet there are no Victorian skyscrapers. Why is this?

Royalty vs. Tall Buildings – Battle Commences

The answer has been torn down. Around 1879, a banker called Henry Hanley started building Queen Anne's Mansions, a block of flats in Queen Anne's Gate, Westminster. Relying on his own designs,

Port of London authority building

Queen Anne's Mansions

Hanley personally supervised the construction, making it up as he went along. A haphazard pile of red brick rose higher and higher, set randomly with sash windows, chimneys and fire escapes. At some stage, he did in fact call in an architect, ER Robson, and in 1888 the block was completed. With fourteen storeys reaching forty-seven metres, this was the tallest residential building in the world, and deserves to be called a skyscraper. It triggered a fear that London was about to be overwhelmed by tall buildings. Across St James's Park in Buckingham Palace, Queen Victoria complained that it obscured her view of the Houses of Parliament. This was the first of many interventions by the Royal Family in the debate about building height vs conservation of views – Prince Charles would be fighting high-rise a century later. Queen Anne's Mansions were demolished in 1971, to be replaced by chunky Home Office buildings by Basil Spence, who incidentally was also the skyscraper architect who gave us *Knightsbridge Barracks.*

There was a practical reason for limiting height as well. Victorians had lots of local height regulations based on how high firemen's ladders could reach. These often changed, not least because the Victorians

did not have a city-wide fire brigade. Finally, in 1894, the London Building Act set a height limit of a hundred feet (30m). This did not stop the heavy Port of London Authority Building, designed by Sir Edwin Cooper in 1912, towering 51m over Trinity Square, by Tower Hill station. But this is still not a skyscraper – there are only four floors of offices, and half the height is a monumental structure housing a statue of Neptune. In a fire, there would be no-one to rescue from these upper levels.

London's traditional world-city rival was Paris, built to Haussman's mid-nineteenth century master plan. It kept within his height restrictions of 37m, which still apply. But in the twentieth century, a new world city was challenging London: New York. There, and in the Mid-West boomtown of Chicago, the Americans had been inventing the skyscraper as we know it.

Made in the USA

Skyscrapers are possible because of two things – steel-frame construction and lifts. Using steel frames rather than stone walls to take the load of a building allows larger internal spaces and higher construction. Steel frames are descended from the first iron-framed building, Charles Bage's Dotherington Flax Mill in Shropshire, built in 1797. (Steel frames would be temporarily superseded by concrete equivalents in the 1950s and 60s.) The American Elisha Greaves Otis invented the elevator by developing a fail-safe mechanism for hoists whereby, if they suddenly fell, they would not plunge down but brake automatically. He demonstrated this in 1852 in New York.

In Manhattan, from the mid nineteenth century, rising land prices encouraged developers to get more return from plots by building high. The Chicago Fire of 1871 was the real spur in skyscraper development. The lakeside city, at the centre of rail and water transport between the Mid-West and the East Coast, was experiencing massive growth from continent-wide trade, and huge enterprises were gravitating there.

Suddenly, following the fire, it all had to be rebuilt in mid-boom. By 1885, William le Baron Jenney's Home Insurance Building in Chicago was leading the way in replacing iron frames with stronger, more fire-resistant steel structures. The nearby Masonic Temple reached an incredible 92m in 1892.

New York, though, was not to be outdone, and right up to the 1970s it competed with Chicago for height. By 1895, New York's eighteen-storey Manhattan Life Insurance Building was the world's tallest office building at 106m. Cass Gilbert's 240m-high baroque Woolworth Building (the world's tallest from 1913 until 1930) was partly inspired by the Houses of Parliament. Initially, American skyscrapers were fancy-looking towers dressed in classical styles, but the stress on ornamentation and complex structure was giving way to stripped-down façades enclosing maximum volume. Stacking up floor after floor, each to the edge of the site, maximised the developer's profit. As Cass Gilbert said: 'A skyscraper is a machine that makes land pay'. Mammoth, massy blocks rose like vast cliffs, blocking light on neighbouring sites. After the monster Equitable Life Building by Ernest Graham in 1915, New York zoning laws required buildings to taper with height. This created the distinctive set-back stepped shapes of the skyscrapers' golden age in the 1920s. By the 1930s,

American skyscrapers were evolving into the 'Modernistic' style, with fairly plain stone façades punctuated by windows and shaped and embellished with Art Deco touches. New York continued to break world records, peaking in the magnificent 319m Chrysler Building by William van Alen (1930) and the 381m Empire State Building (1931) by Shreve Lamb & Harmon. The skyscraper had become the most spectacular architectural genre of the twentieth century, and a symbol reflecting the supremacy of American capitalism.

Not many skyscrapers were to be found across the Atlantic at this time. The first was W Aubrey Thomas' Royal Liver Building on the Liverpool waterfront, a massive office building with twin towers topped with the golden Liver Birds and reaching 90m. When completed in 1911, it was the UK's first skyscraper, and its use of concrete and steel frames were state of the art. After the First World War, Germany became the European centre of skyscraper activity. As we shall see, Mies van der Rohe designed a revolutionary skyscraper for Berlin in 1921, but it wasn't built. An architect called Wilhelm Kreis designed what would have been Europe's tallest, a cylindrical skyscraper rising twenty-seven storeys and 106m for Graf-Adolf Platz in Düsseldorf, but that wasn't built either. However, his 56m-high Wilhelm-Marx-Haus a few blocks away was finished in 1924 (and has influenced *25 Cabot Square*, a London skyscraper built fifty-eight years later). The same year, Jacob Koefer's austere Hansa Hochhaus in Cologne reached 65m.

Even taller towers were going up elsewhere in Europe – the 87m KBC Tower in Antwerp in 1923, and Madrid's 88m Edificio Telefonica in 1924. These neo-classical buildings would not have looked out of place in the US. The most modern European high-rise was not a skyscraper, but a viewing platform – the Tate Tower in Glasgow, a 92m Art Deco slab with four platforms cantilevered from otherwise blank walls, built for the city's British Empire Exhibition. Sadly it

Woolworth Building, Manhattan

Liver Building, Liverpool

Adelaide House

came down in 1935. In the Far East, Hong Kong-based British colonial architects Palmer & Turner built up a portfolio of fairly tall grand buildings along the Bund in Shanghai.

In London, as we have seen, there were height restrictions, but Adelaide House (built 1921–25) by Burnet & Tait on the City side of London Bridge, had all the ingredients of a skyscraper. This eleven-storey office block rises sheer to 45m, and the look and feel of it is distinctly pre-1915 American, with its Egyptian-style cornice jutting out around the top, and vertical lines of recessed windows.

Thoroughly Modern London

In many ways, London in the 1920s was becoming thoroughly modern – in other words, American. While a General Strike challenged the first Labour government, this was nevertheless the Jazz Age. The Charleston was all the rage, and radio and movies were fresh pleasures on offer to all. In 1924, Selfridges brought to London the kind of unstuffy, sophisticated shopping already to be found on New York's Fifth Avenue. A year later, the Great West Road was opened, a fast urban highway just like those in America. It was easy to imagine a high-rise future for London.

Fritz Lang's *Metropolis* is the film that distils perfectly the twenties futuristic vision of buildings rising dizzyingly over canyons spanned with highways vaulting over more highways, and the air above abuzz with aircraft. However, *Metropolis* showed an imaginary high-rise city. The 1929 British movie *High Treason* (directed by Maurice Elvey, a fascist who had surgery to keep his monocle in place) shows a future London rather than a hypothetical megalopolis. Massive twenty-storey-plus blocks rise along the Embankment, dwarfing Big Ben (which means they would have had unfeasibly high ceilings). The finest London vision, however, was that of painter Montague Black. He foresaw the city dominated by fancy towers hundreds of metres high, among which

London 2026 AD 'This Is All In The Air' by Montague B Black, 1926

plied air traffic, from local taxis to dirigibles carrying mail from India. His amazing 1926 painting *London 2026 AD* can still be viewed in the London Transport Museum. Sooner or later, someone just had to build a real London skyscraper.

This almost happened on Piccadilly, opposite Green Park, where the Duke of Devonshire was calling it a day with the ancestral mansion and turning the site over for development and a quick buck. In the architectural competition of 1923, two skyscraper schemes emerged. CFA Voysey, a leading architect in the Arts and Crafts movement, a group that promoted traditional craftsmanship, proposed two thirty-storey residential towers that looked like the Tower of London extruded vertically upwards. Edmund F Tomlins had a more attractive proposition: a wall of a building that stepped gracefully up to

twenty-one storeys, parallel to an eight-storey slab, between which were gardens.

In the end, the new Devonshire House that was built was a vast imposing office building with a stone exterior built onto a steel frame, American style, but with only nine storeys. The new BBC headquarters at the Aldwych, Bush House (1922–25) by Helmle & Corbett, also looked American, despite its use of the traditional London medium, Portland stone. This was superseded by another steel-framed BBC headquarters – Broadcasting House (1930–31) – by George Val Meyers. Even when the style was not American, the scale of 1920s blocks was. Gigantic buildings were appearing in places such as Berkeley Square and over Baker Street station. Other buildings were reaching high – at the end of the decade, the Oxo Tower, designed by Albert W Mere, reached 61m over the

South Bank, and Triton Court, City offices in Finsbury Square, had a spire reaching 67m. However, like the Trinity Square block, these were basically buildings of normal height topped with empty ornamental constructions.

The Owl and the Ghost Storeys

Eventually, London's first true skyscraper, reaching over 50m, was completed in 1929: this was London Transport's headquarters at *55 Broadway*, just across the road from Queen Anne's Mansions. Its architect was Charles Holden.

Holden was born in Bolton in 1875, and studied and taught at the Manchester School of Art and Technical College, where he submitted his first architectural design under the name 'The Owl'. His sympathies were with the Arts and Crafts movement, which promoted the skills of craftsmen rather than industrialised processes. His first major building was a headquarters for the British Medical Association (now *Zimbabwe House*) on the Strand, finished in 1908. It was mounted with statues by Jacob Epstein – Holden would later say that he saw sculpture not as mere decoration but as 'the bone and sinew of good architecture'. His style then was typically Edwardian,

drawing on classical models, but things were set to change. The first steel-frame buildings were starting to go up in London, such as the Ritz Hotel in 1906. That meant that walls didn't need to be solid stone, although Portland stone and brick would remain the medium for many grand London buildings.

Holden, however, developed away from Edwardian-style urban buildings because, from 1917, he began to work for the Imperial War Graves Commission. Here, he came in contact with Sir Edwin Lutyens, one of the greatest British architects of the time. Like other architects, Lutyens had started by recycling classical architectural forms, but developed a more abstract, monumental style, which would later bloom in the magnificent official buildings for New Delhi in the 1920s. In that decade, Holden, now a partner in the practice of Adams Holden & Pearson, started working for Frank Pick, the man running London Transport, which from 1912 had been drawing together the capital's jumble of private bus, tube and tram enterprises into a huge joined-up public organisation. Pick and Holden were both members of the Design & Industries Association, successor to the Arts and Crafts movement, which valued craftsmanship and stressed functionalism. Holden was given the big project of station design for the southern extension of the Northern Line to Morden. His stations were magnificent – solid, chunky stone entrances like ancient mausoleums, yet warm and modern and meticulously detailed inside. Holden had revolutionised the cosy architecture of suburban stations and elevated the suburbs to locations for heroes. He would go on to design new stations for the Piccadilly Line's great 1930s extensions; examples such as Arnos Grove station and the great circular roundabout of Piccadilly Circus station are now considered design classics. Between work on the extensions, Pick commissioned Holden to design the London Transport headquarters at *55 Broadway*. As we shall see, this is a masterpiece of design and a showcase for British sculpture. By virtue of this building Holden

Charles Holden

became the first architect anywhere to integrate an underground railway station into a skyscraper, pioneering the shopping arcade there for good measure.

Holden's last major work would have an even bigger tower. *Senate House* was a commission he won against distinguished competition, including Sir Giles Gilbert Scott (grandson of Sir George Gilbert Scott), who had designed the red telephone box and Battersea Power Station. Reaching a fantastic height of 64m, *Senate House* would remain London's tallest skyscraper for twenty-two years after its completion in 1937. Curiously, Holden rejected the steel-frame method of carrying the building's load. He also drew back from sculptural ornamentation, creating a huge, heavy but almost bare landmark building. He embraced innovations like hidden lighting and services. Both *55 Broadway* and *Senate House* got around the height restriction of the London Building Act by allocating the upper storeys' ghost floors to archives.

Why is Holden such an important architect? His buildings were so strong they redefined their locations, yet contained features on the scale of the hand that were like a craftsmen's work. Even though he was a traditionalist, many of his ideas were way ahead of his time. Some went too far – in 1943, he proposed replacing Tower Bridge with a glass-enclosed construction housing offices and flats, to be called Capital Bridge. Luckily we still have Tower Bridge.

Quite apart from the two skyscrapers, he also had a very modern view of how a modern metropolis should work, especially as to its reliance on the new arteries of mass-transit systems and the relationship between new suburbs and city centre. Others made plans about this, but Holden built the buildings that made it a reality. Holden did receive the Royal Institute of British Architects (RIBA) gold medal in 1936, and was offered a knighthood, but, architecturally, he is still not ranked where he should be –

alongside the greatest of his British contemporaries, Lutyens and the younger Scott.

The only other contemporary London skyscraper was Shell's handsome corporate HQ (now *80 Strand*) by F Milton-Cashmore, finished in 1932. Next door to it, there were also the massive Adelphi offices by Colcutt & Hamp, which, to much outrage, replaced the Adam brothers' fantastic eighteenth-century Adelphi terraces in 1938. These rise only 40m on the river side, but feel like skyscrapers. More might have happened

on London's skyline, but the shadow of war was drifting across Europe again...

In any case, quite different architectural ideas were brewing in the twenties and thirties. The Berlin skyscraper Mies van der Rohe visualised in 1921 was an entirely new sort of office building, clad not in stone but instead sheathed in glass. In France, Le Corbusier was developing concepts for a new sort of urban living, where cities were machines and the needs of the people were serviced in concrete blocks.

When Charles Holden died in 1960, he would have seen the first examples of high-rise resulting from these ideas going up in London. No-one realised then what these new styles would unleash. Blame van der Rohe for the bland glass box, and credit Le Corbusier with the high-rise sink estate.

55 Broadway, SW1

Tube St James
Height 53m, 12 storeys
Completed 1929
Architect Charles Holden

London's oldest skyscraper is the solid, imposing master-piece of London Transport's headquarters over St James's Park station. Although only a sixth as high as the world's tallest building finished in the same year, New York's Chrysler Building, 55 Broadway was mind-bogglingly tall and massive for 1920s London. It is a visual feast of Jazz Age architecture and sculpture above you.

Formed in 1912 by merging the private London Omnibus Company and the Electric Railways of London Company into a publicly owned body, London Transport, like the metropolis itself, was expanding rapidly in the 1920s, and it needed new headquarters. Joint Managing Director Frank Pick wanted a building to reflect the organisation's ethos of 'Service and Responsibility'. The man for the job had to be his friend Charles Holden, who had already designed tube entrances in central London, such as Bond Street in 1924 (remodelled in the seventies), and whole new stations, starting with those on the southern extension of the Northern Line in 1926. 55 Broadway replaced the higgledy-piggledy old headquarters of the Electric Railway Company. Like others in the new generation of London offices rising in the 1920s, it echoed the style of the huge commercial buildings going up in America, but uses the traditional London medium of Portland stone. It's basically a cruciform building, with stepped wings that create terraces on the eighth and tenth floors, on

some of which there are now roof gardens. Small arches at the seventh level bridge the corners between the wings, and London Transport roundels are mounted on the drainage high up. The floors of the central tower, distinguished by a stately loggia, a clock and a flagpole, remained unoccupied until the World War Two because of LCC fire regulations – it was too high for ladders to reach. These floors are now used to store London Transport archives.

In 1944, Holden said how excited he was when he 'realised the full possibilities of the cross-shaped plan – good light, no interference with neighbour lights, short corridors, and a compact centre containing all services'. Holden not only created one of London's great 1920s landmark buildings, he also designed a public space inside the building. It combined a new ticket hall and access to the platforms below, entrance to the offices above, and even pioneered the shopping arcade. The shops and the rush of Londoners are modern, but the warm marble floors, the pillars (similar to his work at Piccadilly Circus station) and the Art Deco embellishments have been faithfully restored.

As well as the building and the arcade, Holden is responsible for a third masterstroke. He wanted wall carvings on the new building, and persuaded a veritable Who's-Who of British sculptors to work on it, even though some had reservations about getting stuck in with the scaffolding and workmen all over the structure. The most controversial of these sculptures are above the ground floor, by Sir Jacob Epstein (1880–1959), the New York-born artist whose work is characterised by stocky figures with an almost primitive solidity. His style was considered revolutionary at the time, and whipped up such hatred that the works were sometimes vandalised. At 55 Broadway, a pot of paint was chucked at Epstein's

St James Park station is integrated into 55 Broadway

work. Here, his *Night* seems to depict a mother with dead child on her lap, while *Day* has a stern, bearded father being embraced by a naked child with a remarkable ability to twist his neck.

High up on the building's wings are wall reliefs in Bath stone depicting the Four Winds, the idea inspired by the Tower of the Winds in Athens. The William Blake-like figures are by different artists, including Eric Gill (a Catholic eccentric who dressed like a monk) and Henry Moore. The latter's *West Wind* (on the north side of the east wing) was his first, and for thirty years, his only public sculpture. It crucially marks the stage where his works' figures become exceedingly chubby – this style would propel him to international fame.

Nowadays, London Transport is called Transport for London, and they occupy offices in different locations, including the nearby *Windsor House*. They have done a great job maintaining and promoting the 55 Broadway heritage, including brilliant illumination at night. The whole building is floodlit, casting gloriously gothic shadows up the central tower, like something out of Gotham City.

80 Strand, WC2
(Shell-Mex House)

Tube Embankment
Height 52m, 13 storeys
Constructed 1930–32
Architect Messrs Joseph

Shell-Mex House stands like a vast stone mantelpiece clock overlooking the Thames. This bulky cubist building, one of London's largest pre-war office blocks, is Grade II listed and has the largest clockfaces in London.

The site has a lot of history. The riverbank used to come right up to where the building stands at Savoy Place, and from Elizabethan times the location was home to various Earls of Salisbury. In 1886, the Cecil Hotel by Perry & Reed went up, the largest hotel in Europe with 800 rooms. Anglo-Dutch oil company Shell, needing a site for a new corporate HQ, paid over £1m for the building and demolished most of it in 1930, but kept its front part on the Strand. This is now Cecil Chambers, and the whole complex is entered through the original Victorian brick arched portico.

Shell-Mex House was designed by F Milton-Cashmore of architects Messrs Joseph. It is a steel-framed building clad in Portland stone. The façade

Shell-Mex river façade

facing the river is actually the back of the building, but because the site slopes sharply down towards the river, the building's main entrance is two floors above the back entrance. This is a very deep structure, with vast floor areas on an American scale – nowadays it would be called a groundscraper. It avoided the height restrictions of the times because the clockhouse would have been classed as occupant-free, and the height at the Strand end (rather than at the Savoy Place elevation) would have just scraped in.

From Ivybridge Lane along the building's side, its great depth is clearly visible. By the service entrance there is a Victorian lamp-post, which burns twenty-four hours a day, powered by fumes from the sewerage system below the Embankment. During World War Two's blackout it had to be specially cloaked!

Shell-Mex House, like the contemporary *55 Broadway*, is embellished with occasional arches and sculpture – for example, lion-heads above window recesses two storeys below the main roofline. The crowning glory is the monumental Art Deco clockhouse, topped with a distinctly Art Deco stepped roof. There are actually two clocks, the one facing north almost invisible from nearby streets. Each clock is the largest in the UK – the hands are 366cm and 274cm long, moving across faces 762cm in diameter (76cm wider than Big Ben's and matching the Edwardian clocks on the Royal Liver Building in Liverpool). The hands weigh 154kg in total, and are driven by an electric motor about the same size as a car engine. The clock doesn't chime, because that would have upstaged Big Ben. On the riverside, two

dreamlike slender stone figures about 5m tall look balefully down from either side of the clock – these are the only London statues by WCH King.

In 1947, a two-storey office extension was added on the Shell-Mex roof behind the clock, bringing the floor space up to about half a million square feet. Shell remained in the building, even after relocating their HQ to a new and even more massive riverside building, the *Shell Centre*, in 1963.

In 1983, Shell embarked on the largest restoration of an occupied building in Europe, calling in architects GMW and the original building contractors Trollope & Co. Shell described the task as converting 'a low-tech wet-heated building into a modern high-tech air-conditioned building'. Two floors at a time were tackled, starting from the top, and hundreds of the 1,500 workers were relocated at any time in temporary offices nearby. There were problems clearing asbestos, and the steel frame caused drilling into walls to reverberate through the whole building. An attempt to add conspicuous projections on the roof was heartily resisted by the Thirties Society. The job was completed in 1988.

Shell sold the building for £170m to Ivybridge Investments, part-owned by American real-estate company Wickloff Group, who had a taste for classical landmark skyscrapers – they also owned New York's Woolworth Building and Daily News Building. Shell themselves quit in 1998, although Stasco, the Shell International Trading & Shipping Company, still occupies two floors. The building had a £32m upgrade by Gensler architects in 2000, with a new glass entrance, and was rechristened 80 Strand. The main occupants now are media conglomerate Pearson, who can access small garden terraces at the top of the building, and Pearson-owned book publishers Penguin. Ivybridge doubled their money when they sold it for over £350m in 2002.

This big stone giant with its clock is one of those landmarks that everyone recognises yet never looks at – a shame, because not only is it magnificent period building, but its clock is trustworthy enough to check your watch against.

Senate House, WC1
Malet St

Tube Russell Square
Height 64m, 19 storeys
Constructed 1932–1937
Architect Charles Holden

Senate House is the centrepiece of the University of London and looms above the leafy squares of Bloomsbury. It is the last of Charles Holden's design to be built, and for twenty-two years was the tallest skyscraper in London. It is now listed Grade II*.

Founded in 1826, London University is the oldest in England after Oxford and Cambridge. In 1926 it paid £525,000 to the Bedford Estate for a swathe of Georgian terraces behind the British Museum. The University wanted to build adminstrative buildings, libraries, a students' union and no less than seven educational institutions. The brief they drew up specified a central tower.

A university committee short-listed fourteen architects, and four went through to the final round, including Holden and Sir Giles Gilbert Scott. This final four were interviewed over a black-tie dinner at the Athenaeum Club. Holden's previous skyscraper at *55 Broadway* had shown that he could tackle big-scale prestige projects, and he got the job. He unveiled his master plan in 1932, called Spinal Scheme 1 because it massed buildings extending out from a seven-storey spine on the same axis as the British Museum. Although strongly horizontal, it contained two towers, the northern one rising twelve storeys. Holden expected construction to take thirty years and cost £3m, and the buildings to last five hundred years. King George V liked the scheme and on 26 June 1933, with his wife Queen Mary, he laid a stone on the Senate House façade facing Malet Street, wielding a silver trowel handed to him by Holden. In 1934, the LCC forbade permission to fill in any floor above the eighth, but changed their mind the following year.

Sir Edwin Dellar, Principal of the University, took pride in showing visitors around his new building during construction. He was killed in November 1936 when a builder's trolley fell down a lift shaft onto him. A year later, the southern end of Holden's big scheme was largely complete, a million pounds had been spent, and it was decided to leave it at that for the time being. Senate House was crowned with a flagstaff in August and floodlit in November 1937.

Senate House's height is due to the Book Tower, which starts on the fourth floor. Like *55 Broadway*, the initial impression of Senate House suggests a twenties modern American stepped skyscraper, but there is something different about it – it feels a lot heavier, like the Constructivist architecture of the USSR. The windows are remarkably narrow, and each long side of the tower has fat stone buttress. This is because, unlike contemporary London buildings, Senate House is not built on a steel frame – all the weight is carried by the stone structure itself. Holden did not trust steel frames to stand for five hundred years. The use of load-bearing walls requires them to be thicker the higher the building is. However, Senate House does use steel decking for floors, and in the Book Tower there is an internal steel frame box that distributes the weight of most of the two million books.

Above the granite ground floor, Holden chose Portland stone because he thought it 'would wash its own face' with rainwater. Of course, it would later stain. Third floor spandrels are emblazoned with '18-81' – not a date, but a stylised plan of the complex, in which the tower is represented by a bridge between the 8s. Otherwise, there is little decoration – Holden had drifted to the Modernists' desire for simplicity over embellishment. He even claimed that the slogan 'when in doubt leave it out' was his own.

Inside the building, Holden concealed heating, gas, water and wiring in the walls, and placed recessed heaters below windows. Everywhere in the fixtures and fittings there is Holden's personal attention to detail. On the magnificent staircases to the Libraries, wooden direction signs hang on chains.

Below the centre of the tower is a lobby used as a pedestrian route from Malet Street to Russell Square – it is hushed even when busy, except when motorbike couriers nip through. This leads off to a two-storey ceremonial hall lined in travertine marble, with wrought-iron balconies and a grand staircase. Off this hall are the Macmillan Hall, now a cafeteria, and the William Beveridge Hall. These halls pioneered air-conditioning as well as new-fangled fluorescent lighting concealed around the ceiling. The School of Slavonic & East European Studies and the Institute of Historical Research are housed in the building's wings.

On the fourth floor, the Libraries have various Reading Rooms. Goldsmith's Library of Economic Literature has a cypress-wood ceiling and windows designed by Hungarian exile Ervin Bossanyi. The Victorian Sir Edwin Durning-Lawrence, who stirred the controversy over whether Francis Bacon really wrote Shakespeare's works, has his English literature collection housed in another library named after him. Two other libraries were named after Middlesex because the county was so generous with funds for the building.

In the seventies, a mainframe computer was put in the basement, requiring structural alterations. A major 1997 restoration recovered much of Holden's interior. In 2002, the new Dr Sang Tee Lee Centre for Manuscript and Book Studies was connected to Holden's building.

George Orwell found Senate House's heaviness sinister, and based his 300m-high Ministry of Truth in *1984* on Senate House. The Ministry of Information had actually taken the building over in the Second World War, and employed Holden's wife Eileen there. More sinister than *1984* is the revelation that, had Hitler invaded London, Senate House would have been his Nazi headquarters.

The Georgian architecture guru Sir John Summerson wrote in the eighties that Senate House 'brood(s) over Bloomsbury with a melancholy air as if to tell us that there is little joy in university life, only the perennial grind of graduation'. However, students nowadays are just as likely to be having fun at gigs and bars in the students' union venues nearby. The solidity and internal tranquillity of Senate House is a perfect contrast to students' ephemeral pleasures.

Massive Buttressing

Signs and stairs

Chapter 2:
Glass Boxes –
Post-War London

In 1950s Britain, things were looking up. The trauma of the Second World War was fading, and the burdensome Empire was being consigned to history. A glamorous young Queen had ascended the throne in 1952 and food rationing ended in 1954. London was coming alive, and getting back to business.

Office blocks started to break cover above the historic rooflines of London in the late 1950s. An orgy of high-rise office building followed, mainly in the International Style. It ran unabated until 1964, when perhaps the finest London skyscraper of them all, *Centre Point*, and the most iconic tower of the century, now the *Telecom Tower*, were both topped out.

Why did this outbreak of skyscrapers happen? What were their architectural roots? Who was behind their development?

Legal Highs and Boring Lows

Before considering these questions, remember that the pre-war London Building Act had limited buildings to a height of 30m, and before the Second World War, only three skyscrapers managed to get around the restriction. Of Central London's pre-war office stock, 8 million square feet (900,000m²), over ten per cent, had been destroyed by the war – about the current volume of the whole Canary Wharf Estate. The City's office space alone was down by a third.

The Third Schedule of the 1947 Town and Country Planning Act allowed office rebuilding with an extra ten per cent on pre-war volumes in three dimensions. By lowering ceiling heights, even more of an increase in two-dimensional floor space could be generated. It was mainly government offices that benefited, because building work had to get a licence to go ahead. Lord Holford and Charles Holden, London's first skyscraper architect, had just prepared

a plan for the post-war City of London, but now the Act required even the City to consult with the LCC, London's city-wide authority. Their amended plan was approved in 1951, just in time for legislation that would incentivise the private developer. Holford introduced the idea of plot ratio-to-building regulation, which would lead to open spaces beside buildings.

After Churchill's Conservatives were returned to power in 1951, they decided to tackle the commercial office shortfall. In 1953 they abolished building licences and taxes based on improvement. Immediately, high-rise office plans started coming off the drawing boards. JS Lacey came up with plans for a fifteen-storey block at London Bridge, while Ernö Goldfinger conjured up a twenty-seven-storey block for Moorgate, but neither of these was built. Campbell Jones started designing *Bucklersbury House*, which would be the City's first skyscraper.

The Tories also extended the ten per cent volume increase from rebuilding pre-war buildings to new buildings that were actually already under construction. If planning authorities refused the increase, they had to pay the developer for lost profits, and at market rates. The LCC were preoccupied with public housing and road 'improvements', so they had better things to do with their money than pay developers not to size up. In 1956, the red light on skyscrapers turned to green – the London Building Act was repealed and the LCC could now consider tall building proposals on their own merits.

But could London's ground physically support skyscrapers? Unlike Manhattan, London does not sit on hard granite, but is spread across the soft alluvial flood plain of the Thames. People thought that tall buildings would sink into the London clay. Imperial College's Professor Alec Westley Skempton was the man who tackled this problem. His work on the bearing capacity of London clay and building settlement led to him developing new bored-piling techniques in the 1950s. It was reckoned that, using these methods, towers as tall as 120m would be supported. Nowadays, London skyscrapers usually sit on concrete rafts that are positioned by piles driven into the ground using Skempton's ideas. The bottom line, literally, with London's skyscrapers is that they are Skempton skyscrapers.

Van der Rohe invents the Glass Box

Modern office blocks are all about concrete and glass, and when it comes to the latter material, the big vision was that of Ludwig Mies van der Rohe. From 1905, this German architect worked in Berlin, and after the First World War he became associated with radical designers who wanted to breathe new energy into German arts. The architectural guru Walter Gropius started the Bauhaus movement in 1919, and proclaimed that the building of the future 'will rise one day toward heaven … like the crystal symbol of a new faith'. This is precisely what van der Rohe came up with when he designed a nineteen-storey skyscraper for Friederichstrasse, on a triangular site in the heart of Berlin. The project, never

Mies van der Rohe

actually built, was revolutionary because it replaced stone walls with façades of glass – a solution that would later evolve into the glass curtain-wall.

Van der Rohe loved glass. He wrote: 'I discovered by working with actual glass models that the important thing is the play of light, and not the effect of light and shadow in ordinary buildings'. Van der Rohe saw offices as places of clarity and organisation, in service of which he designed open-plan floors, another of the defining features of post-war offices. These ideas were similar to those of the great American architect Frank Lloyd Wright, who had effectively designed an open-plan office floor in Buffalo, New York, as early as 1904. Wright would also design glass-skinned buildings in the twenties, and his seven storey Johnson Research Tower (1944) in Wisconsin is an elegant indication of how a thin glass-covered tower could look.

But glass was not the only obvious feature that would come to govern the look and feel of modern office blocks – there was also the flat roof. Flat roofs were characteristic of many New York skyscrapers from Edwardian times, but they still had ornamentation high up. The 'International Style' was to dump all of that. The term was first applied to George Howe and William Lascaze's flat-roofed 150m Philadelphia Savings Fund Society skyscraper of 1932, but it was van der Rohe's work in the 1920s that defined it. In 1933, van der Rohe won the design for the new Reichsbank in Berlin with bold plans for three ten-storey slab blocks standing in parallel. Each slab was identical, rectangular on all sides, and scarily bare of any features at all. This was a taster of the post-war world: flat-roofed glass curtain-walled slabs that made a virtue of being plain. Van der Rohe had invented the glass box.

There was one other big structural change that would characterise post-war buildings. We have already seen that the great pre-war skyscrapers of Manhattan were constructed on steel frames, but, later, frames were generally made of concrete,

860 Lake Shore Drive, Chicago

spread across the world in the 1960s. The first was the UN Secretariat Building, completed in 1953. A committee of eleven international architects, led by the American Wallace K Harrison, started designing the UN complex in 1947, and it was Le Corbusier (as we shall see, the inspiration behind high-rise housing) who conceived the Secretariat. This was a massive slab, thirty-nine storeys and 154m high, curtain-walled in glass and aluminium on its long sides, and with sheer, white concrete side-walls. These blank side-walls are not just aesthetic, they also help brace the building from the force of the wind. Plant machinery — lift engines, air-conditioning, water tanks etc — was placed on the roof, but the building sides were extended up in a grille of vertical beams to disguise these services in a skeleton floor and thus maintain the pure geometry of the rectangular slab. Blank wind-bracing walls and skeleton floors in fifties London slabs such as *Eastbourne Terrace* follow from this.

The second key New York tower was the Skidmore Owings and Merrill (SOM) twenty-four-storey Lever House on Park Avenue, designed in 1952. New York skyscrapers had since 1916 been characterised by step-backs, but the zoning laws allowed a straight-up

which, unlike steel, would not warp and bend in fires. The use of concrete reinforced by steel rods was pioneered at the end of the nineteenth century, notably by the French engineer François Hennebique, who encased hooked steel rods inside concrete to create joints. The first skyscraper built on a reinforced concrete frame actually dates back to 1902 in Cincinnati — the 63m-high Ingiss Building by Elzner & Anderson. The International Style emerged as reinforced concrete frames became standard, and it would not be until the 1980s that steel frames would be in vogue again.

Despite having tried to work for the Nazis, van der Rohe left Germany in 1939 for America. In Illinois, he designed influential structures, the best known being his 860 Lake Shore Drive blocks in Chicago, a design from 1948. They look like chunky office towers but are actually apartments. But, as had happened during the 1920s, the skyscraper action was shifting from Chicago to New York, and van der Rohe was left behind.

Three buildings here define precisely the International Style of office skyscraper that would

UN Secretariat, New York

Gollins, Melvin and Ward

building provided it occupied no more than a quarter of its plot. The SOM team under Gordon Bunshaft used this quirk in the rules, creating a two-storey podium building covering the site, over which floated their narrow curtain-walled glass slab. This formula of podium and slab arrived in London with buildings such as Castrol House, by Gollins Melvin & Ward (GMW), on Marylebone Road in 1960, which looks very like Lever House, but on a more modest scale.

Before we leave New York, van der Rohe himself did leave an International Style office tower there – the Seagram Building, the third building that defines the new style. It's a thirty-nine-storey, 160m-high slab

Lever House, New York

that he designed in 1954, with Philip Johnson and Kahn & Jacobs, and completed in 1958. At the time, it was the most expensive building ever built. It looks like a bigger version of Lever House just across Park Avenue, but crucially disposes of the podium. Instead, it floats above the ground on pillars made from the support columns rising into the curtain wall. The building is sheathed in unprecedentedly dark glass to reduce solar gain, and gives most of its site to the public in the form of a plaza.

Architects like to talk about vocabulary, and the vocabulary of the International Style was now set: curtain walls, flat roofs, podiums and plazas. The formula of the UN Secretariat, that is, a slab with blank side-walls, was initially a more popular variation of the International Style than that of van der Rohe. In England, this new architectural vocabulary was a refreshing, clean and shiny contrast to the fussy architectures of the past – in particular, the grim, heavy Victorian buildings with poky insides. Victorian buildings looked grim partially because they were stained by industrial pollution. After the Clean Air Act of 1956 outlawed coal fires in London, old buildings still remained blackened by soot and grime for decades. That may have helped the glass box to have its first heyday in London.

Speculators and Road Schemes

As we shall see, local authorities, inspired by socialist ideals, were already planning high-rise housing in London and elsewhere: now it was the turn of the capitalist developers to apply high-rise to offices.

Three concrete-framed office blocks over 50m high had been topped out by the end of 1958: *Bucklersbury House* in the City, *Bowater House* in Knightsbridge and Eastbourne Terrace in Paddington. They were developed by the pioneers of what would become a new oligarchy of speculative developers. These men usually knew the property market because they had been estate agents, and they worked out profits based on experience and rule of thumb.

In the fifties their confidence in borrowing was convenient to the established landowners, who were conservative and instinctively keen to shield themselves from risk. Pioneer developer Max Rayne was principally a financier. The Church Commissioners owned land on Eastbourne Terrace and took Rayne on to develop it, and his integrated office complex included a bold UN-style nineteen-storey office slab. The scheme was praised at the time for its modernity and would make Rayne a cool £3.5m. Like many of the developers, he would become an establishment figure, eventually becoming a peer, known for his support of the arts, from saving Hampstead Theatre to giving a Cézanne to the National Gallery.

Harold Samuel had been an estate agent and, unusually for a developer, was also a qualified chartered surveyor. His company, Land Securities Investment Trust, started buying London property as soon as the war finished. Its first high-rise development was *Bowater House* in Knightsbridge, incidentally developed at the same time that Samuel bought Queen Anne's Mansions for later re-development.

The Knightsbridge development was a springboard for Land Securities to become one of the UK's biggest property companies, with a portfolio in 2005 of over £11bn.

In 1959, the LCC proposed that Knightsbridge become a road junction where pedestrians would be separated from cars on raised decks, with a residential block over 100m high above it, designed by Samuel's architects Guy Morgan & Partners. Creating a roundabout there would 'complement' the underpass at Hyde Park Corner. This was a time when car ownership was on a steep climb and traffic was taking over cities. The LCC was obsessed with roundabouts, underpasses and road-widening schemes, and saw towers as markers of traffic intersections on the urban landscape. Under the LCC's Hubert Bennett, who had turned Elephant & Castle into a double roundabout with a stumpy International-Style office tower, the Knightsbridge scheme was revamped in 1963 with no fewer than three towers. That scheme was finally abandoned in 1965.

The most successful developer of the fifties had been Jack Cotton. Resident at the Dorchester Hotel, he was an emotional man who always wore a bow tie and kept deals in his head. His skills dated back to the thirties, when he bought land from farmers to sell to suburban developers. In 1954, he bought the Café Monico at Piccadilly Circus for £500,000 from Express Dairies. Backed by Legal & General, his City Centre Properties wanted to build a thirty-storey tower on the site, and it was approved by the LCC in 1959, subject only to car parking being finalised. Thinking his scheme was in the bag, Cotton proudly exhibited the plans in 1960 – to be met by the first public outcry against skyscrapers, in the shape of the vocal Save Piccadilly campaign. The loss of the old 'Heart of the Empire' was too much, even for those times. The RFAC, who had given Cotton the nod, did a U-turn and condemned the plan, which, but for the car parking, would by this time already have been under way. Nevertheless, plans for Piccadilly Circus would

Seagram Building, columns and plaza

not die and, in 1962, a traffic scheme from Lord Holford featuring a 54m concrete 'campanile' tower was aired, and again defeated. (By 1968 the plan had expanded into a comprehensive redevelopment in which Regent Street would have been rebuilt as a covered pedestrian arcade, with traffic running underneath and emerging below a pedestrian deck at the Circus, which would have had a 133m office tower on the south side, designed by Dennis Lennon.)

By that time, Cotton had been elbowed out of his property company by Charles Clore, and the only mark he left on London's skyline was *Campden Hill Towers* at Notting Hill Gate, the site of another LCC road-improvement scheme. He died in the Bahamas in 1964. Strangely, Cotton made a bigger impact on the Manhattan skyline by developing the Pan Am Building.

Charles Clore's property moves also date back to the 1930s. When the Prince of Wales Theatre, on Coventry Street, was up for auction, no-one was bidding anywhere near the reserve price of just a few thousand pounds. Clore got it for £800. After the war, he took charge of J Sears, which gave him a shoe company upon which to build his fortune, and eventually acquired Selfridges. In development, though, as with Cotton, front-end money came from a Francis Winham, who owned huge chunks of Cardiff but didn't want to be a developer himself. Clore was seen as a hard-nosed womaniser, but he liked hanging out with wartime singer Bud Flanagan. He invariably approved a design when there was an architect's model to show. In 1956, he started the lease acquisition – the art of gradually accruing a site for development by buying out all the small leaseholders on it – that would lead to the *Park Lane Hilton.*

Scaling Up

By 1959, construction was under way on four London skyscrapers that would reach 100m. These were the capital's first truly massive skyscrapers on an American scale. None of these giants follow exactly the then-prevailing Manhattan slab-and-podium formula.

The trailblazer was the *Empress State Building* in West Brompton, designed by AA van Nuffelen. This was a building with a three enormous curved sweeps of façade twenty-seven storeys high, topped with a strange look-out post. It was also the last major office block to be completed without air-conditioning. Air-conditioning had been invented by the American Havilland Carrier in 1902, but it took a long time to come to Europe. In an air-conditioned building, there is no need to open windows, so the curtain wall of metal and glass could become an unbroken skin around a building. This was the case with the Vickers Tower (now *Millbank Tower*), designed by Ronald Ward, who curved the curtain walls rather than have the usual plane façades.

The other two fifties giants, the *Shell Centre* and *Portland House*, don't have curtain walls at all. Critics were outraged that Sir Howard Robertson should reject the International Style for the *Shell Centre*, which was London's first great air-conditioned block. It looks almost like a pre-war building, with windows 'punched' through a façade of white stone. *Portland House*, designed by Howard Fairbairn, also had punched windows, but did look modern with its façades of concrete and granite. *Portland House* was part of the massive Stag Place development by Harold Samuel.

The 1950s were the last decade in which the Royal Family had absolute privacy throughout the grounds of Buckingham Palace. By 1963, *Portland House* and Charles Clore's *London Hilton* on Park Lane both overlooked the gardens there, and also broke above the skylines visible from St James's Park and Hyde Park, both Royal Parks. These parks were considered sacrosanct – Hyde Park was a swathe of pastoral land in the heart of the metropolis where sheep had once grazed, while the landscaped garden of St James's Park were framed by palaces and grand government offices. The new skyscrapers thrust the modern world into these spaces. Only with *New Zealand House* did the Royal Family manage to limit the damage to their privacy. Here, architect Robert Matthew compromised directly with the Duke of Edinburgh on the building's height.

Fenston and his protégé Hyams

Developers such as Clore were good at lease acquisition, but Joe Levy was probably the master. Levy had been a fireman during the war, and knew the location of London's bombsites. After the war, he became an estate agent. In 1956, Levy's company, Stock Conversion, started acquiring leases on the north side of the Euston Road. Here, the LCC wanted to build an underpass. What would ultimately emerge there would be the massive Euston Centre, with London's tallest International-Style skyscraper, *Euston Tower*, but, in the event, this did not top out till over a decade later.

Just down the road, at St Giles Circus, where Tottenham Court Road meets Oxford Street, the LCC had another road scheme, this time for a roundabout. The LCC was making a hash of the lease acquisition. As if out of nowhere, an extraordinarily discreet man with a Spanish-style goatee and a sharp cut of suit stepped in to the rescue. His name was Harry Hyams.

Cotton may have been considered as the role model for London's speculative developers, but Hyams was the protégé of ultimately a far more influential developer, the now forgotten Felix Fenston. Hyams was born in 1928, and after the war entered estate agency. He worked for Joe Levy for nine months, then became a negotiator for estate agents

Hamptons. Hyams was seldom to be found there, and, according to Oliver Marriott in his 1967 book *The Property Boom*, once failed to collect his wage packets for four months. For much of that time, Hyams was hanging out with Fenston at the latter's base in Hill Street in Mayfair, where Marriott recalled seeing a stuffed lion in the entrance hall.

Fenston enjoyed big-game hunting, despite having a tin leg and a heart condition. He was a cultivated man, and liked his friends so much that he cut them in on his developments. He had shared a desk at college with Jack Rose, and so the Rose brothers' real-estate business, Hamptons, got a share, as did the exiled Polish Prince Stanislas Radziwill. Fenston also owned the building contractor Kyle Stewart. In 1957, Fenston, Hyams and Radziwill bought a club in St James's, and let it stay empty for years. Hyams would have gathered the importance of being in business with a builder, and what could happen to the value of empty property.

In the mid 1950s, Fenston employed an architect called Richard Seifert to design a headquarters building on the Marylebone Road. With that commission, Seifert set up his practice in a basement in Princes Street, off Hanover Square, just a few minutes walk from Fenston's flat. The new Maxwell House was completed in 1959, when Castrol House (now *Marathon House*) was making the area hot for commercial property. It was soon leased through Hamptons to Woolworths and became Woolworth House. It was criticised for being quite a conventional building, but it packed a lot of space behind a Festival of Britain-style concrete façade.

Felix Fenston, 1959

Fenston was now developing the *Empress State Building*, the key development which literally upped the skyscraper game. As it was coming to fruition, Fenston did two very strange things. First, he fell out irretrievably with Hyams. Secondly, he decided he was tired of the property business, and promptly disappeared overseas, devoting himself to game hunting and other gentlemanly pursuits.

Why had Hyams and Fenston fallen out? This remains a mystery, but it may just have been about Seifert, who would become the architect of Hyams' developments throughout the sixties. In 1958, Hyams asked Seifert to design the skyscraper for St Giles Circus. That same year, now in new offices in Great Ormond Street, Seifert established a partnership with George Marsh and Tony Henderson.

In exchange for the land to enable the LCC to build its roundabout there, Hyams had got permission to build at an extraordinary plot ratio of 10:1. In January 1959, Hyams brought a property company called Oldham Estates that owned low-rent cottages and moribund mills in Lancashire – this would be the vehicle for what turned out to be any developer's most

remarkable streak of landmark buildings. He let building contractor George Wimpey take forty per cent of the shares – this would finance the building programme. Hyams had his formula in place – an architect he trusted, and a contractor inside the business. But time was running out. A new Town and Country Planning Act was coming in August 1959, which would outlaw the granting of planning permission on unsecured sites. Just a few days before it came into force, Seifert submitted plans for London's tallest skyscraper yet – *Centre Point*.

Woolworth House

The Colonel's Recipe

Richard Seifert was born in 1910 and studied architecture at the Bartlett School of Architecture at the University of London. He went into practice in 1933, designing suburban houses for £3/10s (£3.50) per plan, which he was not always paid. During the war, he was posted to India with the Royal Engineers, and rose to the rank of lieutenant–colonel. Thereafter, he would be known as Colonel Seifert. He was a conservatively dressed figure, distinguished by his round glasses and a pipe, who liked to play the violin when home in suburban Mill Hill. His first significant commission was for a Luxram light bulb factory in Rochester, followed shortly by Fenston's Marylebone project. As his widow recalled in 2005, 'he was criticised for making Woolworth House look old fashioned'.

In the late 1950s, he embraced the new possibilities of the International Style. This was not because he shared the fashionable enthusiasm for Mies van der Rohe – he 'wasn't so keen' about him, his widow recalls. More likely, it was because of his interest in the technology of building. Seifert's first skyscraper was commissioned in 1957, for a site on the Edgware Road (now *Capital House*). Here, he took a lead from London's pioneering glass box on a podium, Castrol House.

Seifert exploded on to the property scene in 1959. Now under the patronage of Hyams, and working on a fee of 5.5 per cent of construction costs, commissions tumbled onto his desk. Over at *London Wall*, the City of London Corporation planned its first cluster of office towers, each allocated to a different developer. Fenston had won the tender for one, and Clore another. At the time when he fell out with Fenston, Hyams had Seifert design his *London Wall* tower. All had to fit into the straitjacket of the City of London's building envelope requirements –

each had to be the same height and the same shape. Later, in 1962, the City would decree that its central area around Bishopsgate would be suitable for different skyscrapers to cluster, but at *London Wall* the Corporation gave little room for variation. That meant that Seifert's tower looked pretty much like the others there. However, it was the cheapest to build because it used pre-cast concrete H-frames behind its curtain walls. This ingenuity showed that Seifert could save a developer on construction costs as well as making bold designs. In 1960, Seifert designed a twenty-two-storey skyscraper, *Tolworth Tower*, in the distant south-west suburbs. Here, the tower seemed to stand on huge tapering 'dinosaur legs', which would become a distinctive Seifert feature, and an early sign that his style would become quite expressionistic, or, as critics would later say, 'flashy'.

Hyams went on to commission further towers, including Space House (now *One Kemble Street*), *New London Bridge House* and the sublime *Drapers'' Garden*. But it was *Centre Point* that would be forever synonymous with the Seifert name. This was a fantastic wafer-thin tower that looked like no other skyscraper anywhere in the world. The celebrated sculptor Eduardo Paolozzi described it as London's first Pop Art building.

Centre Point did not have a curtain wall, nor punched windows in a solid façade, but rather a highly distinctive honeycomb-grid exterior that was also an engineering feat – it was load-bearing. Although probably no-one realised it at the time, it was entering a three-horse race with two American buildings that were also breaking new ground on how a skyscraper carries its load. At SOM, Bengali-born Fazlur Khan invented revolutionary techniques to give tall buildings rigidity against the wind, famously a major factor in Chicago where he was based, as well as making them cheaper to build.

His revolutionary 'tube-in-tube' idea made the building perimeter a load-bearing tube, liberating the space between it and the central core tube from any need for columns. This was first tried in the Chicago's Brunswick Building (now Cook County Administrative Building) – effectively a thirty-four-storey concrete box. Meanwhile, an influential designer called Eero Saarinen had been working on a thirty-eight-storey skyscraper on New York's Sixth Avenue. Saarinen had designed the Tulip Chair in 1956 that would define the retro-future feel of 1960s furniture. He was deeply impressed by van der Rohe's Seagram Tower, but did not want to copy it. His New York design in 1960 was for a 'rectangular donut' of concrete, which, as with *Centre Point* and the Brunswick Building, would carry load on the exterior. He sheathed it in black granite, and the CBS Building became known as the 'Black Rock'.

These three buildings were all topped out in 1964, so the race was effectively a draw. But it did show that, in London, Seifert was at the same cutting edge that was being pushed forward in the twin homes of skyscrapers, Chicago and New York.

White Heat and Brown Ban

With the completion of *Centre Point*, 1964 was a high-water mark for London skyscrapers. A year before, Beatlemania had swept the UK, and, much to everyone's surprise, the Beatles, Mary Quant and the whole ensuing Swinging London phenomenon would soon transform the knackered post-imperial capital into the world's grooviest city. Yet London architects were stuck in the ideas of Mies van der Rohe and Le Corbusier, now four decades old. New buildings were failing to match the style revolutions in popular culture. All except Seifert's… and a design from the Ministry of Public Building and Works.

At the time, there was an avant-garde movement of British architects named after their magazine, *Archigram*, started in 1961. Their vision was inspired by technology, science fiction, and taking modular construction to extremes. Their ideas would surface in the High-Tech architecture of the 1980s, although none of their stuff was actually built. However, the Ministry of Public Building and Works-designed Post Office Tower (now *Telecom Tower*), topped out in 1964, looked like something designed by a committee of mad scientists, exactly the sort of thing Archigram aspired to.

When Harold Wilson won the 1964 election, he appointed as his Postmaster-General Anthony Wedgwood-Benn (later Tony Benn), who transformed the post into that of a minister for technology. Wedgwood-Benn promoted Britain's 'White Heat of Technology', in which high-tech businesses would work with unions and academics to drive an export boom. A new quango, the National Economic Development Council, would mastermind this, and was duly installed in the Vickers Tower (now *Millbank Tower*). These were heady days, dominated by headlines about Soviet spies and spaceshots, and Britain was determined to be a player in the space-age US-Soviet power games. The Vickers Tower became a node in a virtual configuration of British power and technology buzzing above

Cook County Administrative Building, Chicago

London's skyline – the Houses of Parliament were just up the road, MI6 at Century House (now *Perspective*) over the river, military and communications staff were in the *Empress State Building* to the west, while, most visibly, the great technology symbol of the Post Office Tower to the north connected the whole country by microwave.

Another Harold Wilson appointment was George Brown as Minister for Economic Affairs. Labour had promised to tackle the 'profiteers' who were driving up land prices, and in November 1964 Brown placed a ban on new offices. Furthermore, a Location of Offices Bureau was established to encourage businesses to move office workers from Central London, which is exactly where it was based – in Chancery Lane. The 'Brown Ban' killed new skyscraper plans and marked the end of London's first great office skyscraper boom. But, by squeezing the supply of new offices, the Brown Ban would boost rents, leading to a bonanza for speculators who had plans already approved.

Vanishing Slabs

In the twenty-first century, the survival of London's early post-war office skyscrapers is patchy. They have been rendered redundant by modern office requirements, and their lousy energy efficiency makes them bad news from an environmental viewpoint. *Millbank Tower*, the *Shell Centre*, *New Zealand House* and *Centre Point* are now listed, but the others are wide open to being transformed into new structures or even to demolition. Century House and Castrol House have been converted to flats. Seifert's first skyscrapers, at Edgware Road and *London Wall*, have been lost. Of the classic fifties-designed office slabs with concrete side-walls and skeleton floors at the top, looking like junior versions of the UN Secretariat building, only *30 Eastbourne Terrace* remains intact.

London's rich urban fabric has always resulted from the accumulation of layers of styles from different times, so that the city's history itself is in its buildings. But few clues may remain to the particular layer created when London's skyline first broke free of the old height restrictions.

Centre Point

CBS Building, New York

Bucklersbury House

30 Eastbourne Terrace

Bucklersbury House, EC4
Queen Victoria Street

Tube Mansion House
Height 51m, 14 storeys
Constructed 1954–58
Architect Owen Campbell-Jones & Sons

The developer, Sir Aynsley Bridgland, didn't like modern architecture, and the original plan was for more traditional buildings on the site. The LCC and RFAC, however, wanted something bold and modern, and a new design was ready for the lifting of the 30m height limits of the London Building Act, which took place in 1954.

Just a couple of weeks prior to the new regulations, the remains of a Roman temple, dating from about 245 AD, were found in the excavations. The temple was dedicated to Mithras, a Persian god popular with Roman soldiers. Mithras, the legend goes, slew a bull in return for glory after death. Building around the temple would have added half a million pounds to the construction costs, so the temple foundations were shifted to a different alignment.

Bucklersbury House is a very plain building, basically a slab running between Queen Victoria and Cannon Streets, with three six-storey wings. A virtual clone building called Temple Court was quickly added to the site, the only difference being it had blue spandrels instead of grey. Temple Court houses Legal & General, who had financed the whole project.

In 2004, Legal & General commissioned the legendary French architect Jean Nouvel (designer of Barcelona's Torre Agbar) to design for the site's redevelopment – his shopping complex has now been approved. Mithras will be glad that his temple alignment is being restored.

30 Eastbourne Terrace, W2
(John Adam House)

Tube & Rail Paddington
Height 61m, 19 storeys
Constructed 1957–58
Architect Cecil H Elsom & Partners

30 Eastbourne Terrace stands as a great example of a fifties office slab. All of its contemporaries except *Bucklersbury House* had been recycled into new buildings by the century's end. This mini-UN Secretariat-style tower time-warps us back to the optimistic post-Festival of Britain days when modern skyscraper architecture was first applied to commercial developments. The site was developed by Max Rayne for the Church Commissioners, and his company London Merchant Securities borrowed the money to build from the Norwich Union. Rayne made £3.5m, a harbinger of the skyscraper fortunes that would be made in the sixties.

The slab is in a frame of pre-stressed concrete with exposed aggregate. This rough surface was actually considered attractive as well as practical – architects of the time utterly failed to anticipate the way exposed concrete stains. The façades have typically fifties blue-green spandrels beneath sash windows. The lifts were amazing at the time, zipping up at a rate of up to 210m/minute. The reinforced concrete end-walls brace the block against wind. The top storey is a 'skeleton floor', basically a half-empty frame, barely disguising undecorated partitions behind which lurk lift motors, boiler flue outlets etc. This is an interesting way of dealing with the necessity to house service structures. In 1956, JM Richards wrote in *Architectural Review* about 'Lumps on the Skyline' – he meant the small blocks that were appearing on London's new flat roofs to house lift machinery, ruining the clean modern shape of the buildings. He endorsed taking the external walls up an extra storey to screen such 'lumps', as Lever House in New York had done. The architects did this at Eastbourne Terrace, but still left the service clutter visible.

Owners Land Securities own the whole development along the entire 300m length of Eastbourne Terrace alongside Paddington Station. The original development brutally tore Eastbourne Mews apart. Nineteenth-century mews houses each suddenly faced a car park and a bland wall of offices from which the out-of-scale tower looms. Until recently it looked quite shabby, but refurbishing has smartened it up, giving it a retro-modern classic cool. For all its faults, it is a rare glimpse of the heady fifties days of a new, modern, commercial London.

Bowater House, SW1
Knightsbridge

Tube Knightsbridge
Height 52m, 17 storeys
Designed 1958
Completed 1959
Architect Guy Morgan & Partners

This massive scheme, with 24,720m² of offices, could have been the first step in the destruction of Knightsbridge as we know it.

Bowater House was developed by Harold Samuel's Land Securities Investment Trust, and replaced boutique shops that had helped make Knightsbridge such a fashionable shopping centre (they are beautifully evoked in Jacques-Emile Blanche's 1913 painting *Knightsbridge* in the York City Art Gallery). The building is dull but different – a ten-storey 112m-long bland cliff facing Hyde Park, bridging Edinburgh Gate, with two parallel wing slabs, one of seventeen storeys, the other 12 storeys, and a four-storey bridge of offices on the Knightsbridge side.

The architects had big plans for Knightsbridge, backed by the LCC, who planned a roundabout covered by a pedestrian deck. As Bowater House was being completed, Guy Morgan designed a twenty-nine-storey, 102m-high block of flats, and in 1963 the 'Knightsbridge Green' scheme was further revamped into a 126m residential tower, a 99m hotel and an 85m office block. Luckily, the plans were finally abandoned in 1965.

At the back of Bowater House is Sir Jacob Epstein's *Rush of Green*, depicting a naked family dashing for the park, pursued or encouraged by Pan, notable for his animal legs. Epstein was working on the sculpture when he died. Epstein's public work had started on London's first skyscraper, *55 Broadway*. It's strange how his career was marked by London high-rise.

Bowater House is due to be replaced by 106 luxury flats designed by Richard Rogers, which will certainly be an improvement for this key location.

Thorn House in the eighties

Orion House, WC2
(Thorn House)
Upper St Martins Lane

Tube Leicester Square
Height 61m, 16 storeys
Designed 1956
Constructed 1957–59
Architect Basil Spence & Partners
Remodelled 1988–90 by RHWL.

This shiny white office block was the first old London skyscraper to be recycled.

The original fourteen-storey Thorn House was commissioned in 1956 by one of the UK's blue-chip companies, Thorn Electrical Industries. Architect Basil Spence, famous for Coventry Cathedral, also later designed the Home Office building that replaced Queen Anne's Mansions, and *Knightsbridge Barracks*. Thorn House was a classic fifties skyscraper, using the slab-on-a-podium formula in the style of the UN Building in New York, topped by a skeleton floor and with blank end-walls to brace it against wind. Here, the tower rose from a long two-storey frontage along Upper St Martin's Lane, which contained a 250-capacity demonstration theatre to show off Thorn's technology. The spandrels were a distinguished powdery dark blue, and the north face had big white letters spelling THORN at the top. Thorn's company boardroom was on the top floor, giving power views over Westminster from below the water tanks and lift machinery – imagine the mechanical sounds in the background of board meetings!

On the eastern façade was mounted a fantastic welded bronze sculpture – *The Spirit of Electricity* (1958), by sculptor and later Royal Academician Geoffrey Clark.

Bowater House

Orion House

The Spirit of Electricity

Marathon House, NW1
(Castrol House)
Marylebone Road

Tube Baker Street, Marylebone
Height 49m, 16 storeys
Designed 1955
Completed 1960
Architect Gollins Melvin & Ward with
Hugh Casson and Neville Condor

This modernist block of flats began life as the first curtain-walled office high-rise in London, and one of the key buildings that brought the International Style to the UK.

Architecturally, the most exciting commercial office in the early 1950s anywhere was Lever House in New York, which introduced the idea of a tower rising from a podium building. Edmund Ward, the W of London architects GMW, was one of those who went over to look at it, and was the first to bring curtain wall to London with an office block on New Cavendish Street. When the Marylebone Road site came up for redevelopment, Festival of Britain planner Sir Hugh Casson proposed the podium-and-tower concept for it. Initially, the idea was to build to twenty storeys, but that was turned down by the RFAC – nothing above the height of Marylebone Town Hall (opposite) was allowed. GMW designed a thirteen-storey tower, with one set-back floor underneath, and all mounted on a two-storey podium clad in white Sicilian marble with black mullions. Along with the plant machinery, the top floor also held a caretaker's flat, executive lounge with roof access, and bedrooms for visitors. This was London's own Lever House. The tower's curtain wall of aluminium, set with green spandrels, was a first, and would be endlessly copied throughout 1960s Britain.

Castrol House was headquarters for major oil company Castrol, and the whole building and its steel-trimmed, marble-floored reception gave a clear message of breaking with the past of stolid old companies in stuffy Victorian buildings. At night, lighting gave the

This is a seven-tonne boat-like sliver with structures representing light bulb filaments and electric arcs, set on a vertical spine 23.5m long. Clark had produced works for Coventry Cathedral and in 1959 was further commissioned to do a huge relief in Castrol House.

In the 1980s, RHWL used the old steel frame to create a new building, clad in white as shiny and smooth as a brand-new fridge (similar to the cladding used in the recycled tower block *Parsons House*). The skeleton floor was filled in with another two recessed storeys, and the lifts relocated. This is a classy refurb, and set a standard for subsequent office-block recycling, such as that at 388 Euston Road.

The Spirit of Electricity has been remounted on the new liftshaft bulge on the north façade, and now reflects the paparazzi flashes as the rich and famous are snapped at The Ivy restaurant on West Street below it.

Marathon House

impression of a stack of trays in a box of light. A huge
7 × 15m metallic mural from modern sculptor Geoffrey
Clarke was commissioned (see *Orion House*).

When Castrol was subsequently brought by
Marathon Oil, the building became Marathon House,
but by the 1990s it was redundant. Developers
Hammersons commissioned a new 'organic' building
from GMW, but when Westminster council turned it
down, they decided to sell it. Marathon House was refurbished as flats in the nineties by Bristol architects
Leighton Carr, and marketed as retro-chic, the first
London block to celebrate sixties modernism as cool.
GMW may be unhappy with the marine-blue re-
cladding, but it does give an idea of the bright clean feel
of this pioneering building.

Capital House, W1
(Foster Wheeler House)
Chapel Street

Tube Edgware Road
Height 59m, 17 storeys
Commissioned 1957
Completed 1960
Architect Richard Seifert & Partners.
Reconstructed 1991 by Fairhurst Architects

London's greatest twentieth-century skyscraper architect
was Richard Seifert, and here was his first skyscraper.
However, that highly significant building has been obliterated by an oddly jazzy nineties refurb.

The location of Century House is significant. A few
blocks to the east is Seifert's first major London building,
Woolworth House on the Marylebone Road. It was
influenced by the Festival of Britain buildings, but by
the late fifties that sort of block was old hat. This is the
first of Seifert's slab-and-podium projects, with a
skeleton floor on the roof and blank wind-bracing
sidewalls, just like Eastbourne Terrace in nearby
Paddington. The tower was occupied by American engineering conglomerate Foster Wheeler.

Capital House now

The one-storey podium followed the line of Chapel
Street, and a five-storey block was mounted on it on the
Edgware Road side, as if to hide the tower behind.
Marks & Spencer took the ground floor, and are still
there. On the wall above M&S was a statue of a naked
man, which made many people cross the Edgware Road
for a closer look. Lord Sieff of Marks & Spencer called
Siefert down to scrutinise it – Seifert couldn't see
anything wrong, but agreed that a fig leaf might be in
order. The statue now carries a sporran.

Later, as the slab-and-podium formula fell of favour,
one of the first to stick the knife in was John Betjeman,
who in July 1971 wrote a sarcastic eulogy to this particular building for *Private Eye*.

Capital House's refurbishment is unusual. The dark
glass, the angular cornering, the prism stair bays and the
sloping glass mini-atrium entrance are a sort of eighties
compromise between simply recladding with darker
glass and adding some Post-Modernist touches to sex it
up. The result is already dated. An excellent sculpture,
The Window Cleaner, by Allan Sly, stands by the
entrance, looking up at the tower with an expression
that clearly says: 'Blimey, guv, that curtain wall's a
big job!'

Foster-Wheeler House in the sixties

Empress State Building, SW6
Lillie Road

Tube West Brompton
Height 100m, 30 storeys high,
plus a 17m spike on the roof
Completed 1961
Architect Stone Toms & Partners
Remodelled 2001–03 by Wilkinson Eyre

The extraordinary Empress State Building was London's first skyscraper to reach 100m, and is now refurbished as a unique retro-future landmark. This was the building that trailblazed London's sixties skyscraper boom. At the opening party in April 1962, the developer Felix Fenston, who originally wanted to build a hotel here, was present with the up-and-coming developer called Harry Hyams. They had recently fallen out, and may not have talked.

The original design, by AA van Nuffelen of architects Stone, Toms & Partners, was fantastic. He named it the Empress State Building. A massive 32,520m² of floorspace was created in a Y-shape; three wings extending 37m from a central core to equilaterally placed satellite cores. Van Nuffeln's first masterstroke was to build continuous sweeping curves between the wings, creating three vast, breathtaking concave façades twenty-seven storeys high. These pre-dated the curved façades of *Millbank Tower*, which became London's tallest just a year later. This was one of the last big London buildings not to be air-conditioned, so all the windows opened. The spandrels below them created long horizontal arcs of sky-blue. At each extremity, the building is clad in white stone, with a still-visible pattern of vertical slits. Twelve lifts were split between covering the lower half of the building and whizzing straight up to the fourteenth floor and above. At the end of each wing, toilets alternated by floor between gents and ladies. The eleventh floor was a sick bay and the twenty-seventh a canteen.

Empress State Building, 1965

Van Nuffelen's second masterstroke was at the top of the building. A two-storey structure housed, as well as plant machinery, a games room offering table tennis, billiards and darts. At the very top was an odd glass observation deck with outwardly sloping windows and a streamlined roof, looking rather like an airport control tower. It was easy to imagine as you looked at it from afar that a crisply-dressed man in Her Majesty's Secret was looking back at you through binoculars. This may indeed have been the case...

Who was in the Empress State Building? The Royal Crest over the entrance and Union Jacks fluttering on the wings were a clue, but few people who had not signed the Official Secrets Act knew anything except that the Admiralty was there. In 1962, they moved staff from Queen Anne's Mansions and also installed the Naval Historical Library, the world's largest naval library, with 125,000 books. The Admiralty was followed in 1964 by the new Ministry of Defence's Arms Procurement department. But the most mysterious occupants were spies. Although MI5 (see *Euston Tower*) was thought to be there, it is more likely that the tenant was a London branch of Government Communications Headquarters (GCHQ), based in Cheltenham. GCHQ's mission is to provide 'signals intelligence', which effectively means eavesdropping. The 'Composite Signals Organisation Station' in the ESB is said to have

Remodelling

On the terrace

occupied several upper floors and specialised in intercepting diplomatic traffic from London embassies.

The building gradually emptied in the nineties. When the Procurement Agency moved out to Bristol in 1997, the ESB fell silent.

Land Securities acquired the building, and, to update it, hired an A-list practice – Wilkinson Eyre, who had just designed the City's biggest skyscraper for Fenchurch Street (never built) and were about to win two Stirling Prizes from RIBA (for Yorkshire's Magna Science Adventure Centre and Tyneside's Gateshead Millennium Bridge). Consent came in 2001 to expand the building. The task was not only to turn a knackered sixties hulk into twenty-first century offices, but also to evoke the original's astounding visual impact.

Because they were building on the old concrete frame, the floor heights had somehow to squeeze in air conditioning, network cabling and other services that normally make modern floor heights a metre higher. The concrete floors were replaced with steel decking, and 6km of Multi-Service Chilled Beams, carrying all office services, were woven into the building. The great sweeping façades were panelled in charcoal grey. The south side was built out by 5.5 metres, with new support columns on which was hung a screen of aluminium louvres to reduce solar gain and create a fashionably diffusive surface. This is the widest expanse of brise-soleils anywhere, and won the 2003 Aluminium Imagination Award. The new supports also help carry the weight of a further three full-size floors, where the games rooms had been. All this expanded the block's floor space by nineteen per cent. At ground level is a vast airy double-height marble-clad reception.

On the roof itself, Wilkinson Eyre placed a circular structure called Orbit, topped with a 17m-high mast. This is a stroke of pure Flash Gordon architecture. Orbit is basically a revolving bar, London's first since the *Telecom Tower*'s old revolving restaurant. A 24m-diameter ring of floor turns at up to twelve degrees a minute, and floats on pneumatic suspension.

The futuristic remodelling was finished in July 2003. In October, an outdoor sculpture, *Fall*, by Diana Edmund, was installed. Suspended high on a 14.5m-high steel frame are two giant curving leaves, caught as if in mid-fall. In 2004, the Metropolitan Police were the first major tenant, continuing the legacy of state security tenants. As in 1961, the Empress State Building today is a very strange skyscraper. It looms over nearby neighbourhoods as if it were the vanguard of an alien invasion sliding across the rooftops. At night, blue lighting makes it float over the nearby dark railway lands and Brompton Cemetery like a ghost of the future. In keeping with its original developer, the ESB is enigmatic and, quite simply, brilliant.

33 Cavendish Square, W1

Tube Oxford Circus
Height 70m, 20 storeys
Commissioned 1957
Completed 1962
Architect TP Bennett & Son

This is one of London's most overlooked office skyscrapers, despite its being totally out of scale in an exclusive square laid out in 1719 where grand aristocratic houses once stood. Considering its height and mass, it manages to be suitably discreet in its sensitive location. It follows the podium-and-slab-tower formula, but in this case there are two slabs intersecting at right angles. Its dark marble vertical bands and stone spandrels give it a distinguished look — you could just about imagine Cary Grant stepping out from it in an early sixties film, exuding modern class.

Exactly how much class became clear in 2005, when the Coal Board Pension Fund put the whole city block up for auction. The starting price was £315m, including Oxford Street shops and the London College of Fashion, designed by LCC Architects. A consortium around the Abu Dhabi royal family, recently stung by being outbid for a Knightsbridge block, saw off seventeen other bidders by putting a whopping £425m on the table. Just shows, 33 Cavendish Square is a pretty big deal.

33 Cavendish Square

Shell Centre, SE1
Belvedere Road

Tube Waterloo
Height 107m, 26 storeys
Designed 1955–56
Completed 1962
Architect Sir Howard Robertson & Ralph Maynard Smith

The Shell Centre was Europe's first major air-conditioned block, and a highly controversial design for the 1950s.

After the Festival of Britain closed, the Ministry of Works declared the South Bank a good place for a tall tower. Shell acquired part of the site and commissioned their consulting architects Easton & Robertson to design a complex to house 5,000 office workers. The architectural practice was famous for the Art Deco Royal Agricultural Halls in Westminster, completed in 1928. Sir Howard Morley Robertson was on Le Corbusier's team designing the UN buildings in New York, but had serious doubts about glass skyscrapers, which he thought were energy inefficient. That sort of thinking was heresy at the time, but is similar to current doubts about all-glazed buildings. Robertson worked on the Shell Centre with partner Ralph Maynard Smith, who in private life was a moody surrealist artist. Their plan of a slab topped with a skeleton floor, along with a great bank of eleven-storey buildings, was exhibited at the Royal Academy Exhibition of 1956. People hated it. It was too heavy, and everyone was flabbergasted that the chance of building a gleaming International Style block was being squandered.

Robertson faced the critics down, although he amended the design. Introducing air-conditioning meant that the tenth floor was occupied by plant machinery, with more stacked away behind an open viewing terrace on the top floor, which was open to the public in the 1960s. Curiously, the building has a pitched roof. Otherwise, the tower looks like a pre-war skyscraper, stepped at the top, with recessed bays and windows punched through a stone façade. Like Shell-Mex House (now *80 Strand*), Shell's old headquarters across the river, the Shell Centre was clad with Portland stone, enhancing its solid, stately air. A new tube exit for Waterloo was built into the Shell Centre, making it only the second skyscraper project integrated with the Underground since *55 Broadway*.

Robertson died in 1963 and Smith a year later, both with reputations in doubt after the Shell Centre. The building is quite stodgy and bulky, but, since 2000, the London Eye stands in front of it, so it no longer dominates the South Bank. The lower buildings have been converted into apartments. The Shell Centre tower is sometimes used as a backdrop for giant projected images, notably on Remembrance Day.

There's interesting sculpture at the base of the tower: the *Shell Fountain* (1961), a 9m-high spiralling shell by Franta Belsky; the *Motor Cyclist* by Siegfried Charoux, and, over on Belvedere Road, the *Shell Ball*, a 1.8m ball decorated with rings of stone and granite and carved shells, by Eric Aumonier.

London Wall, EC2

St. Alphage House
Tube Moorgate, Barbican
Height 69m, 20 storeys
Completed 1962
Architect Morris Sanders Associates

City Tower
(40 Basinghall Street)
Tube Moorgate, Barbican
Height 69m, 20 storeys
Completed 1964
Architect Burnet Tait Wilson & Partners
Refurbished 1985 by GMW

London Wall was where the City of London built its post-war vision of a modern business quarter, but it turned out to be a disaster. In 2006, of its original five skyscraper blocks, only two survive.

In 1959, the 'South Barbican' plan, by the City of London and the LCC, was approved for the area which had previously hosted London's rag trade and been entirely blitzed in 1940. The plan was about circulation and offices. Pedestrians would circulate on a podium level 5.5m above street level, with bridges spanning London Wall, which was to be upgraded into a four-lane highway. The traffic-free level of pubs, restaurants and plazas was to be a new environment alive with businesses and advertisements that would ultimately extend to cover the whole City. Le Corbusier had envisioned separating pedestrians from traffic. The City stipulated strict dimensions for five parallel office towers, each let out to developers on tender, to create a dramatic urban perspective of clean, modern blocks grouped together, with three north of the highway and two to the south. The London Wall blocks were staggered at an angle to the highway; each was to be 67m high, have a floorplan of 42.7x17.9m, and even the window widths and possible spandrel colours were specified. The idea of identical parallel slabs dates back to van der Rohe's plan for the German Reichsbank in 1933, and London Wall was also inspired by Stockholm's Hötorget redevelopment scheme, which had similarly proportioned office slabs in the city centre.

Not surprisingly, the blocks looked identical. The first to be completed was *Moor House* in 1961, developed by Charles Clore and designed by Lewis Solomon, Kaye & Partners, who would design the *Park Lane Hilton*. It was followed in 1962 by St Alphage House and Richard Seifert's first City skyscraper, Royex House, which was initially called New Ocean House and was developed by Harry Hyams. Although Royex House looked like all the rest, it was built, uniquely, with precast concrete H-frames, a construction trick that saved money and would make it the most profitable tower here; 40 Basinghall Street and Lee House followed in the next couple of years. Lee House was named after a sister of Jackie Kennedy (later Onassis) who was married to Prince Radziwill, one of the developers in Felix Fenston's consortium. It was by Burnet, Tait Wilson & Partners, who had also designed the UK's tallest building in 1962, the CIS Tower in Manchester.

Hötorget, Stockholm

St Alphage House

London Wall, 1962

The podium level soon became a deserted, windswept area where businesses in leaky concrete kiosks failed. The towers became a byword for blandness, amplified by the way they were grouped. In Manhattan, the mind-numbing visual effect of parallel International Style office slabs became known as the Sixth Avenue Syndrome. London Wall was London's very own version of this, but on a meaner scale. The effect was more like a set of matchboxes.

What really killed the orginal vision completely was the demolition of Lee House to build *Alban Gate*, which closed off the view down the London Wall axis. 40 Basinghall Street was reclad with dark blue reflective windows and vertical aluminium lines by GMW, who would become masters of bringing dead City blocks back to life. It became City Tower and now looks quite slick. *Moor House* was demolished in 2001 and is replaced. Royex House was demolished in 2004 for a 71m, eighteen-storey tall tower by Eric Parry Architects.

This leaves only St Alphage House in its original form, looking particularly dilapidated. There are plans to replace it with a massive twenty-one-storey building by KPF (see *10 Upper Bank Street*). The strata of London's post-war skyscraper history are all contained on London Wall, from early International Style to Norman Foster's new curvy blocks, and St Alphage House is the last survivor of the bottom layer in the strata. Now robbed of its original confidence, it has even begun to take on a period charm, but it soon will also be lost.

London Hilton, W1
Park Lane

Tube Hyde Park Corner
Height 101m, 28 storeys
Constructed 1960–63
Architect Lewis Solomon Kaye

They tried to stop this hotel being built because it would rise over the trees of Hyde Park, but Harold Macmillan's government forced it through because they needed dollars.

Park Lane in the 1950s still contained stretches of elegant Regency terraces, and developer Charles Clore bought a bomb-damaged section in 1956. He went on to buy out 170 miscellaneous interests before the site was his to do as he wanted with. When he proposed to build a modern, American-style skyscraper hotel, the reaction was universal horror – Hyde Park would be hemmed in by walls of high-rise, like Central Park in New York. Hyde Park was not just like a refuge of tranquil country-side, but a Royal Park. The Queen worried that the top floors could look into Buckingham Palace. The RFAC and the Ministry of Works objected to the plan, but they were overruled in the Cabinet by the Ministry of Housing and Local Government, under pressure from the Board of Trade, who wanted the foreign exchange.

In 1960 BOAC (a forerunner of British Airways) had £150m of planes on order but worried that passengers might not come because of London's hotel shortage. The Hotel Corporation of America was already building the eighteen-storey Carlton Towers Hotel on Sloane Street.

That year, demolition at the Park Lane site began. During construction, Clore invoked 'The Third Schedule' to go from twenty-five to twenty-eight-storeys. The hotel opened in 1963, initially leased to Hilton for twenty-five years. As well as 530 rooms, the Hilton had a shopping arcade, 360 car park spaces and could accommodate 1400 banqueters. Just off the lobby is Trader Vic's, a branch of a Polynesian-themed American bar chain that invented the Mai Tai cocktail. A *Breakfast at Tiffany's*-style rooftop restaurant and bar, exploiting the spectacular views, was designed by leading architects Casson, Condor & Partners. The five-star hotel immediately became a London bridgehead for the jet-set, challenging the traditional haunt of celebrities, the Dorchester, just up the road.

The design of the Hilton is modern but not in the International Style. Three wings allow open views from more rooms than a slab or cross-plan building would have accommodated, and the rooms facing the park have balconies on a curved façade. Initially, this narrow façade was designed flat, but it was then curved to echo the Regency bow-fronted façades in the block to the north. The tower rises from a three-storey glass-fronted podium. The Hilton is one of London's most under-rated sixties buildings, a lot more elegant and sensitive than the modern neighbours that followed, the plain Londonderry Hotel and the Brutalist concrete Playboy Club (by legendary Bauhaus architect Walter Gropius).

The Park Lane Hilton

In 1973, Howard Hughes left Las Vegas and checked in with his entourage, taking the highest guest floor. Of course, no-one saw him, but he did emerge in June to pilot a Hawker Siddley 748 around Hatfield Aerodrome, naked. Two months later, he broke his hip on a night-time bathroom visit.

On 5 September 1975, the *Daily Mail* received a ten-minute warning of an IRA bomb in the Hilton. The Metropolitan Police sent three officers and were just ordering evacuation when the explosion ripped through the lobby. It killed two people and injured sixty-three. In 1982, a basejumper died when he got tangled in his parachute, but Gary Connery, a professional stuntman, successfully basejumped the Hilton in 1995 and 2006.

Nowadays, there are lots of Hiltons in London, but the Park Lane one is easily the most prestigious. The hotel group has a lease until 2033. Trader Vic's is still there, as well a casino and conference facilities, and the rooftop restaurant is now called Windows. The Hilton was London's first really tall hotel and, architecturally at least, it's still the best.

Millbank Tower, SW1
(Vickers Tower)
Millbank, Westminster

Tube Westminster, Pimlico
Height 118m, 32 storeys
Constructed 1959–63
Architect Ronald Ward & Partners

Just down the road from Parliament is a Grade II-listed skyscraper. In 1963, the Vickers Tower was London's tallest skyscraper, and a statement about Britain's aspiration to technological power in the 1960s.

This was to be a prestigious skyscraper on an almost American scale, forward-looking and radiating confidence. There was only one way to express that as the sixties kicked in: a curtain-walled tower in the International Style, rising from a podium. But architect Ronald Ward gave it a twist – he broke the convention of flat façades and instead alternated them between concave and convex. His curves may have been influenced by his home, a converted circular coastal bunker in Hythe built to guard against a Napoleonic invasion. Ward's only other skyscraper, the contemporary St George's Tower in Croydon, is a conventional slab.

Construction started in June 1959. The Vickers site includes a smaller office block and some flats. Because this was an early air-conditioned tower, the windows were not designed to open. The plant machinery at the top is enclosed in a curved steel box.

Vickers, then a booming British defence and aerospace conglomerate, was riding high after the launch of their VC10 airliner in 1962. A year later, they were able to move into their new HQ and set up their boardroom on the thirteenth floor. After Harold Wilson came to power in 1964, his Postmaster-General Anthony Wedgwood-Benn (later Tony Benn) promoted Britain's 'White Heat of Technology', in which high-tech businesses like Vickers would work with unions and academics to drive an export boom. A new quango to mastermind this, the National Economic Development Council, was installed in the Vickers Tower. The skyscraper became a key location in Labour's power machine, and Wedgwood-Benn became a frequent visitor.

In the sixties, a sinister force threatened Britain: the Cybermen were ruthless silver androids who had pipes sticking out of their heads and seemed to play chest-mounted accordions when they communicated. In the 1968 season of BBC TV's *Dr Who*, 'The Invasion', they teamed up with the International Electromatic company, whose HQ was the tower. With Cybermen roaming around the sewers, London was about to fall. Luckily the doctor, then played by Patrick Troughton, was in town at the time, and despatched them. In 1975, when the tower had become Millbank Tower, Dr Who (now played by Tom Baker) returned to deal with the Loch Ness Monster a.k.a. the Sygon Skarasen. The creature rises from the Thames outside the skyscraper, just as the TV show's parallel universe Prime Minister is hosting an international energy conference there. Dr Who tosses a tracking beacon down the monster's throat.

Back in the real universe, the Labour Party in 1997 had not had a real Prime Minister for eighteen years, but things had changed. This was New Labour, a reinvigorated machine that had shed its submission to trade unions and ancient class divisions. In charge of the media machine to sell it was the formidable Peter Mandelson. Labour moved out of the rabbit-warren of its old Georgian HQ in run-down Lambeth, and took two floors of open-plan offices in the skyscraper. Here, Mandelson installed the legendary Excalibur computer, basically a search-engine with a vast database of press-clippings, which was able, virtually instantly, to generate rebuttals to anything the Tories said in the election campaign. The result of Mandelson's 'Operation Victory' was a Labour landslide.

Like Wedgwood-Benn, Mandelson saw the skyscraper as a modern, forward-looking base, handily just down the road from Parliament, from which to drive the nation into a bright science-fiction future, symbolised this time by the Millennium Dome rather than the *Telecom Tower*. Labour went on to mastermind a second election victory from Millbank in 2001.

When landlords Tishman-Speyer refurbished in 2000, Labour quit rather than pay a tripled annual rent of £900,000. The building still hosts occasional trade union meetings, and is the London base of the International Labour Organisation, as well as some United Nations agencies up on the twenty-first floor.

Millbank Tower thus remains a Power Tower after forty years, if not as powerful as it was. Still, its

Westminster location suggests it's unlikely we have seen the last time it plays a part in making political history. In 2005, the BBC's Andrew Marr started presenting a Sunday TV magazine programme with the view from the top as its backdrop – his interviews with politicians temporarily made Millbank Tower a political platform again.

New Zealand House, SW1
Haymarket

Tube Piccadilly Circus
Height 69m, 19 storeys
Completed 1963
Architect Robert Matthew,
Johnson-Marshall & Partners

It's not particularly tall or spectacular, but this Grade II-listed building is considered one of London's most important sixties skyscrapers. This is because of the way the architect, Robert Matthew, deals with the prevailing podium-and-tower formula, pushes glazing to the extreme, and pays meticulous attention to internal space and fittings. It also has the UK's first modern atrium, and is the only skyscraper anywhere that can be entered from a Regency arcade.

Robert Matthew was the chief designer of the Royal Festival Hall (1948–51) and the head of the LCC Architects Department, the team that introduced Corbusian modernism to the UK with early council estates. He approved the demolition of the Carlton Hotel at the bottom of Haymarket in 1948, and a year later New Zealand bought the site for a new High Commission, having outgrown their old one in the Strand. Matthew went into private practice in Edinburgh in 1953, and wanted this commission, even travelling out to New Zealand to lobby the government there. He won it in 1959, against competition including Sir Basil Spence, who had just designed Thorn House (see *Orion House*).

Matthew travelled to New York with the New Zealand Government architect Gordon Wilson. Seeing Lever House, they decided to go for the tower-and-podium formula. The idea of a skyscraper here was approved by the Cabinet, but the Royal Family objected to one so close to Buckingham Palace and Matthew had personally to reach a compromise with Prince Philip to reduce the height, which had originally been about 95m, including a mast. This compromise was still higher than any building in New Zealand itself. Matthew commuted down to London on weekends to oversee the design work being done in his practice's London branch. He became president of RIBA in 1962.

What was built was a four-storey podium building in scale with the old buildings of Haymarket, mounted by a fourteen-storey square tower of offices floating one storey above the podium's roof terrace, which has tranquil, semi-enclosed courtyard gardens. At the back of the site is the Royal Opera Arcade by John Nash (1816), which had fallen into disrepair – the arcade was bought by the NZ government and restored, and a rear entrance to the new building made from it. The columns that support the concrete structure are covered in stainless steel at street level and on the terraces above the podium and the roof. Because of its location, the hospitality suite terrace at the top probably has the best views from any West End skyscraper. From the ground, however, New Zealand House would have been more exciting if the tower had not been so set back, making it look stumpy rather than the elegant glass tower it actually is.

New Zealand House is big on glazing. The huge double-glazed street frontage was built as a shop window for New Zealand, with a gap big enough for a window cleaner to squeeze in. The tower's floors have unprecedentedly large areas of plate glass, down to below knee level, which leaves the building wide open to solar gain – curtains often need to be drawn to prevent the internal greenhouse effect. There are no spandrels below the windows, just narrow stone bands of Portland stone. Matthew worried that workers might get vertigo, so he created wide window sills.

New Zealand did not stint with the budget for their flagship building. Even when it was running over budget, Matthew had no problem persuading the High Commissioner to cover it. Fittings from door handles to cupboards were custom-designed by the architects, and New Zealand woods used for panelling and skirting. New Zealand 1960s art decorates the entrance, including a 15m-long mural by John Drawbridge. The atrium manages to fit in a 15.5m-high Maori *pouihi*, or totem-pole. This was carved on site by Inia te Wiata, who was also a great classical singer. He led a double life and would pop in to work on it in breaks from the Royal Opera House.

Robert Matthew's practice is now called RMJM, and they carried out a light renovation in the 1990s, leaving New Zealand House more faithful to its original form than any contemporary skyscrapers. The World Bank is now one of its tenants. Interestingly, RMJM are returning to skyscraper design, with a 2005 proposal for a twenty-five-storey eco-tower in their hometown of Edinburgh.

Millbank Tower

New Zealand house. Curtains prevent solar gain too

Metro Central Heights, SE1
(Alexander Fleming House)
Newington Causeway

Tube Elephant & Castle
Height 55m, 13 storeys
Designed 1959
Constructed 1960–63
Architect Ernö Goldfinger
Converted into flats in 1998

The legendary Hungarian-born Brutalist architect Ernö Goldfinger had designed skyscrapers before, but they had never materialised. When he was taken on to design a key building for the LCC's comprehensive redevelopment of Elephant & Castle, it was his big break.

Elephant & Castle was wrecked by the Blitz, and because major roads radiate across South London from it, in 1956 the LCC indulged in a grand scheme of roundabouts, pedestrian subways, offices, homes and a shopping centre. The LCC themselves designed the landmark tower block *Draper House* for it. Goldfinger designed a new headquarters for the Ministry of Health, named Alexander Fleming House after the discoverer of penicillin. The site was previously the Trocadero, Europe's largest cinema. (Later, Goldfinger designed the nearby Odeon Cinema, now also demolished.)

Two curtain-walled towers (above the shopping centre and at the London School of Printing) would also go up in Elephant & Castle, but Goldfinger dismissed the International Style – 'buildings with masks like those stockings burglars use'. Goldfinger wanted to show off a building's structure – in this case, a concrete frame which is clearly visible as an exterior grid. Some of the windows slotted into this are recessed from the grid, and some project out a little. In the bay window by the stair tower in the tallest block, there's even a hint of the famous cantilevered head of the *Trellick Tower* he would later design. In the main block, ministerial suites were installed on the twelfth and thirteenth floors. Two further blocks of seven and thirteen storeys are connected by seven-storey glazed passageways, and create an internal quadrangle. There was an automatic conveyor system for post from a loading bay. The pre-war pub The Elephant and Castle was rebuilt. In 1967, Alexander Fleming House won a Civic Trust Award.

In the years that followed, Elephant & Castle slid into a hell of life-threatening pedestrian subways, traffic, seedy shops and dilapidated buildings. After the ministry was absorbed by the DHSS, the department created a vast benefits office in Alexander Fleming House. When the building fell victim to sick building syndrome, it was abandoned.

In 1997, residential developer St George cleaned out the building, converted it into luxury flats and brightened the exterior with white paint and blue spandrels. A gym and sauna were installed, the courtyard had a pond put in, and the development was sealed off with security gates. Many flats were taken by Hong Kong Chinese, anxious about the colony's handover to Beijing. The marketing suggested the re-named Metro Central Heights was a prime site – Elephant & Castle is actually Greater London's geographical centre – but when the flats were ready in 1998, new occupants were less than happy to find themselves living in a low-rent traffic nightmare. Nowadays, residents still complain about things like cooking fumes from the Nando's there, but the area is improving. Elephant & Castle is due for a wholesale redevelopment anyway, and St George have twice applied to add another block to Metro Central Heights, the second time with a design from Broadway Malyan (see *St George Wharf*).

As with the *Trellick Tower*, socialist Goldfinger's building has ended up prospering in the private sector.

Portland House, SW1
Stag Place, Victoria

Tube Victoria
Height 102m, 29 storeys
Designed 1959
Completed 1963
Architect Howard Fairbairn and Partners

In 1956, Gio Ponti published plans for a thirty-two-storey, 127m tower for the Pirelli company in Milan. The Pirelli Building, finished in 1960, was a distinct break from standard rectilinear skyscrapers – although curtain-walled, in cross-section the concrete slab was a long octagon. Its shape and remarkable engineering (by Pier Luigi Nervi) created an architectural sensation, and directly inspired two similar blocks, both built by London developers – one in Manhattan, the other this behemoth towering over Victoria. Jack Cotton hired the legendary Walter Gropius and Pietro Belluschi to design the forty-nine-storey, 246m-high Pan Am Building (now the MetLife Building) over Grand Central Station. Meanwhile, Harold Samuel's huge Stag Place development would be dominated by Portland House. It and the Pan Am Building were both finished in 1963.

Samuels planned a big pure office development for 5,000 workers on the site previously occupied by the Stag Brewery, but the LCC insisted on a block of flats as well

New York's MetLife is bigger

and reduced the overall plot ratio from 5:1 to 3.5:1. Nevertheless, a massive office tower design emerged, which would impact on the views from St James's, Green and Hyde Parks. The RFAC objected and the Ministry of Works pressed for a lower tower, but the LCC overruled them. Plainer blocks, including *Westminster City Hall*, followed at Stag Place.

Unlike the Pirelli Building, Portland House has no curtain walls, but punched windows in façades of concrete with grey Cornish granite aggregate. The top floor was built as a viewing gallery but never opened to the public, probably because it directly overlooks Buckingham Palace. Above that, rooftop plant structures are screened by concrete slabs with narrow gaps between them. The block is 62m wide, and 25m deep at the centre. This great concrete lozenge is a taster for the Brutalist skyscrapers that would emerge in the next ten years.

Portland House had refurbishments in the eighties and nineties but its overall look has not changed. This century, Portland House's entrance has been brightened by colourful street installations. It is a mixed-occupancy tower, popular with government departments and quangos, including the ODPM and English Heritage's Education Service. Much of the rest of the Stag Place development has at last been replaced by far better contemporary buildings, such as the sweeping Cardinal Place retail and office development designed by EPR. The beefy hunk of Portland House still lurks behind, but somehow manages to fit quite handsomely into the new, improved environment.

The Economist Building, SW1
St James Street

Tube Green Park
Height 54m, 17 storeys high
Commissioned 1959
Completed 1964
Architect Alison & Peter Smithson

The strange thing about the Economist Building is that the architects were leading Brutalists, yet this, their most popular work, is a very human-scaled complex. They didn't like the International Style, yet they used a lot of its formula, from the glazed tower to the plaza below it.

Alison and Peter Smithson were flamboyant Northerners who enjoyed mixing in avant-garde circles. They established their Modernist credentials with a school in Hunstanton, Norfolk, but in 1953, just before it was finished, they led a revolt against Le Corbusier's prevailing ideal of zoned cities with tower blocks and wide spaces. They argued that a slum street can give more of a sense of belonging to a place than spaced-out redevelopments. When they were commissioned to design new offices for *The Economist* in 1959, they had become entranced with the alleys and hidden courtyards of the City. The idea of intimate space made them create a new interpretation here.

The site is next to the long-established gentleman's club Boodles on St James's Street, and the Smithsons designed three new buildings on the site, grouped around a raised piazza. The type of Portland stone used there is Portland Roach, which exposes the fossils of Jurassic marine invertebrates of 140 million years ago. The buildings are all octagonal, and although the main one is a skyscraper, it manages almost to hide in the old streets of St James's. The smaller buildings contained housing, a banking hall and an art gallery. Like the magazine, the Smithsons described their buildings as

The Economist

Suburban excitement

'didactic' (i.e. well-informed) and 'dry', and they promised 'no fake antiquarianism'. They spent some time observing how *The Economist* journalists worked, endearing themselves to the editor, Sir Geoffrey Crowther.

Unlike virtually every other 1960s skyscraper in London, no-one has ever had anything bad to say about the Economist Building. It is now a Grade I-listed building. It was refurbished by SOM in 1990, with the tower lobby enlarged and glazed, but preserving the overall original appearance. When architects Fletcher Priest designed the trendy Che bar and restaurant in the ex-bank building, they recovered walnut veneers and mosaics from Smithson's original designs, and exploited the whole sixties aspect by installing Warhol and Lichtenstein prints.

Tolworth Tower, KT6
Ewell Road, Tolworth, Kingston

Rail Tolworth
Height 81m, 22 storeys
Designed 1960
Constructed 1962–65
Architect Richard Seifert & Partners

While *Centre Point* was going up, about to establish Seifert's practice as a household name, his first great landmark tower was completed in a distant south-western suburb. His partner George Marsh was in charge of the project. The site, overlooking the Kingston By-pass, was previously an Odeon cinema. When topped out, Tolworth Tower was the sixth-tallest skyscraper in London.

This slab is not like the fifties-designed mini UN Secretariat slabs we have seen – but this design is crisper and carries exciting Space Age architectural features. Instead of blank end-walls, massive mosaic-covered

tapered columns splay out at the base like upside-down Ys. These 'dinosaur legs' would become Seifert hallmarks on which his skyscrapers would be mounted, allowing the space underneath to be free for other purposes – in this case a raised two-level car park. The columns repeat through the slab, carrying the weight of the concrete structure. A staircase rises up into the block at the western end between these legs. On the main service core, which breaks through one of the wide curtain-wall façades, odd trapezoid mosaic-covered loops like half-punched staples link the concrete of the floors either side. A long five-storey North Wing podium building emerges, also floating above a two-storey car park.

As with Seifert's first skyscraper, *Capital House*, Marks & Spencer have a big shop in the podium building. Recent refurbishments have given it a new marbled entrance. Local station Radio Jackie mounts its antenna on the tower. Tolworth Tower featured briefly in the classic British comedy film *The Sandwich Man* (1966) starring Michael Bentine, and more recently in the book *Boring Postcards* by Martin Parr.

Seifert was influenced by the Brazilian architect Oscar Niemeyer, architect of the then new capital Brasilia. Tolworth Tower demonstrated that Seifert, too, was a unique expressionist despite the limited possibilities of individuality in the International Style. It brings excitement to an otherwise bland suburb, and it is still as clean and crisp as the day it was finished.

Early Seifert legs

New London Bridge House, SE1
London Bridge Street

Tube/rail London Bridge
Height 94m, 25 storeys
Completed 1965
Architect R Seifert & Partners

This classic Seifert skyscraper faces demolition, On first glance, it seems a typical sixties office slab, but it has characteristic Seifert touches. First, it stands on tapered 'dinosaur legs', and secondly, a vertical crease folds the façade at a shallow angle so that the plan is not actually rectangular at all. The angularity of the design owes something to the Pirelli Building in Milan, which, like other architects, Seifert greatly admired. He later paid homage to it in his 1970 design of Birmingham's Alpha House, which would be that city's tallest for the rest of the century. Finally, New London Bridge House's top floor is a viewing gallery, although never opened to the public.

Developer Harry Hyams took his time before letting it, as he had at *Centre Point*, in this case until 1973. Standard Chartered had offices here into the new century. The block did get a refurb in the nineties, with a crude service tower added to the south, clad in the wrong colour. In 2003 the block was sold for £39.5m to the Sellar Property Group, developers of Renzo Piano's *Shard* next door. In 2005, Piano himself was brought in to tackle the site, now called No 1 London Bridge, He talked of 'bringing sunlight to adjacent Joiner Street that is a kingdom of darkness'. His design, a fifteen-storey glass office longer than it is high, has a curved profile, in contrast to *The Shard*, but, like it, will be an exercise in glass.

The Shard will be good news but it will be sad to lose New London Bridge House. The best skyscraper clusters contain a variety of styles, and this potential cluster, with Guy's Hospital, could have encompassed the International Style, Brutalism and the twenty-first century.

Telecom Tower, W1
(General Post Office Tower)
Howland Street, Fitzrovia

Tube Warren Street, Goodge Street,
Great Portland Street
Height 177m excluding mast, 26 storeys, 34 levels
Constructed 1961–1965
Architect Ministry of Public Building & Works

Once described as looking like an extraterrestrial rectal probe, the Telecom Tower is the most bizarre tower built in the 1960s. It's as if a committee of mad boffins had been allowed to build their own fantasy tower in the heart of London. Curiously, this is half true – communications engineers worked with the Ministry of Public Building and Works in the design. But the credit goes to the Ministry's chief architect, Eric Bedford, and his architect-in-charge, GR Yeats.

Lots of cities worldwide have communications towers, usually bare concrete shafts mounted with tele-vision transmitters and, sometimes, observation decks. These do the same job as London's then tallest structure, the 222m-high Crystal Palace television mast erected in 1950. They are not skyscrapers, but the Telecom Tower is – it has operational, enclosed floors for most of its height. Its main purpose, however, was to provide phone lines.

Microwave Dialogues
From the 1920s, the demand for long-distance 'trunk' calls was booming, but laying the trunk lines to carry them meant digging to bury cables, which in London was expensive and disruptive. The General Post Office (GPO), which was then in charge of the phone system, had tried carrying calls by microwave as early as 1934; after the war, the GPO planned a national network of concrete microwave towers. Transmitting microwaves across London would involve towers on the surround-ing hills, or a central tower at least 107m high. They had the perfect site for the latter.

London telephone numbers used to begin with three letters related to their location, and near the British Museum was the MUSeum exchange. It was only a few hundred metres from the BBC in Langham Place, so the site would be good for switching televi-sion feed as well. Finally, Bedford reckoned the locals wouldn't create problems defending the architecture around there – little in the decrepit Georgian jumble of Fitzrovia (as it would later be known) was then considered worth protecting.

The new New London Bridge House

New London Bridge House, 2005

The first plan for a Museum Radio Tower in 1956 was a square obelisk, housing equipment, topped with the aerials, with a medium-rise slab housing the telephone exchange. The plans evolved as Post Office engineers negotiated their technical requirements with the men from Ministry. In 1959 they made the tower circular in plan, to reduce lateral wind pressure, improving rigidity and probably giving it a chance against a Soviet atomic bomb shockwave. A bare concrete column supported a four-storey cantilevered cone housing equipment, with a Perspex-covered aerial structure above – a shape similar to many European communications towers. The 1960 plan looked like a huge fountain pen: equipment was now housed in floors wrapped around the concrete shaft, and above a brief gap were covered aerials. The government then decreed that there should be public viewing galleries. The final design that we see has the extraordinary 'rotunda' head, bristling with mysterious technical attachments. The design was wind-tested in the National Physics Laboratory, where it was found that it would sway just 19cm in 160km/h winds.

Structure

Construction started in June 1961. As the unfeasibly thin reinforced concrete core rose into the air, ring platforms for the floors were mounted around it, like stacked dinner plates. High above these, a new structure emerged, resembling nothing ever seen before. This rotunda was assembled without scaffolding, everything hoisted up in a square cage just 168cm on each side. The GPO Tower was topped out on 5 July 1964. Building contractor Peter Lind advertised in big letters around the top. From foundations 7.5m deep a cone of reinforced concrete rises from a 90cm-thick raft. The buried cone becomes a tube rising through the podium building housing the exchange. Above this it is exposed, but then disappears into 69 vertical metres of cantilevered floors, tapering gradually within from 10.5m diameter to 6.05m. The floors are curtain-walled in 4,500m² of triple-layer Antisun glass a centimetre thick, to keep equipment at a constant temperature. There is a roof at 109m.

Moving up, we find a 30.5m stretch of 'aerial galleries', where the microwave horns are mounted. Each horn is a transmitter, 8.25m high and weighing just over a tonne. The 2–6GHz microwaves emanate from a waveguide at the base of the horn and are reflected by the parabolic-reflector-shaped surface facing the mouth. The shiny purple skins across the mouths keep the horns airtight and keep birds and weather at bay. They have a capacity of 150,000 trunk calls and make the tower the hub of a network of 157 microwave relay stations, with the main link to a sister GPO Tower in Birmingham.

The cantilevered rotunda starts at 145m, with its roofline at 177m. This six-storey structure was designed for three floors of observation galleries tapering outwards, then a restaurant on the widest floor (20m in diameter), a cocktail bar above that, and kitchens on the top floor. The restaurant had a rotating floor that turned

Telecom Tower over Foster's British Museum roof

every 22 minutes. The 3m-wide revolving element weighing over 23 tonnes rolled on nylon tyres. The *Empress State Building* would have a similar rotating floor installed forty years later.

There is a final cantilevered structure above this, housing lift equipment and water tanks. Above that is the Meteorological Office's 12m storm warning mast. The tower included a National Television Switching Centre (NTVSC), to distribute (but not transmit) television around the UK among broadcasters, studios and transmitters. The BBC and ITV, foreign broadcasters, ad agencies and others all generated television feed, so the centre was built to handle forty channels.

Two lifts reached the top in just thirty seconds, and they would last thirty-nine years. The whole tower and foundations weigh 13,208 tonnes. The construction costs had been a mere £2.5m, or £9m including equipment. The GPO Tower was hardly a discreet building, but under the Official Secrets Act its location was officially a secret, until MP Kate Hoey blew its cover in Parliament in 1993.

Power over London

On 8 October 1965, Prime Minister Harold Wilson and his wife Mary opened the GPO Tower with Sir Billy Butlin. The Butlins family business, famous for low-cost British family holiday complexes, had taken the restaurant franchise. From the third floor, Wilson made a microwave call to the Lord Mayor of Birmingham, who was probably too polite to complain that his city was getting a 152m-high sister tower that was merely a bare, square concrete stick.

On 19 May 1966 the Queen opened the public viewing galleries. The Postmaster-General, Anthony Wedgwood-Benn, gave her a 22-carat 5cm gold model of the tower. The galleries were an instant success – queues snaked out from the Cleveland Mews entrance and 1.5 million

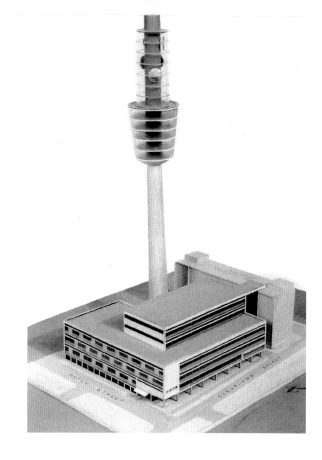

Museum Tower proposal

visitors were clocked up in the first year. The galleries remained open till 9.30 at night. Above them, 'The Top of The Tower' restaurant ran a brisk business, especially with its £2.50 set lunch, including 40p for the lift ride. A photographer floated around. Customers who spent too long in the toilet might be confused to find their table had moved right around the room when they came out.

The sixties were the heyday for the tower, and VIP visitors included Soviet premier Kosygin and world heavyweight boxing champion Cassius Clay (later Muhammed Ali). Paul McCartney organised a press reception for *Postcard*, the album by Mary Hopkin, just signed to the Beatles' own record label, Apple. His future wife Linda Eastman attended, along with Jimmy Hendrix and Donovan. In May 1969, aircraft circled the tower as well as the Empire State Building in New York, to complete the Daily Mail Air Race.

The GPO Tower symbolised Britain's 'White Heat of Technology' which Wedgwood-Benn fostered at the Vickers Tower (now *Millbank Tower*). It suggested a new world, where technology was taking on a life of its own, on a different level to the day-to-day life in the street. It was almost as if a machine was up there, watching over London and making silent plans. This was precisely what Wotan, the evil computer in the 1966 BBC *Dr Who* adventure 'The War Machines', was up to. As soon as Dr Who (then played by William Hartnell) stepped out of his Tardis, he felt something sinister in the air, and looked up to see the new tower. It confirmed his unease. Up in the rotunda, Wotan was masterminding its War Machines, which looked like giant shoe-cleaning automats rampaging through the streets of London.

Wotan was nothing on the giant mutant cat that actually wrestles the tower down in The Goodies' *Kitten Kong* TV episode. Strangely, it was broadcast just a fortnight after an IRA bomb exploded in the lowest viewing gallery one night in October 1971. The tower's

Rotunda and horns

core was barely scratched, but a void was blasted in the rotunda's skin. After restoration in 1973, the viewing galleries never re-opened to the public. A total of 4,632,822 visitors had enjoyed them. The restaurant stayed open until its lease ran out in 1980.

The Post Office Tower ceased to be the UK's tallest when the NatWest Tower (now *Tower 42*) was topped out in 1977. British Telecom was spun off from the Post Office in 1981, and became Mrs Thatcher's pioneering privatisation in 1984. The tower became the London Telecom Tower, then the British Telecom Tower, then the BT Tower, before settling down as the Telecom Tower. The rotunda is now The Tower Suite for BT's corporate entertainment. Nowadays, optical fibres carry trunk calls, but the microwave links are still in use.

Retro Future Now
What is the architectural significance of the Grade II-listed Telecom Tower? Bedford has a sketchy architectural record – his only other skyscraper design was the despised Ministry of Environment on Marsham Street. These three twenty-storey slabs were perhaps the ugliest in London, ever, and were demolished in 2003. Yet in 1965, *Architectural Review* had compared Bedford's GPO Tower's profile to a Wren steeple, and its horns to Wren's cupolas. It was admired as engineering-led 'innocent' architecture – innocent of the style pretensions of architects. It was modern, but of a technological modernity rather than Modernism. The Telecom Tower was about the future – and it turned out to be the future of architecture as well as communications.

Only Archigram made designs like the Telecom Tower, but they were never built. It was also London's first round skyscraper. Circular design would resurface in 2003 at *30 St Mary Axe*. The Telecom Tower was also London's first structure in which, above the podium, all the floor space is cantilevered, like *Tower 42*. The meteorological mast was a precedent for the 'aerial farms' that would crowd skyscraper roofs when mobile phone networks spread in the 1990s. The sealed triple-glazing climate control anticipates the triple glazing of vented façades in green skyscrapers from the 1990s onwards.

Finally, the exposure of technical equipment on the outside anticipates the High Tech Post-Modernism of Richard Rogers, where service structures such as pipes,

lifts and water tanks are on show: this would come to London two decades later in the *Lloyd's Building*. High-Tech, like the Telecom Tower, celebrates components by making them a building's signature.

Nowadays, the Telecom Tower's signature has become brilliantly sci-fi retro, but in detail, it really did preview much future that is now the present.

Centre Point, WC1
St Giles Circus

Tube Tottenham Court Road
Height 121m, 35 storeys
Commissioned 1959
Constructed 1962–65
Architect Richard Seifert & Partners

Some hate this building, yet it's probably the best twentieth-century skyscraper in Europe. Even at the height of Centre Point's notoriety, a few critics could see through the controversy to recognise the sheer quality of the design. The artist Eduardo Paolozzi said it was London's first Pop Art building, and it still dazzles like no other from the Swinging Sixties. Centre Point is not like its International Style contemporaries – it challenges the monotony of stacking endless identical floors by housing them in a huge, hypnotic honeycomb façade. Nor is it another box – this is a slender blade of a tower, so slender that even slabs look fat against it. Centre Point invites the wind to blow the building over, and each floor is so thin it can only accommodate about forty people. Yet its wide façades are not flat, but subtly convex. Its podium is no bog-standard low-rise, but a crazy mix of 'dinosaur legs', concrete slits and a glass bridge so vast, it's a functions venue in its own right. Centre Point is also brilliant engineering, marking a major advance in the way the load is carried. Finally, it is the quintessence of the 'landmark building' – in 3m-high letters it spells out exactly what it is, London's 'CENTRE POINT'.

The area has a less-than-salubrious history. St Giles was once a leper colony, then an ale stop for men on their way to be hanged at Tyburn; it was the inspiration for Hogarth's Gin Lane, then for the noisome slums of Dickens' *Bleak House*. Across the road lies Soho and its sex businesses, while below Centre Point is Denmark Street, a.k.a. Tin Pan Alley, where once pop charts were manipulated through payola bungs. Centre Point, too has a sketchy past...

Notorious
Why is Centre Point so notorious? First, developer Harry Hyams got permission to build through a dubious deal, and, secondly, he became very rich by leaving the building empty for fifteen years. Of all London's property speculators, Hyams was the master. In 2005, the *Sunday Times Rich List* valued Hyams at £320m, much of it derived from Centre Point...

The story starts in 1956, when the LCC decided St Giles Circus should become a roundabout. To do that, they needed property owned by the Pearlberg family, who operated their Ve-ri-best Manufacturing Company

GPO Tower under construction

there. However, two compulsory purchase notices were served, and the decision as to which was valid got bogged down with the Lands Tribunal. In 1958, Hyams was introduced to the Chairman of the LCC's Town Planning Committee, Richard Edmonds, and proposed a deal. If Hyams could deliver the whole site for the roundabout, the LCC would allow him to build offices with an amazing plot ratio of 10:1, twice the maximum allowed. It was illegal to sell planning permission, and a new Town & Country Planning Act was coming in which would also make it illegal to grant planning approval on unsecured sites. Thus, the deal was never written up. In August 1959, just a few days before the act came into force, Seifert submitted architectural plans. Hyams felt confident about finishing the land acquisition because he could buy out at market rates rather than the pre-war rates set by the LCC. By 1962, the whole site had been collected, and Hyams sold it to the LCC for £1.5m, and leased back the building plot for £18,500 annually for 150 years. Construction started immediately.

Centre Point was topped out in 1964, just as the Ministry of Transport decided they didn't want a roundabout after all. It had cost a huge £5.5m to build. At its base, a massive sign proclaiming 'TO LET' was mounted… and stayed there. For fifteen years. In fact, Hyams was gaining on two fronts – there were no rates to pay on an empty building, and Centre Point's capital value was rising faster than inflation. Since the value was based on potential rent, and rents were rising in the sixties, to let it would be to freeze the value of it. In 1973 it was valued at £20m, at the peak of the market.

All this made people angry about Centre Point. But what of the building itself?

Credit

The original design had quite plain façades. Seifert's widow, Josephine, said in 2005: 'It was me who scrapped it. It was ordinary. My husband decided to start all over again'. In 1989, Seifert's partner George Marsh said it was he who had drawn up Centre Point, and that 'the aesthetics were to get away from the box architecture of the time'. His signed drawings had been published in an Italian architectural magazine in 1968. Since he was in charge of the project, he obviously would have executed drawings. Recently, Jonathan Glancey in *The Guardian* has portrayed Marsh and Seifert as rather like Ken Shuttleworth and Norman Foster (see *30 St Mary Axe*), or even Christopher Wren and Hawksmoor (who really designed odd bits of St Paul's?). The suggestion is of a quiet genius working in the background while the credit goes elsewhere. But this was not the case with Centre Point. The key to the design dates from 1961 – pre-cast concrete T-sections framing the windows, with the horizontal arms of the T angled like wings, creating the façade's honeycomb-like illusion. David Esdale, a Seifert draftsman at the time, clearly remembers Seifert coming in at 7.30 one morning, with the original sketches on foolscap paper of the T-sections which he'd designed overnight. Josephine Seifert is quite clear: 'George Marsh did not design it'.

These concrete T-sections were bolted together, and so the construction was 'dry' rather than 'wet', which meant there was no need for scaffolding and construction was rapid. It was designed as the tallest pre-cast concrete structure in the world. Although Centre Point has two narrow service cores inside, the façade also carries load. This makes Centre Point's structural concept similar to the 'tube-in-tube' idea of Fazlur Khan, pioneered in Chicago's Brunswick Building. Another tower pioneering load-carrying perimeter concrete walls was Eero Saarinen's CBS Building in New York, whose design, interestingly, is echoed in a later Seifert skyscraper, *Windsor House*. The Chicago and New York towers were built simultaneously with Centre Point.

The 'dinosaur' legs below the tower are covered in mosaic. At its top are two viewing gallery floors, sadly never opened to the public, but on the open one, accessible only by stairs, the big neon CENTRE POINT letters are now mounted. The site also included the notorious on-off blue fountain pool on the Charing Cross Road, which makes it impossible to cross the road. Originally a bank, shop and pub sat beneath the glass bridge, where the popular Point 101 bar is now. Finally, a seven-storey block with thirty-six maisonettes is mounted above a podium of showrooms behind the tower, to meet the LCC's demand for housing there.

After the Seifert design was originally presented, the RFAC objected, but since the LCC had not referred the design to them for approval, there was nothing they could do. The RFAC would have pressed for a height reduction, a dull call they would invariably make with Seifert skyscrapers thereafter. A long time later, the RFAC would finally get it, and praise Centre Point's slender tower as comparable to a Wren spire. In 1990, the first attempt was made to list Centre Point. On the third attempt in 1994, environment secretary Virginia Bottomley listed the building Grade II.

Two views of Centre Point

Gimme Shelter

In the 60s, Hyams claimed he was waiting for the right single tenant. British Steel were talked about. Centre Point's rent was set at £1.25m annually in 1968, but negotiations with music giant EMI failed the next year. Tiny Rowland's African trading vehicle Lonrho almost moved in, but decided in 1971 that the air-conditioning was inadequate. In his book *Beneath the City Streets* Peter Laurie wondered if Hyams didn't have a tenant all along. He speculated that Centre Point comprised secret government offices on standby for a chemical or biological attack – because it was air-conditioned, perhaps it could be sealed off from the atmosphere.

In 1973, Camden Council, with a long waiting list of council tenants, started a campaign to acquire the empty flats. Meanwhile, the pedestrian subways, connecting to Tottenham Court Road tube station, became shabby and haunted by the homeless. A charity for young rough sleepers was actually named after the building in 1969, and set up in the subways in the 1970s. The outrage about empty offices and homeless people came to a head in a headline-grabbing event in 1974...

Burns International Security Services were employed to patrol the building. In late 1973, two men signed up as guards, using the false names Jones and Donovan. They enabled two accomplices posing as engineers to pass in and out of the building unchallenged. The 'engineers' were inside on 18 January 1974. At 5.05pm, a woman contacted them at the entrance, then crossed over to the tube station. There, 50 activists, including nurses, lawyers and Labour councillors, had converged from different directions to avoid attention. At 5.20, she gave them the signal: 'All systems go'. Jones and Donovan entered the building at 5.29, informing the real security guards that they were taking the building over. For a moment, the guards understood that as meaning the night shift had arrived, but when they saw the crowd piling in behind them, one pulled out a cosh. He withdrew it when he understood that this was a peaceful protest. The leaders, Jim Radford and Ron Bailey, issued a statement that concluded: 'This building ... is a symbol of corruption in this society'.

The squatters spent most of the time debating, and complaining about the cold as they bedded down in sleeping bags on the concrete floors. Outside, police surrounded Centre Point. Negotiations began; after two days, the squatters voted to accept a police offer to take no names. When they stepped out, a crowd of 2,500 outside cheered.

Hyams seemed to get the message. He dropped his insistence on a single tenant, and in 1975 a Greek shipping company called AGELEF took the fifth floor, the sole tenants. Hyams was officially exonerated of any malpractice, but was cleared. Only in 1979 did a big tenant appear – the Confederation of British Industry, who moved into fourteen floors a year later, spending £3m on upgrading the facilities. From the tower, they could overlook their traditional adversaries the Trades Union Congress, a few blocks away.

Hyams sold Oldham Estates in 1988, getting £150m from a property group called MEPC. They commissioned architects Allies & Morrison to refurbish the block, but their plan to replace the concrete entrance never bore fruit. The CBI quit in 1989. MEPC were taken over in 2000, netting Hyams another £98m. When Centre Point was refurbished in 2002/3, English Heritage worked with architects Gaunt Francis Associates to see that the building's features remained intact. After that, Centre Point was sold for £90m.

Despite its protection, there are fears that excavations for Crossrail, the giant rail scheme that also threatens *The Barbican*, could literally undermine Centre Point in the next decade.

London's Greatest Skyscraper?

Nowadays, *30 St Mary Axe* is considered London's most exciting skyscraper. It and Centre Point have a lot in common, such as their state-of-the-art engineering, even the controversy about which architect deserves credit. But there are also many differences – not least, their locations. The City is about making money, while the West End is about spending it, and Centre Point is like a huge marker for all the shopping, drinking and clubbing focused intensely below it. With the surging night crowds and wailing police sirens, all beneath the looming height of a great skyscraper, it's as near as London gets to Midtown New York. But this is a Pop skyscraper, uniquely local, and with a lightness of touch none of its contemporaries can match.Only the blind or terminally grumpy can fail to be dazzled.

Chapter 3:
The Rise and Fall
of the Tower Block

Almost all skyscrapers everywhere are either offices or homes, and most high-rise housing is the type of social housing usually referred to as tower blocks. In the UK, tower blocks were planned and built by local authorities from the 1950s. They spread to virtually every corner of the UK in the sixties. Even historic towns such as Bath built them, but in the big cities, such as Birmingham and Leeds, veritable forests of tower blocks grew. When the idea of tower blocks was finally abandoned in the late sixties, almost 350 had been built in London of 50 metres or higher. In 2004, about 290 still stand, accounting for over sixty per cent of all skyscrapers across the city, and housing about 1 per cent of the city's population. This is a lot, but approximately half of all the UK's twenty-storey-plus tower blocks sit in Glasgow, and about ten percent of the city lives in blocks of ten storeys or more.

We all know that London emerged from World War Two victorious, but exhausted and battered. Hundreds of thousands were homeless – in Greater London, 106,000 houses had been obliterated and over ten times that figure needed repairs. Even if there had been no war, there was another problem – the appalling state of working-class slums. Overcrowding and bad sanitation conditions, not unlike those in third-world cities today, were commonplace. According to the LCC, which administered the inner London boroughs and Woolwich, eighteen per cent of households had to share a bathroom, while forty-four per cent had no bath at all; additionally, thirty-five per cent of households had to share a toilet and sixteen per cent a kitchen sink. That was as late as 1951. For the new Labour government under Clement Attlee in 1945, housing was high up on the socialist agenda. Initially, the government could only administer a massive band-aid solution of house repairs and one-storey prefabs, many of which latter would remain for decades.

However, the 1947 Town and Country Planning Act placed London's planning in the hands of the LCC.

The Blitz had left huge tracts of London in ruins – in the old boroughs of Islington, Finsbury and Shoreditch, nineteen per cent of the built-up area had been destroyed, while Bermondsey and Greenwich had lost fifteen per cent. This devastation was to provide a clean slate for the LCC to tackle public housing on a huge scale. The LCC's Architects' Department under Robert Matthew (who would later design *New Zealand House*) became key in introducing the new in-vogue architectural style of Modernism to the UK at the Festival of Britain on the South Bank in 1951.

The new generation of LCC architects had a strong Utopian socialist vision of housing schemes, and a deep urge to build a new Jerusalem for Britain based on that vision, which was drawn chiefly from the ideas of, Le Corbusier.

Le Corbusier

Who was Le Corbusier, and what were his big ideas? Born Charles Edouard Jeanneret in a Swiss watchmaking town in 1895, his first house design in local style was built when he was just eighteen. However, a series of key encounters ignited a unique vision. In 1907 in Lyons he met Tony Garnier, a radical socialist architect who in 1904 had first proposed a planned Utopian industrial city for workers. Le Corbusier was blown away by such ideas. Meanwhile, in Paris, Auguste Perret had built a pioneering block of flats supported not by masonry or steel but by reinforced concrete. Le Corbusier worked with Perret there in 1908, and was converted to the wonders of concrete. Henceforth, much of his work was to be about grand urban planning and creating concrete forms. A third crucial influence followed in 1910, when Le Corbusier

visited Germany and saw how modern production technology was giving industry a world-beating edge. This made him think in terms of seeking solutions through engineering, and ultimately he would see his designs as machines. By 1915 he had developed and refined the idea of building from pre-assembled standard units, giving modern architecture the basis of modular construction and structure.

In 1922 Le Corbusier went into practice with his cousin Pierre (who kept the Jeanneret family name). That year they revealed plans for a Ville Contemporaine, a theoretical city for a population of three million, to be laid out on a spaced-out grid centred around two dozen sixty-storey cruciform-plan office blocks. Particularly influential were his projected twelve-storey walls of housing, with double-height flats overlooking communal rectangles of greenery. Socialist thinking at the time was that both worker and intellectual would be collectively empowered by delivering everyone work, decent housing and cradle-to-grave welfare, and Le Corbusier was offering an architecture for that. In 1930 he designed a highly zoned Ville Radieuse where every-thing, including the roads, floated above the ground,

and flats were stacked in long glass curtain-walled terraces. His most celebrated public housing actually built was the Unité d'Habitation, completed in 1952 in Marseilles. It's an eighteen-storey slab raised on fat concrete legs; across the plane façades, divided by the grid of the block's concrete frame, concrete brise-soleils reduce the impact of the solar gain (sunshine heating a building up). Various concrete shapes resem-bling objects in a Surrealist painting sit on the roof, which is a communal facility and includes a children's swimming pool. Concrete formed into shapes became characteristic of the Brutalist style.

When we look at the worst architectural aspects of bad council estates (the so-called 'sink estates'), most of them can be traced back to Le Corbusier. Walkways above the ground, monotonously repeating modular flats, flat roofs, rigid rectilinear lines, concrete every-where and sheer scale – these are the design aspects that make many council estates dehumanising. Although often opposed by socialist intellectuals, Le Corbusier's large-scale plans were in fact about achieving socialist ideals through social engineering, even if this could only come about by being imposed on the people. Still, his intentions were good, and it's difficult to argue against, for example, providing space and light for all, or making construction more efficient by using industrially produced building elements. Despite effectively being responsible for inventing the sink estate, Le Corbusier's ideals did work in early post-war housing schemes.

Unité d' Habitation

Churchill Gardens

New LCC Estates

The first major post-war estate to build high was at Churchill Gardens, by Powell & Moya, commissioned in 1946 with the backing of Communist councillors in the City of Westminster who hoped to slip a working-class enclave in just down the road from Parliament. Work started in 1950. Positioning ten-storey blocks to catch the sun between open spaces met Corbusian ideals of airy communal living, but the brick-clad

blocks are dull and reminded one contemporary observer of German housing projects.

In 1953, a plan by architects Hosburgh & Kadleigh to build residential towers 103m high on Paddington Goods Yard was aired, but nothing came of it. In the same year, the Modular Society was named after Le Corbusier's 'Le Modular' system, promoting the idea of uniform modular building elements. This would lead to the system-building construction of council estates.

Still in 1953, Matthew's deputy John Leslie Martin took over the LCC Architects Department, and Corbusian housing schemes moved from the imagination to the construction site. The first medium-rise blocks by the LCC went up on the Alton Estate in Roehampton, southwest London, planned under Matthew and completed in 1956. It has a mix of traditionally scaled low-rise houses, long slabs where flats are built along a linear spine, and 'point blocks', which stacked flats around a central service core. Roehampton's 39m-high eleven-storey point blocks were set in open spaces, and the whole estate still feels like a Corbusian masterplan.

Tower blocks really took off after a decision by the Conservative government in 1956 to give public high-rise flats a subsidy three times greater than that on new houses. In elections, Labour and Conservatives started to compete to outdo each other with ever-higher targets for new public housing. They reckoned the tower block was the only way to achieve high population densities for London and still provide open space – an argument similar to the views of many twenty-first century architects.

Most high-rise schemes were to rise amid the slums of East and South London, where the Blitzkrieg had done most damage. Here, local borough councils often competed with the LCC to build new estates. They tended to be Labour boroughs – in the west, Tories held local councils and they were less keen on tower blocks. Initially, Corbusian slabs rather than point blocks dominated plans. In 1955, eleven-storey slabs started to go up on the Loughborough Road Estate in Brixton.

Somerset Estate towers

The borough of Camberwell, since absorbed by Southwark, had London's highest amount of public housing construction between 1946 and 1962. The council's own architects under FO Hayes designed the long fifteen-storey slabs of Sceaux Gardens Estate, finished 1960. Meanwhile, in Bethnal Green, the fifteen-storey *Keeling House*, a revolutionary cluster point block, had been completed in 1959. Here, the architect Denys Lasdun fully expected that the sense of community of the old East End would find a new home in his vertical street.

System-Building Addiction

The first truly high-rise tower block – reaching over 50m – was *Great Arthur House*, completed in 1957. Its designers Chamberlain, Powell & Bon came together when one of them won a competition to design high-density housing for the City's Golden Lane Estate, in which *Great Arthur House* is the centrepiece. It's a brilliant realisation of Le Corbusier's ideas, even down to the sculpted concrete form and pool on the roof of the tower. As soon as it was finished, the partnership began work on *The Barbican*, of which more later.

Warwick Crescent Estate

Golden Lane was a small estate with just one tower, but elsewhere, on larger estates, tower blocks would not only get higher but also appear in groups, each a clone of its neighbour. The LCC's *Brandon Estate* in Camberwell was completed in 1959 with six towers 52m high. In 1961, over in West London, the LCC started work on six twenty-one-storey towers stretched out along Maida Vale's Warwick Crescent Estate, each 62m high, the last not being completed until 1968. In 1963, Lewisham Council Architects went to twenty-six storeys and 78m in their designs for the three tower blocks of the Pepys Estate (one of which was the *Aragon Tower*). At about this time, the LCC were publishing plans for an estate in Erith in Kent that would include thirty-one-storey towers, built with modular sections of four storeys that cantilevered from their cores. These had a futuristic look, like model buildings in a Gerry Anderson sci-fi TV set. They were never built, but that basic design formula would be recycled in the twenty-one-storey Canada Estate at Canada Water in Southwark, the Somerset Estate in Wandsworth, and, later, the twenty-two-storey Wyndham Estate in Southwark.

In 1965, Harold Wilson's Labour government passed the Housing Act, which reduced the subsidy on tower blocks. A 'Housing Cost Yardstick' was introduced to limit council spending, but there were also new cash incentives for slum clearance. The tower-block bonanza moved from sites that had been blitzed to built-up neighbourhoods where old houses could have been upgraded. In the same year, the LCC became the Greater London Council (GLC),

Cotton Gardens Estate, Lambeth

extending its manor from the inner city into the suburban boroughs. The LCC had built about one hundred point blocks, and their taste for them was inherited by the GLC. Tower blocks were trumpeted as great social advances, and dignitaries would be wheeled out to make speeches on their opening.

The sixties were the heyday of the tower block. Corbusian ideals lived on in the sixties, but were fading fast. Applying the Housing Cost Yardstick meant that humanising Corbusian features such as roof terraces and community facilities were dropped. However, Corbusian modularity thrived. The construction industry was becoming increasingly professional, recruiting qualified civil engineers, who absorbed functionalist ideals from architects. 'System building' did for building what Ford had done for cars. It formalised fast-track construction methods, such as the Swedish Larsen-Nielsen and Albetong systems, which were licensed to building contractors. Larsen-Nielsen used industrially produced components ranging from wall panels to fitted kitchens, and made its UK debut in Greenwich in 1963. Wates had their own system for pre-cast panels, co-developed by engineers Ove Arup, helping them build twelve per cent of all UK tower blocks from 1963–73 (Wimpey built the most tower blocks in this period – twenty-four per cent of the total constructed). These systems made tower blocks ever

faster and apparently cheaper to knock up. In fact, subsidies disguised the fact that it was generally cheaper to refurbish old buildings, or build on a traditional scale, than go high-rise.

The architect's mission had changed from creating decent dwellings for the common man to packing in as many families as quickly and cheaply as possible, and councils had become addicted to housing targets. To fulfil them, the cartel of national building contractors was keen to keep councils dependent on tower-block projects that only system-building methods could deliver. This created a sort of dealer-junkie relationship, with builders as the dealers. While design declined, corruption and shoddy construction were on the rise.

There were a few notable exceptions to the decline of design standards. Away from the reality of actually having commissions, Warren Chalk of the Archigram group, radical architectural fantasists of the time, imagined a modular block in his Capsule Tower of 1963. Inspired by the Post Office Tower (now *Telecom Tower*) he designed modules to stack over cantilevered ledges, but these were never built.

In the real world, the LCC architect Hubert Bennett retained his idealism while other local government architects became agents of the construction cartel. His work includes *Draper House* in Elephant & Castle, and, later, the dazzling *Luxborough Tower* near Baker Street, not completed until 1972. Lambeth Council also came up with good designs. Under E Hollamby, it built Brutalist concrete tower blocks in Kennington and Stockwell that have a similar complexity to *The Barbican* towers (see pp 102–03).

The most ambitious tower-block scheme was Lambeth Council's Brixton Town Centre redevelopment. In 1967, they proposed no less than fourteen tower blocks averaging thirty storeys, grouped around a new main road that was virtually a motorway. The scheme was amended two years later to have just eleven towers, and, as the years passed, it was gradually chipped away until in 1982 the only remaining element left was a supermarket site redevelopment.

Goldfinger, the Last Idealist

London's greatest tower block architect was Ernö Goldfinger. He was born in Budapest in 1902 and studied in Paris from 1923. There, like Le Corbusier, he fell under the concrete spell of Auguste Perret. Goldfinger became a structural rationalist who believed that 'it must always be possible to see how and feel how a building is supported'. The biggest influence was Le Corbusier himself – Goldfinger took on board his ideas such as double-height apartments, grid boxes to slot them into, and concrete exteriors. He disliked suburban sprawl, and thought that city dwellers should be concentrated in tall blocks. As early as 1933, he designed a twenty-three-storey housing block that incorporated a nursery, infants' school and communal restaurant – it was not built, but it predates Le Corbusier's Unité d'Habitation, which is pretty much the same concept. The same year, Goldfinger helped organise the Congrès International d'Architecture Moderne, which regularly brought together many of Europe's leading Modernists. This congress was held on a cruise ship, and from it Le Corbusier issued the Athens Charter spelling out the group's socialist-inspired visions of zoned cities.

In 1927, Goldfinger had designed a Modernist shop for Helena Rubinstein in Grafton Street, but it wasn't until 1934 that he moved to London. He was a Marxist, and his works in the thirties included commissions for the British Communist Party and the *Daily Worker* newspaper. As the war started, Goldfinger took up residence in a house of his own design in Willow Road, Hampstead. He even designed the furniture to make his house a total Modernist experience. After the war, he was well placed to contribute to London's rebuilding, but commissions were slow. A 1955 plan with HT Cadbury-Brown to build a twenty-seven-storey office block at Moorgate came to nothing, probably because he rejected the emerging International Style, but shortly afterwards he was commissioned to design a government ministry headquarters (now *Metro Central Heights*) at Elephant & Castle. However, it is his social housing that marks Goldfinger out as a giant amongst architects. He applauded the emerging tower blocks, declaring in 1962 that slabs 'are cheaper to build, more economic to rent, and show a higher investment [return] on a long term'.

His breakthrough was in 1965 in Poplar, where he designed an estate that separated the housing blocks from service towers incorporating lifts and stairs, along with boiler houses – some perched in rather odd places. The estate's tower block, the *Balfron Tower*, for example, mounted its boiler house at the top of the lift tower. Goldfinger recycled this form on a larger scale in his last design, the *Trellick Tower*. The service tower there creates the stunning icon that dominates North Kensington, and is almost certainly the most famous tower block in the world. Goldfinger had such faith in his housing visions that he moved into the *Balfron Tower*, although he soon returned to Hampstead, where he stayed until his death in 1987.

Even with designs as good as those of Goldfinger, there were increasing signs that the inhabitants of the new tower blocks were not happy. The social problems of sink estates and tower blocks would explode in the 1970s.

Tower Blocks Fall

It was exploding gas that turned the tide. On 17 May 1968, a shoddily built Larsen-Nielsen system twenty-three-storey block in Canning Town called Ronan Point hit the headlines when all the floors on one corner collapsed like a stack of cards, following a gas explosion in a kitchen. Five people were killed. The GLC evacuated 5,000 tenants from blocks whose construction meant that the disaster could be repeated, and the government swiftly abolished its handouts for building tower blocks.

Tower blocks had become vertical slums. Broken lifts trapped elderly tenants unable to tackle stairs, and mothers lived in fear that their small children

would fall out of windows. Common areas were vandalised and filled with rubbish and anti-social types. A new sort of tenant was thriving in the crannies behind the concrete wall panels – the cockroach. It was not actually the point blocks that hosted the worst problems, but medium-rise slab estates, where high-level walkways and open stairs became adventure playgrounds for adolescent gangs, and muggers and drug dealers established bases in corners thick with the stench of urine. The sense of community had been destroyed along with with the tight low-rise urban fabric that council estates had replaced. Tower blocks were the obvious symbols of a failed social experiment, none more so than the *Trellick Tower*, with its junkie-infested graffiti-decorated landings and lifts that felt like gang-rape boxes.

The arrogance of socialist architects in forcing people to live their utopian ideals is at the heart of the failure of tower blocks. Richard Seifert, the greatest commercial skyscraper architect of the sixties, was against high-rise living, and, as his widow recalls, always maintained that 'it's alright if you're a millionaire'. When James Bond author Ian Fleming met Goldfinger, he so disliked him that he named a Bond villain after him, although whether that was because of Goldfinger's arrogant character or arrogant ideals is not clear. Goldfinger would later say 'I built tower blocks for people to live there, and now they have messed them up – disgusting'.

Already, the architectural challenge of social housing had moved to medium-rise social housing, such as Patrick Hodgkinson's Brunswick Square complex from the early sixties, or Neave Brown's linear Alexandra Road project in Swiss Cottage, designed in 1968. However, tower blocks already approved were yet to work their way through the system. The last major tower block scheme, the World's End Estate in Chelsea, was not completed until 1977. Its warm brick cladding is very different from the slapdash finish of prefabricated panels, which would have been unthinkable by this time.

The collapse of Ronan Point

By 1979, the first tower block demolitions started in Merseyside. That year, the Conservatives came to power, and the entire ideal of public housing was rejected. Tenants were soon encouraged to become homeowners with right-to-buy schemes, which offered them their homes at prices way below market rates. In the eighties, one-fifth of London's social housing became private property. Mrs Thatcher's market-orientated economy created new 'loadsamoney' working-class entrepreneurs, and a reinvigorated 'yuppie' middle class was there to buy their services – and the homes they had lived in.

However, tower-block flats were only a small part of this property privatisation. A tower block was just as likely to be a temporary transmission base for the early eighties' rise of pirate radio stations broadcasting unlicensed music. Stations like Alice's Restaurant and Thameside mounted rigs on tower blocks, which gave more reach than transmitters on conventional roofs. Especially in South London, black stations such as LWR reached a hungry street-wise inner-city audience below. Sadly, the pirate radio scene started to turn ugly, with thugs breaking into bedroom studios to steal their rival's kit mid-broadcast. In 1990, when Kiss FM gained an official licence, London's great tower block radio era was over. Pirates still pop up on tower blocks (see *Shearsmith House*), but it's rare. In the nineties, it was mobile-phone operators who requisitioned tower block roofs for radio, and local authorities created a new income stream from the base-station rents.

Hackney Council blew up more tower blocks than any other borough – nineteen by 2003. Rachel Whiteread is an artist always concerned with urban living spaces, and she photographed some of this from 1993 to 1996 in her *Demolished* series, and commented that the tower block was 'something that is going to be completely forgotten – the detritus of our culture'. Her pictures can be seen in Tate Britain.

In this century, tower blocks are not blamed for social problems. Everyone now acknowledges that concentrating people into ghettoes with inadequate youth facilities, bad schools and thin employment opportunities is asking for trouble.

The Other Welfare Towers

Tower blocks were not the only signature of the welfare state on city skylines before Mrs Thatcher's time. There was also the National Health Service. The 1960s saw hospitals planned and built in numbers unseen since Victorian times, on a bigger scale, and with the intention of bringing state-of-the-art technology to the sick, both in medical equipment and building infrastructure, which was far more complicated than social housing or offices. Big hospitals needed to circulate air and heat on an industrial scale, as well as deliver rarer services such as distilled water and vacuum. Plant machinery and installation could amount to a fifth of hospital construction budgets.

Two behemoths punctuated the London skyline, both costing about £10m to build, and both concrete monsters. *Guy's Hospital*'s new tower became the tallest medical building in the world, while the new *Charing Cross Hospital* dwarfed its surroundings in Fulham. By coincidence, they were both opened by the Queen within a month in 1974.

Taking a Shine to Tower Blocks

The key event to kick-start the revival of the tower block was the 1988 re-cladding of *Parsons House*, a brick-clad disaster on the Edgware Road with typically atrocious structural problems. The architect appointed to refurbish it, Peter Bell, had a pioneering record of re-cladding houses to look like fridges. After his attentions, the drab tower re-emerged not only with a new shiny skin, but also with red mullions and an exuberant red roof superstructure that metamorphosed it into an eye-catching icon. Thenceforth, the worst tower blocks might just have a future!

Tower blocks elsewhere have since been similarly restyled with weatherproof panels and new roof structures, as with Camden's Mornington Crescent towers. Some have been crowned with pitched roofs, such as Wandsworth's Arndale Centre towers or Tower Hamlets' Westferry towers (which try to echo the pyramid roof of nearby *One Canada Square*). Such physical improvements really started to make a difference in the nineties. Hackney's refurbishment strategy pioneered change of use — it spent £10m on a tower called Grange Court in the Holly Road Estate to make it a kid-free zone for the over-fifties.

Even the worst tower-block council estates that were once no-man's-lands now have some police presence. Examples include the Broadwater Farm Estate in Tottenham, where PC Keith Blakelock was hacked to death during riots in 1985, and the Stonebridge Estate in Brent, a notorious hell of drug dealing and gangs. The estates still have problems, but the security of the buildings themselves has been transformed with buzzer-entry doors and concierges.

Some of the better-designed estates, such as Camberwell's *Brandon Estate*, have now been listed by English Heritage. No tower sank socially more than Goldfinger's *Trellick Tower*, but, by the time it was listed in 1998, it was already one of the coolest places to live in London and one of the hottest blocks to buy into. A tenants' association had turned the place around, installing security and cleaning the place up. The changes were so effective that crime rates fell even *outside* the building. That pattern has been repeated with tower blocks all over London.

Demolishing a tower block can cost a tenth as much as refurbishing it, but there are good reasons for spending the extra money. Tower blocks have a small footprint on the increasingly precious land, they are generally located near local borough town centres, they can be made energy efficient, and, with security, make good locations for elderly communities. They are also suitable for a younger sort of person, without children to keep an eye on...

Le Corbusier for the Rich

The refurbishment of tower blocks has enabled the biggest twist in their history — their colonisation by yuppie tenants. Tower blocks may once have been a bleak prospect, but, especially where the original architecture was good, there's now no shortage of middle-class demand for them.

Refurbishment has seen many blocks follow the *Trellick Tower* in creating a mix of council or housing association tenants and private owners. Flats at the top of some of Lambeth's Brutalist concrete towers have been sold for big money, which has subsidised the rest of the blocks. Some blocks have been sold in their entirety by the council to private developers; examples include Tower Hamlets' *Keeling House* and, as we shall see later, *Aragon Tower* on Lewisham's Pepys Estate.

It is ironic that Le Corbusier's socialist design ideals now work best in blocks where private money moved in, but then again he did see workers and intellectuals living in shared urban space.

There is one estate where that was the plan from the start. Perhaps the most successful estate in the UK built during the tower-block era is still the City of London's *Barbican*, by the same team of Chamberlain Powell & Bon that had designed the Golden Lane Estate. The three 126m towers were finished in 1976, and became the UK's tallest residential blocks. The whole estate owes a lot to Le Corbusier, and the long medium-rise terraces in it look very like his Ville Contemporaine. *The Barbican* was in fact never intended as social housing, but as luxury flats to attract a new sort of community to the City. A smaller YMCA tower there was intended for 'young workers'. This makes *The Barbican* the precursor to London's next wave of high-rise residential towers, built by private developers, which began to rise along by the river in the late eighties.

As we shall see later, London's first elected mayor Ken Livingstone has now made affordable housing provision for key workers a condition for upmarket developments. A convergence between social housing and luxury living continues in today's residential towers built for the rich.

Great Arthur House, EC1
Golden Lane Estate, Golden Lane

Tube Barbican
Height 51m, 17 storeys
Designed 1954
Completed 1957
Architect Chamberlain Powell & Bon

Kingston-upon-Thames is an unlikely place for one of the UK's greatest high-rise architectural teams to spring from. Here, three lecturers at the Kingston School of Architecture – Geoffrey Charles Hamilton Powell, Christof Bon and Peter Chamberlain – were in thrall to Le Corbusier's modern ideas, as were almost all of their generation of architects. Bon had worked with Modernist idealists in Switzerland and Italy. In 1952, the three entered a competition to design high-density housing on a bombsite, and made a pact that should any of them win, they'd form a partnership to build it. Powell won and redeemed this pledge. Chamberlain, Powell & Bon took on the Golden Lane Estate commission for the City of London.

Their original plan involved bulky medium-rise blocks, but these were considered too oppressive. The site was expanded and it was decided to have fewer but taller blocks. The final design was for an estate of 557 flats and maisonettes, centred around a sixteen-storey block, to be called Great Arthur House, containing 120 two-room flats, each with a projecting balcony, and which would have 'hobby rooms' and a laundry on the ground floor.

Medium-rise social housing, as in the nearby eleven-storey Peabody Estate buildings, was emerging in the 1950s, but Great Arthur House is London's first housing to reach over 50m. Effectively, it was London's first tower-block skyscraper. It has pick-hammered concrete end-walls, with mustard-yellow spandrels beneath the windows radiating a bright, summery feel. The crowning glory is a distinctive concrete wave structure on the roof, which juts westward like a jauntily upturned cap brim. Behind the overhang, it arches up above the boiler house, water tanks and lift machinery; a roof terrace for the tenants, furnished with a decorative pool, seats and plant boxes, completed the rooftop landscape. This is exactly what Le Corbusier intended for his flat roofs, and is directly inspired by his Unité d'Habitation in Marseilles.

Golden Lane became Chamberlain Powell & Bon's practice run before tackling the huge Barbican Estate next door to it. The estate is proof that Corbusian ideals in post-war social housing can work, although, today, Great Arthur House is hot on the private flat market.

Great Arthur House

Keeling House, E2
Claredale St, Bethnal Green

Tube Bethnal Green
Height 43m, 15 storeys
Constructed 1954–1957
Architect Denys Lasdun

This listed tower block is a heroic effort to create a vertical street, and its history is the quintessential story of the London tower block, from post-war idealism to twenty-first century yuppiedom.

While sharing the zeitgeist urge to turn Le Corbusier's socialist visions of housing into reality with other post-war architects, Denys Lasdun had suspicions about the way Le Corbusier saw people as anonymous inhabitants in his machines for living. Lasdun knew that the community of the pre-war East End was incredibly successful socially, and he studied photographs of the streetlife to understand how it worked. His big idea was to up-end the street and create the same social dynamics within the block – neighbours gossiping in communal areas, hanging out washing on balconies instead of backyards, and so on.

Keeling House

Keeling House was a pioneering cluster block, with four wings radiating from communal landings. The flats were two-storey maisonettes, as Le Corbusier planned, but also reflecting the small terraced-house interiors all around it. The concrete balconies all accessed sunlight, and could not be overlooked by neighbours. The block was painted white, a colour to emphasise the break with the bricks of the past.

Sadly, Keeling House failed to recreate the old street camaraderie of the past, and like most tower blocks, it declined socially and physically. In 1993, Tower Hamlets council declared it structurally unsafe and evacuated it. The empty hulk of Keeling House was earmarked for demolition.

However, in 1999, Keeling House was listed Grade II*. A private developer snapped the block up. Steve Marshall of Munkenbeck & Marshall masterminded the refurb for the trendy professional market. Lasdun himself helped design the new lobby, which now has a memorial stone in his memory. The designer-cool flats went on sale in 2001. It is now an exclusive block commanding top prices. A high fence around the building makes it effectively a gated estate.

This is Lasdun's only London high-rise and now has a very different sort of community to that he envisioned. But he was canny, preferring a new twist to demolition of his odd and unique masterpiece.

Brandon Estate, SE17
**Bateman, Browne, Cornish, Cruden,
Prescott & Walters Houses
Otto Street, Southwark**

Tube Oval
Height Cornish House is 58m and
the other buildings are 52m, 18 storeys
Designed 1956
Completed 1959
Architect LCC Architects Department
(under EE Hollamby)

The Brandon Estate lies between Camberwell and Kennington. The area was heavily bombed by the Luftwaffe; after the war, prefabs rapidly sprung up in gaps between the surviving houses. This was a showcase estate developed by the LCC, containing the highest London tower blocks when built. They were topped out in 1959 and the whole estate finished in 1961. The contractor was Wates, establishing itself early in the lucrative trade of tower-block system builders.

The LCC's designs under Edward Hollamby were still very true to Corbusian ideals. The Brandon Estate has wide expanses of grasslands between the tower blocks, as well as the distinctive roof structures with curved concrete shapes crowning the tower blocks. These top floors with their huge arched end-windows look as if they could be special flats, but in fact they just house plant machinery. The flats on the seventeenth floor are accessed by spiral staircases. The six blocks are identical, save for a minor variation in Cornish House, which is next to the boiler complex and carries the boiler flue up through the tower. The tower sometimes looks like a huge mutated cottage when its chimney is smoking.

Cornish House, smoke and sculpture

Brandon Towers

Campden Hill Towers, W11
Notting Hill Gate

Tube Notting Hill Gate
Height 54m, 18 storeys
Designed 1957
Completed 1961
Architect Cotton Ballard & Blow

Notting Hill Gate suffered a heavy attack of post-war planning, which produced Campden Hill Towers. It looks like a council tower block, but waxy plants and subdued lighting in the lobby are clues that it is actually made up of private flats. It is the only major London skyscraper developed by tycoon Jack Cotton, who, despite being acknowledged as the greatest developer of his time, failed otherwise to leave his mark on the skyline.

Notting Hill Gate was originally an ancient toll-gate, and, until redevelopment, the road squeezed into a crooked bottleneck, with separate Central and Circle Line stations on either side. In the 1950s, the heart was ripped out of Notting Hill Gate – 540m of buildings on the north side were demolished, and 135m on the south side. Redevelopment allowed the LCC to widen the road and create an integrated tube station. Cotton took on the development and exhibited his plan in Kensington Town Hall in October 1957. It created a counterpoint between this huge residential slab, astride a long low-rise stretch containing shops, and Newcombe House, a twelve-storey office slab on the south side of the street. Like other first-wave post-war slabs, Campden Hill Towers has wind-bracing bush-hammered concrete side-walls. Two bedroom flats are set in a Corbusian concrete grid, and each contains its own fire escape staircase to a corridor above. The block juts over the pavement, and McDonalds now ply their business below it.

Campden Hill Towers is harsh and massively out of scale with its surroundings. Despite that, the surrounding streets of elegant Victorian terraces have taken it in their stride, and the cool Notting Hillbillies hardly notice it at all.

This is a great estate, now listed. Unlike later tower blocks, the Brandon Estate has not needed major refurbishment. There's a Henry Moore sculpture oddly located between the towers, called *Two-Piece Reclining Figure No. 3* (1961), which is part of his return to public art after a thirty-year gap following his *55 Broadway* work. Commissioning public art for social housing would become rare after this. In the 2005 series of *Dr Who* starring Christopher Ecclestone, his assistant Rose Tyler, played by Billie Piper, lives on the Brandon Estate with her mother.

Campden Hill Towers

Draper House, SE1
Elephant & Castle

Tube Elephant & Castle
Height 75m, 25 storeys
Designed 1960
Constructed 1962–65
Architect Hubert Bennett, LCC

This tower block, with its particularly Brutalist roof structure, was the tallest in London when built. Initially, the plan was to build four-storey blocks here, but it became part of the comprehensive redevelopment of Elephant & Castle, which also includes Goldfinger's first skyscraper (now *Metro Central Heights*).

This design was by Hubert Bennett of the LCC's Architects Department, which as we have seen was inspired by Le Corbusier. After the war, Brutalism was in vogue – a style characterised by bulky blocks of concrete, often looking like crude abstract sculptures. On Draper House, this takes form in the massive plant machinery lump sitting on the top, which suggests a gigantic cannon pointing at the city north of the river, as if challenging it with socialist ideals. A total of 133 double-height flats, accessed from balcony passages, are set in an exposed grid frame of bush-hammered concrete granite aggregate. However, Bennett went beyond the standard materials and used storey-height slabs of white Sicilian marble to create large vertical white bands running up the block, as if to say 'nothing is too good for the people'. The development also included a piazza and shops, as well as a seven-storey wing of flats.

Draper House was well regarded at time – *Architectural Review* said it 'sets a standard of clarity and vigour'. Nowadays, the marble is stained and the block has declined, but its strong Corbusian rectilinear design make it almost as important as the Goldfinger classics, the *Balfron* and *Trellick* Towers. Later, Bennett would explore other unusual exterior finishes with Luxborough House and *Marylebone Tower*.

Water Gardens, W2
Edgware Road

Tube Edgware Road/ Marble Arch
Height 52m, 18 storeys
Designed 1961
Completed 1966
Achitects Trehearne & Norman, Preston & Partners

This triplet set of towers, developed for the then 'middle-income' market, is special because of the way the architects used wide white bands to create huge motifs on their black façades. Justifying the name, developers the Church Commissioners commissioned water gardens from landscape designer Philip Hicks. They are at the back of the podium that connects the towers, and lush plants emerge from rectangular pools mounted above a basement car park.

The bands across the façades are part of a concrete frame that extends to skeleton floors at the top, and are covered with white mosaics. Set back from the narrow ends of the slab towers, the white mosaics also form long

oblongs. The influence was probably Lubetkin's from his nearby Hallfield Estate. The effect is like a Mary Quant dress design – bold, symmetrical black-and-white patterns. The only other architectural practice to put something of Swinging London into high-rise was, as we have seen, the Seifert partnership (see *Centre Point*). Contemporary luxury apartments just a block away look like council tower blocks, but the Water Gardens design is quite different – groovy and now very upmarket.

Balfron Tower, E14
St Leonards Road

DLR All Saints
Height 84m, 27 storeys
Constructed 1965–67
Architect Ernö Goldfinger

Everyone knows Goldfinger's Brutalist masterpiece, the *Trellick Tower*. The Balfron Tower is its slightly older sister at the opposite end of Inner London. It is the centrepiece of the Rowlett Street Housing Project, approved in 1965 for a site by the mouth of the Blackwall Tunnel.

The estate is an extreme example of Brutalism – concrete buildings with uncompromising starkness. It was built when the architectural quality of tower blocks was being sacrificed to cost-cutting system-build construction methods, but Goldfinger stayed resolutely true to his passionate Corbusian ideals, not least by making the flats light and spacious. What really distinguishes the Balfron Tower is the separation of the 146 flats, all set in a grid, from the service tower housing lifts and stairs. Having a distinct service tower was not itself original; it had just been done in the Pepys Estate (see *Aragon Tower*), and is seen in tower blocks of the time across Europe. However, Goldfinger detaches the service tower completely, creating a unique signature shape. A boiler room (with four exhaust flues) is placed near the top, and the stairs and lift lobbies are marked by slits in the exterior. Enclosed concrete bridges every third floor connect to the flats. The same pattern of bridges is used in the estate's ten-storey wall of Carradale House.

The Balfron Tower was opened in February 1967, months before the collapse of Ronan Point turned the tide against tower blocks. Goldfinger lived at the top for two months to prove his faith in high-rise living. He became a local hero, but then moved back to Hampstead. Horace Cutler, the leader of the GLC, was shown around by Goldfinger and was impressed enough to commission the *Trellick Tower*.

Nowadays, the Balfron Tower is Grade II listed and is in still in relatively good repair, although £2.4m of lottery money was allocated to estate improvements. It remained Tower Hamlets' tallest building until Canary Wharf. It has been much slower than the *Trellick Tower* to become a trendy place to live, but it has been used in fashion shoots.

Blocks and bridges of Balfron Tower

Edward Woods Estate, W11
Norland House, Poynter House and Stebbing House, St Anne's Road

Tube Shepherds Bush, Latimer Road
Height Each building is 69m, 24 storeys
Built 1964–68
Arcitect Hammersmith Borough Architects Dept

These identical grey tower blocks are monuments to forgotten local hero Ted Woods.

Woods was a fighter. Born in 1896, he was brought up knowing the poverty of the Latimer Road slums below Notting Hill, where huge families crammed into squalid houses. In 1922, this big bachelor with a Chaplin moustache was elected as a Labour councillor to the Conservative Hammersmith Borough Council. For the next four decades, he tirelessly served the borough, rising to be Mayor in 1942 and earning the nickname 'Mr Hammersmith'. He became an acknowledged authority on local housing and. in 1959, the Vice-Chairman of the LCC. Hammersmith decided to build heroic tower blocks right next door to Kensington, where they could look down on the posh Tories. Public places were seldom named after someone living, but Hammersmith's flagship estate was an exception and, in 1966, Ted Woods officially opened his estate. It was a triumphant culmination to his life's work of decent housing for local people.

A year later and behind schedule, the first tower block, Poynter House, was opened. Like its sister blocks, it was named after a street obliterated by the estate. Each contains 176 flats, with pale-grey spandrels on their long sides and black brick on their split flank walls. Things soon started to go wrong. Lifts failed straight-away. Old ladies were isolated on high floors, and young mothers worried that their children would fall from windows. Public opinion turned against tower blocks. The fall from grace of council estates is even suggested in a 1969 episode of *Dr Who*, where a government minister (played by Geoffrey Palmer) collapses from an alien Silurian virus at the foot of an Edward Woods tower block.

Woods died in 1971, and his estate already had desolate no-go areas where adolescent crime and vandalism laid siege to the tenants. Security guards were installed in 1979, and entryphones in 1981. Today, the estate is safer, but recent attempts to humanise the towers with portico entrances don't really work — it's like giving gorillas fancy little false moustaches. The slabs have a crushing effect over the adjacent nineteenth-century conservation area. On the other side, they look down over the only kilometre built of the West Cross Route, which was to be one side of London's Inner Motorway Box. The GLC finally cancelled that plan in 1973. Standing by the motorway in damp weather, with its heavy juggernauts swooshing down through the wet grit, the towers can look serene and sad, like gigantic grim tombstones to the idealism of post-war social planning.

Peregrine House, EC1
Hall Street

Tube Angel
Height 80m, 27 storeys
Completed 1969
Architect Dr CL Franck of Franck & Deeks

Michael Cliffe House, EC1
Skinner Street

Tube Angel
Height 74m, 25 storeys
Completed 1968
Architect Dr CL Franck of Franck & Deeks

Numerous tower blocks spread across the north of Clerkenwell are all marked by curvy roof structures. Amongst these stand two giants, both until recently notorious for suicides.

Finsbury was one of London's smallest, poorest and densest boroughs. Its council had a reputation for enlightened socialist architecture, especially with the work of the Russian émigré Berthold Lubetkin.

Balfron Tower

Edward Woods Estate, a memorial to sixties ideals

His Tecton practice's Finsbury Health Centre (1938) was a showcase example of his Corbusian-influenced progressive approach to designing accessible facilities for the people, with uplifting curves, space and natural light. Finsbury was absorbed by Islington in 1964, and the latter took over Finsbury's legacy of ambitious housing plans.

Michael Cliffe House, named after a Labour councillor and MP who died in 1965, is a concrete tower of 185 flats and the centrepiece of the Finsbury Estate, which was opened in May 1968. The architect was CL Franck, who had worked on housing with Lubetkin, and later, in 1959, on the Galway Street estate. There, the rooftop plant machinery of its seventeen-storey slabs were covered with curved concrete canopies. In Michael Cliffe House, Franck uses curved concrete not just in a great arc on the roof, but also in a great arch at the main entrance. Above this entrance is a grand stack of open balconies, recessed from the façade of the tower.

The problem was that anyone could get in and access the balconies. The suicides soon started, at an average rate of one a year. Locally, the tower became known as 'Beachy Head', after the seaside cliff where lovers jump. In the nineties, bodies fell by the new children's playground, and sometimes got impaled on the railings. 'The noise of people hitting the ground is different from other bangs you get around here', observed one tenant. In 1998, four tenants objected to a plan for a net to catch jumpers. Michael Cliffe suffered other problems typical of tower blocks – power cuts, heating breakdowns and, in 1990, even a roof fire. When Jack Straw toured the estate in 1999 to launch ASBOs, he got a rough ride from locals, long intimidated by youths. Nowadays the building is secured with CCTV and a concierge.

The City Road Estate contains more tower blocks, and Peregrine House is London's second-highest tower block designed by a local authority. It is almost identical to Michael Cliffe House, except that a central boiler was scrapped to save costs, so the plant canopy sits lower on the roof. It, too, has suffered from suicides, as well as from bizarre water problems – a worm once came out of a tap, while, later, toilets spewed sewage into flats. In 1989, when there was a freeze on building social housing, local housing officer Leo Boland climbed to top to unfurl a computer printout listing 14,000 names on council waiting lists for National Housing Week. It tore in the wind. Soon, new flats at *261 City Road* may look down on Peregrine House.

Clerkenwell is very hip nowadays, but few professionals have bought into the towers. Finsbury's tower formula was not repeated elsewhere and they stand as distinctly local features in the rich architectural history of the area. Curiously, the idea of great roof arcs would return in the late eighties, but on Post-Modernist office blocks such as *Alban Gate*.

Michael Cliffe House

Knightsbridge Barracks, SW1
Hyde Park Barracks

Tube Knightsbridge
Height 94m, 29 storeys
Constructed 1967–70
Architect Sir Basil Spence and Partners

Knightsbridge Barracks contains a tower block where families of soldiers of the Household Cavalry Mounted Division, known as the Blues & Royals, are housed. It was seen by some as a military complex designed to withstand a civil uprising.

The barracks also include low-rise blocks, including stables for horses, which the Household Cavalry ride out into Hyde Park, dressed in traditional uniforms. It replaces Victorian barracks on a thin plot stretching along Hyde Park. As we have seen, architect Sir Basil Spence, a leading post-war Establishment architect, also designed Coventry Cathedral (1962) and Thorn House (now *Orion House*), but his tower blocks at Sighthill, Glasgow, became one of the UK's worst sixties sink estates. Here, his style had developed, and features such as angled concrete planes, lead surfaces and red-brick exterior styling (on the lower-level buildings) mix the textures, making this Brutalist-tinged work somehow quite warm.

In the late sixties, protests against the Vietnam War were growing across Western Europe; in Paris, even revolution seemed possible. The Rolling Stones' song *Street-Fighting Man* is about the protests filling the streets around the American Embassy in Grosvenor Square, only a kilometre away across Hyde Park. The high wall surrounding the barracks was built with vertical slits all the way down to the pavement, as if for defending the place with rifles. Mobs crossing from the park would be confronting an actively defended fortress. The slits are now filled in with black covers. It was also rumoured that a large secret British Army HQ lay under the barracks, and that the tower was a VHF and HF radio relay station. The strange concrete superstructure at the head of the tower would also provide bays for microwave horns, like the ones on the *Telecom Tower*. On the top is an open platform that is clearly an observation post.

Although it did not send troops, the Harold Wilson government backed the US in Vietnam, and saw the threat of civil unrest that this stirred. Crown Immunity Powers were used to overrule both the LCC/GLC and Westminster Council, who objected to the tower's high visibility from Hyde Park. It was completed in 1970, and in October Field Marshal Sir Gerald Templer and Earl Mountbatten of Burma unveiled a plaque beneath a classical-style triangular pediment from the previous buildings. Tragically, Mountbatten, who had turned the tide of World War Two against the Japanese and was India's last Viceroy, was assassinated by the IRA in Ireland in 1972. Three years later, the IRA exploded a remote-controlled nailbomb in the park near the Barracks, killing two Household Cavalry soldiers and seven horses. The horses that survived were called Sefton, Yetti and Echo.

The Barracks tower pops up over large swathes of Kensington Gardens and Hyde Park, as detractors had feared. Towards Park Lane, on clear evenings, it appears in silhouette near the 87m-high Victorian Imperial College tower (by TE Colcutt, 1893). Their slender shafts and complexly structured crowns complement each other, like distant, mighty king and queen chess pieces – a beautiful and fitting view for a Royal Park. (See page 18)

Trellick Tower, W10
Goldborne Road

Tube Westbourne Park
Height 98m, 32 storeys
Constructed 1968–72
Architect Ernö Goldfinger

The Trellick Tower is a global icon for Brutalism and the extreme example of not just the urban hell into which tower blocks sunk, but also how they could be completely turned round and even become the height of cool urban living. Trellick also represents the swansong of the arrogant, inflexible genius, Ernö Goldfinger.

Faulty Tower
We have already seen how the great Hungarian-born architect was a disciple of Le Corbusier, and how Goldfinger realised his first great social housing project, the radical *Balfron Tower*, in Poplar. Horace Cutler, the Conservative head of the GLC, was so impressed by the estate that he commissioned Goldfinger to design housing for a semi-industrial site on Edenham Road, by the Grand Union Canal in North Kensington. This was approved in 1966 and became known as the Cheltenham Estate, with individual buildings, including Trellick, named after Gloucestershire villages,. Work began in early 1968, with Goldfinger on site supervising the start of an extraordinary tower he had first sketched on a piece of butcher's paper.

The Trellick Tower contains 217 flats, including eleven split-level maisonettes. Forty-two of the flats are in a seven-storey wing – the whole building actually has

Military Tower Block

an L-shape plan. Of course, it is the tower that everyone knows. As in Poplar, its most obvious aspect is the separation of housing from services, including lifts and rubbish chutes. These are housed in a column tower marked by the huge cantilevered 'head' containing the boiler, from which four flues rise to the full height of 98m, and a meeting room. Bridges connecting the service tower to the flats rest on neoprene bearings, allowing movement between the two towers of up to 5cm. Goldfinger hated washing lines, so the floor below each bridge in the service tower was designated as a 'drying room', while the floor above was a 'hobby room'. Goldfinger designed the three lifts in the service tower to take coffins, making them narrow and deep.

The residential tower slab is slightly lower, but still as tall as the tallest sixties monster tower blocks in Birmingham and Glasgow. The flats are recessed from a Corbusian grid of bush-hammered concrete, and fronted with cedar panelling by the windows. The interiors were spacious, full of light and warmed by hot air. Doors slid into walls and rooms could be partitioned into different spaces. Bedroom windows were designed to rotate for cleaning. In the lobby, abstract stained glass greeted visitors with optimism.

It was ready for tenants in April 1972, and Goldfinger moved his office there, to a space intended for a pub. He was obsessively interested in the details of his creation. In a lift, he asked a woman what she thought of her new flat. A tenant called Lee Boland said she liked it, but there was no broom cupboard. 'Bloody women' muttered Goldfinger, 'never satisfied'. Boland's subsequent tireless campaigning for the block's welfare proved Goldfinger right about her at least.

Almost immediately, the problems began. In June, a burst fire hydrant caused water to cascade through the building. Delinquents were soon wandering freely in the corridors and lobbies, stealing milk bottles left outside doors and menacing tenants. At Christmas, vandals broke fire hydrants on the twelfth floor, and the water blew out the electricity. The toilets blocked up because they couldn't be flushed. Rubbish chutes choked up. Milkmen and postmen refused to deliver, and the Fire Brigade recommended the evacuation of the tower.

In the New Year, a Tenants Association presented its first demands to the GLC: an emergency generator, police patrols, and a concierge. But the UK was in recession, and funds were tight. The Trellick Tower continued to slide into anarchy. For every tenant who moved in, there were five who refused the place. In 1977, Goldfinger himself retired from the building and from his practice, bitter and frustrated. The GLC caretakers went on strike. That November, the lifts were knocked out again, this time by yet another fire started in the blocked rubbish chutes. A twenty-seven-year-old tenant died climbing the steps. An eighty-year-old tenant, unable to leave her flat, told a reporter: 'I'm in prison.'.

In 1981, Ken Livingstone took control of the GLC, and during the next year spent £343,000 on entryphones and repairs, but the work was shoddy. The alarms installed on corridor doors were soon vandalised. The terror continued. Graffiti, drug debris and smashed glass trashed the common areas. The evening was the peak time for verbal and physical abuse. When they worked, the deep lifts were scary places to be cornered in, especially for the almost one-in-five tenants who were single mothers. In the service tower, lifts still opened on the floors that never did get used for drying or hobbies. A 27-year-old woman was dragged into the disused fifteenth floor and raped. On the same floor, a mother leapt to her death.

In June 1982, five base jumpers reached the top of the service tower. One died when his parachute failed to open. Two years later, when the GLC identified an asbestos hazard in the wall panelling, they couldn't afford to do the work. The Trellick Tower passed to the Royal Borough of Kensington & Chelsea, a Tory council that hated tower blocks and weren't particularly keen on council tenants. Could things get worse?

Turning the Tower Round

One of the first effects of the Tory council takeover was an unexpected outburst of outrage in the architectural press. Along the length of the residential block's roof ran a cornice, a long strip of concrete mounted like a barrier, which was deemed unsafe and removed. Purists fumed at the desecration of Goldfinger's masterpiece. Other architects scoffed that it should matter when his design housed hell. The council at last tackled the asbestos. A new Tenants Association formed in October 1984 and started a relentless campaign of petitions and lobbying to get things moving. Its secretary, Patricia Williams, declared that 'Kensington & Chelsea Council's attitude towards council tenants must change radically'.

Strangely, after a lot of pressure, it did. In 1986, the Safe Neighbourhoods Unit demanded twenty-four-hour security, new entryphones, and new lifts with CCTV. The next year, the Trellick Tower at last got a concierge. The

From Golborn Road

Trellick Tower

council introduced a policy of allocating flats only to those who wanted to live there. In 1988, London Electricity began installing a new Cyclocontrol system, which heated water overnight when electricity was cheap, replacing Goldfinger's oil-fired boiler. This had never been done on such a scale before, and, in 1989, Energy minister Cecil Parkinson came to see it. The garages, popular with drug dealers, were demolished and replaced by a playground. In 1990, a new entryphone system was installed; the next year, a start was made in replacing the lifts by faster models with security cameras inside. Finally, in 1994, the tower got twenty-four-hour security and CCTV at the entrance.

There were still setbacks, such as a fire on the twenty-fourth floor that caused the evacuation of seventy-five residents in 1996, and a gas pipes failure in 1998, but the 1990s were finally seeing Trellick work. A sense of community and pride in the building emerged. Local artists celebrated the building with spectacular lightshows in 1997. Only one in ten of the early tenants ever exercised their right to buy, but by 1998 flats that came to market were hot. The Trellick Tower gradually became a model tower block, attracting the attention of housing ministers from South Africa and Mongolia. The Tenants Association was now led by Lee Boland, the woman who had complained to Goldfinger about accommodating brooms. Goldfinger himself died in 1987 and never saw the turnaround, but Boland vigorously defended his architecture. In 1998, the Trellick Tower was listed Grade II*.

In December 2002, John McAslan & Partners, architects of *25 North Colonnade* and specialists in restoring modern architecture, were commissioned to renovate the Trellick Tower, tackling the pipes, rubbish chutes and cedar window frames that were wearing out. Their aim was higher – to reinstate Goldfinger's details, even to the extent of replacing the lost cornice and Goldfinger's original signage. McAslam's wanted to scaffold the entire block to replace 800 windows, but the residents didn't like the idea of scaffolding or the proposed windows. An abseiling survey suggested only about sixty needed replacement anyway. The Twentieth Century Society challenged McAslam's latest update to the £8.6m restoration plan in 2006, because of their window-frame choice. This story still had some way to run...

Trellick Tower's Been Calling

In his 1975 novel *High Rise*, JG Ballard writes about a tower block that descends into anarchy as different floors wage war on each other. The inspiration was the Trellick Tower. Less than 400m from Westway, the flyover that cut a near fatal scar across the great decaying Victorian tenements of North Kensington, the tower was bound to be a symbol of the way urban Britain seemed to be falling into open class and race warfare, sinister nights of violence, alienation and dreams, all set to a sound-track of whizzing cars and rebel music.

North Kensington was Bob Marley's area, and he was photographed with Trellick behind him, as if the tower represented Babylon. This was also the manor of The Clash and the roots of an exploding local punk scene. The Clash played gigs against a stage backdrop of Westway and the Trellick Tower, painted by their bass player Paul Simenon. As for music itself, it's not until 1995 that the Trellick Tower is actually name-checked, in the Blur song *Best Days*.

The Trellick Tower has been photographed and painted so often that it joins the elite of structures that are known worldwide as being nowhere else but London. Perhaps the best painting is by Nottingham artist Nick Hederly in 2002, capturing the unique profile against a brooding blue haze.

Of course, it was Goldfinger himself who created the original artwork – the building itself. Socialists saw art and design as political tools to shape a better society, and the Trellick Tower was Goldfinger's finest creation in the application of this credo. The Trellick Tower is the most famous tower block of social housing in the world, better known even that Le Corbusier's Unité d'Habitation. The irony is that it was a Tory authority that built it and, after much hounding, a Tory borough that recovered Goldfinger's socialist dream.

Luxborough Tower & Marylebone Hall, W1
Luxborough Street

Tube Baker Street
Height 67m, 23 storeys
Designed 1965
Completed 1972
Architect Hubert Bennett of LCC/GLC Architects

These two startlingly white towers look as though someone's taken a precision cutting tool to a single block, cleaving a thin, clean gap. One tower is academic accommodation, the other social housing. They lurk behind the glassy campus entrance to the University of Westminster, opposite the former London Planetarium.

The university was previously the Polytechnic of Central London, for whom the ILEA (Inner London Education Authority) commissioned the design, including the innovative Teaching Block and two other connected buildings. The northern tower, Marylebone Hall, contains

Charing Cross Hospital, W6
Fulham Palace Road

Tube Hammersmith
Height 75m, 17 storeys
Constructed 1968–73
Architect Ralph Tubbs

The Charing Cross Hospital was founded in 1818, and as far back as the 1930s the building on the Strand was already outdated. In 1957, it was decided to relocate to Fulham and absorb the Fulham Hospital. Architect Ralph Tubbs was appointed because he impressed a committee with his concern for patients – he'd been a sickly child. The plans were presented in 1960, only after the motorbike courier got lost in Elephant & Castle (see *Metro Central Heights*). The first teaching hospital built since the war, this was going to be huge.

Tubbs designed this cathedral to the modern NHS in the plan of a crucifix. The three cross wings would be wards holding 640 beds, with wide continuous balconies to stop patients getting vertigo and to reduce solar gain. There were ten operating theatres on the thirteenth and fourteenth floors. In the long eastern wing were clinical research laboratories, linking to a wider, full-height extension without balconies, housing the medical school. The floor area was a huge 84,000m².

In 1966, three streets were obliterated to clear the site, and 191 piles were driven 14m into the clay. Construction involved 7,000 tonnes of reinforced steel, 46,000m³ of concrete, 600 doors and 160km of wiring; a 600-tonne refrigeration unit and machinery to produce 1,000 litres of distilled water an hour were also installed. Topping-out was in April 1970. The hospital came in on time and to the £11m budget, and contractors Higgs & Hill reckoned its workforce got through a million cups of tea and 250,000 coffees. To the south they built three 45m-high tower blocks for nurses, and a School of Nursing. A Henry Moore sculpture and a water feature are to be found at the front and tiled murals from the Strand are mounted on the first floor. The Queen opened the hospital in May 1973.

The hospital suffered two strikes, in the winters of 1978 and 1979. When pickets blocked the supply of heating oil in November 1979, the head of radiology wheeled out a cancer patient who coughed blood and told them: 'You don't know the meaning of hard work'. In 1988, the main kitchen was closed because of cockroaches.

In 2005, the hospital needed £100m on repairs, and again faces closure, which it had avoided in 1993. Plans to move everything to Hammersmith Hospital in Acton are denied, but demolishing the tower and selling the grounds would raise big money.

If the Charing Cross Hospital goes, few will miss the intimidating grey form that floats above the low terraced houses of Fulham. While this bulky block is one of London's busiest hospitals, with top research facilities and a renowned undergraduate training hospital, it is a mammoth blot on the landscape.

University halls of residence for 178, and is basically a square pillar, with cantilevered windows at the front. It hit the newspapers in June 2005 because a pair of peregrines nested there and raised chicks. These hunting birds, which can reach a record-breaking 320km/h, were close to extinction in the UK in the 1970s. They normally like cliff edges, but skyscrapers are pretty similar and give access to a feast of urban pigeons.

The southern block, Luxborough Tower, is where the BBC set up cameras to watch the peregrines for wildlife voyeur program the *Springwatch*. It houses 115 families, and has longer windows and balconies, some recessed. The blocks were set back from the Marylebone Road to protect views from Regent's Park. They replace Luxborough Lodge, a 1000-capacity old people's home and workhouse.

These towers may be Hubert Bennett's finest work. As with his earlier *Draper House*, he chose a superior cladding, in this case white Portland stone, which gives the towers their brilliant, clean appearance, as if they really belonged in Miami Beach. Luxborough Tower certainly doesn't look like an average council tower block.

Guy's Tower, SE1
St Thomas Street

Tube London Bridge
Height 144m, 32 storeys
Constructed 1968–73
Architect Watkins Gray Woodgate International

Guy's Tower, part of Guy's Hospital, is the tallest medical building in the world – it beats Hong Kong's Queen Mary Hospital by 6m. Its extraordinary cantilevered 'head', its bulk, and its uncompromising use of concrete make it an extreme example of Brutalist architecture. Apart from the *Telecom Tower*, Guy's was London's tallest skyscraper when built, and in 2006 is still the tallest south of the Thames. Soon, however, it will find itself next to *The Shard*, over twice as high as Guy's.

Guy's Hospital is a maze of buildings, the oldest by Thomas Dance, which is listed Grade II. World War Two destroyed warehouses, shop showrooms and cottages next to it, liberating space for hospital expansion. In 1961 the dull New Guy's House was built. The next phase was commissioned in 1963. Architects Watkins Gray Woodgate advised a Building Committee on the design.

Construction started in April 1968. A raft 3.05m thick was laid for the building, but strikes caused major delays, pushing costs from the budgeted £8m to almost £10m. The building was ready in May 1973 and, a year late, on the 250th anniversary year of Guy's Hospital, the Queen officially opened it.

Guy's actually has two linked towers. The 122m User Tower has a regular rectangular floorplate around twin concrete cores. Hospital wards, operating theatres and laboratories occupy nineteen floors, and above them is a dental training hospital. Heavy-looking concrete balconies reduce solar gain and make window cleaning easy. The other tower is the 138m Communications Tower, bundling most of the lifts and major service ducts. This is topped by the signature 'head' structure. Above the distinctive sloping roof, boiler flues rise a further 6m to the full 144m height. The separation of most service infrastructure into a separate tower is the same basic design philosophy that Goldfinger employed in the *Balfron* and *Trellick Tower*s, which coincidentally also have jutting-out 'heads' on their concrete service towers.

The distinctive head is more than just an architectural extravagance – it contains a 150-capacity lecture theatre, entered from the thirtieth floor. The sloped audience seating at the back of the theatre is actually over a sheer drop of almost 120m. Next to the Lecture Theatre is a Hospitality Suite. The décor here is original seventies, and reflects the use of colour and Scandinavian-style furniture throughout the hospital below, an approach which also pioneered big colourful abstract designs on the walls to cheer patients and visitors up. Above all of this is the sloping roof; at its lower edge, tall weeds and plants such as dune-grass used to grow, but were cleared in 2004. Guy's head has been a popular spot with charity abseilers. When cooling equipment needed replacement in 1985, Sea King helicopters brought up parts from Potters Fields, where London's City Hall now stands.

The ten passenger lifts are mostly bundled in the Communications Tower. Half are express lifts for the dental school floors, going straight to the twentieth floor. There are a further nine special-purpose lifts and even three package hoists.

With its mind-bogglingly complex system of medical infrastructure and pipe networks, Guy's is also a triumph of engineering. It has some amazing statistics. Here are some examples, from the original number of fluid outlets around the tower: Compressed Air – 1514; Natural Gas - 1380 (excluding kitchens), Vacuum – 554; Oxygen – 338; NO_2 – 59; Oxygen/NO_2 mix – 26; CO_2 – 20. Since then, even more outlets have been added, pushing up the figures by perhaps another ten per cent! The dental suction system was designed to suck spit from 212 chairs with a maximum flow rate of 1,200 litres/second.

Most visible, of course are the chimneys of the boiler system, designed by engineer Len Schwarz. Some of it can be glimpsed through a glass wall by the ground-floor reception, which shows off some serious-looking big blue pipes and lots of gauges. One of the four basement gas-

Shearsmith House, E1
Swedenborg Square

Tube/DLR Shadwell
Height 82m, 28 storeys
Completed 1972
Architect GLC Architects

Shearsmith House architecture is so uninspired, it's a bit of a stretch to call it architecture at all. However, it is outstandingly tall – the tallest tower block in London actually designed by local government architects. (Although Birmingham, Gateshead and Glasgow boast taller examples.) *The Barbican, Trellick Tower* and *Balfron Tower*, too, are taller, but they were designed for local authorities, rather than by them. Unlike these signature buildings, neither Shearsmith House nor its two shorter tower block neighbours on the estate bear any Corbusian design touches. They all look like stacks of grey bricks.

This tower block is on an estate in Shadwell, still a deprived part of Tower Hamlets. It is named after Richard Shearsmith, who was the landlord of Baron Emanuel Swedenborg, a Swedish scientist who had mystic visions. He lived in the eighteenth-century Swedish community around Wellclose Square, one of the East End's unique old neighbourhoods, subsequently destroyed, not by the Luftwaffe, but by the GLC.

In 2005, Shearsmith House hit the news because of the first ASBO banning someone from a borough's roofs. DJ Slimzee was found guilty of operating a pirate radio station with a transmitter on Shearsmith House's roof. Rinse FM had played house garage music and helped break Dizzee Rascal. Not only was Shearsmith House's electricity being diverted to the radio kit, it was also hooked up to boobytrap the trap door up to the roof, although that particular offence didn't carry in court. Slimzee was banned from all roofs over four storeys up in the borough.

fired boilers is now replaced by a CPH unit. From the basement, exhaust fumes are taken into flues 130m high, freestanding at ground level. These immensely long concrete-ring tubes regularly expand by about 15cm and are secured at their top, connecting to narrower flues above. In the seventies one of the long flues broke free and twisted, then collapsed. The resulting compression force caused walls to buckle so abruptly that a six-tonne X-ray machine was pushed right across a room.

It's hard to like the look of it, but it certainly cuts a powerful profile. If there were neon-light edging on the tower, its shape would be brought to life. This was actually proposed in the late eighties but turned down by Southwark Council. As it stands, Guy's Tower may be a carbuncle, but one day it could have heritage value as a vertical monument to the post-war utopian vision of a National Health Service on the grand scale.

Shearsmith House

The Barbican, EC1

Tube Barbican
Architect Chamberlain, Powell & Bon

Shakespeare Tower
Height 128m, 43 storeys
Completed 1976

Lauderdale Tower
Height 126m, 44 storeys
Completed 1974

Cromwell Tower
Height 126m, 43 storeys
Completed 1973

Barbican YMCA
Height 52m, 17 storeys
Completed 1971

The three triangular towers dominating the City's showpiece Grade II-listed Barbican complex are the tallest twentieth-century apartment blocks in the UK. They were built not as social housing, but for professionals, and so they anticipated the upmarket high-rise living trend of today.

The old urban fabric here, crossed by a swathe of railway lines into Moorgate, was obliterated by the Luftwaffe in 1940. The City of London engaged Chamberlain, Powell & Bon to plan the Barbican in 1954, and their first scheme was for four-storey blocks around courtyards. Then the City included three City schools, so a second plan emerged in 1956 with thirty-storey square tower blocks to incorporate the flats from the space lost, as well as a glass pyramid conservatory. In 1957, the same year as their adjacent Golden Lane Estate (see *Great Arthur House*) was completed, the three partners set off to look at urban developments in Italy and Sweden. They had a big area (24ha) to play with, and a brief to bring back life to the City at night, the silent time of caretakers and cats. The Barbican was to house 6,500 people at a time when the City population was 5,000 and falling. This estate would span over Beech Street, and enclose St Giles church (built 1394, completely restored after wartime destruction). Their detailed plan for a multi-layered, enclosed citadel-like community was approved in 1959 and construction began in 1963.

As at Golden Lane, and the Vanbrugh Estate in Greenwich completed in 1965, CPB's main inspiration was Le Corbusier: towers and terraces, space and light, concrete and gardens, buildings on pillars and pedestrians separated from traffic. The podium-level walkways would connect to those in the *London Wall* scheme of new office towers to the south, in a pedestrian system that the City hoped would extend all over the Square Mile. Later, it was decided to cover the Barbican's podium walkways in glazed brick, in line with the seventies trend to try to humanise new buildings. The water garden weaving through the estate reflects their desire to also emulate Venice.

As the Barbican's second phase, its Art Centre, started construction in 1971, the first Barbican skyscraper was completed on the estate's north-western corner. It is not one of the great apartment towers, but a more modest Brutalist concrete box, originally intended for 'young workers' in the City, almost like today's 'affordable housing'. The 200 rooms in the YMCA were on eight floors for men and four for women. The lucky warden had a penthouse flat. A self-supported concrete fire escape goes all the way to the top.

But it is the three very similar giant towers that marks the Barbican on the skyline. They are triangular in plan, with flats stretched out linearly along each façade. Initially, the towers were going to dazzle with polished spar-infused white concrete, but this was changed to pick-hammered concrete to save costs and reduce streaking. Their angularity is inspired by Frank Lloyd Wright's only built skyscraper, The Price Tower (1956in Oklahoma), and they have complex features. Stacks of balconies make sawtooth profiles at the towers' broken corners. The towers' heads, which house three penthouses per tower, are stepped and marked by battle-ment-like structures and portholes. This look is pure Brutalist, but there's also something medieval about their rooflines. The giants stand in line, but because Chamberlain, Powell and Bon, wanted 'to create a clear sense of order without monotony', they orientated each tower differently.

Cromwell Tower, named after Oliver Cromwell, who was married at the estate's church of St Giles, was completed first, in January 1973. It has 108 flats plus maisonette penthouses. Lauderdale Tower, named after the Scottish earls whose London home was on the estate, was finished next, with 114 flats plus penthouses. Virtually identical to it is the Shakespeare Tower, so named because Shakespeare once lodged nearby. It contains 113 flats plus maisonette penthouses, one on three levels, and was completed in February 1976.

Left: Lauderdale and Cromwell Towers
Centre: Barbican YMCA

World's End Estate, SW10
**Berenger, Dartrey, Whistler, Ashburnhan, Greaves, Chelsea Reach & Blantyre Towers
Kings Road**

Bus 11, 22
Height Each building 54m, 18 storeys
Completed 1977
Architect Eric Lyons, Cadbury-Brown, Metcalfe and Cunningham

This was the last tower-block estate to be built in London, and looks very different to the others. The cluster of seven towers linked by high-level walkways is not another exercise in Brutalist concrete or shoddy system building. The architect Eric Lyons was president of RIBA when the estate was finished, and was very aware of the public contempt for architects and their projects. The estate is clad in warm brickwork and presents complex shapes and plans. Even so, it has suffered from some familiar problems of tower blocks.

World's End is named after the Kings Road pub with a history dating back to the sixteenth century. As early as 1963, Chelsea Borough Council proposed redeveloping the rows of small terraced houses between the Kings Road and the river. Two schemes were drawn up to house 2,500 people, one involving towers 65m high. When a public inquiry examined them in 1965, it worried that the highest floors could suffer from pollution from the nearby *Lots Road* Power Station, which then generated electricity to drive the Tube system. The enquiry's commissioners suggested heating the exhaust so that it might leave the chimneys more vertically! In 1968 a scheme involving eight towers with modular sections around their cores was published. It went back to the drawing board after the Ronan Point disaster. The very different current design emerged in 1969, containing 714 flats, shops and a church, and costing £5,650,000.

Work began immediately but soon began to slip. By 1971, contractors Holland Hannen & Cubitt were demanding a further £1.5m to keep working. By late 1972, when everything should have been almost ready, only 18 per cent of the brickwork had been laid. In 1973, Cubitt officially closed the site. A hundred-strong deputation barricaded the (now merged) Kensington & Chelsea council offices till midnight, demanding answers about this fiasco. The council sued Cubbitt and appointed Bovis to finish the job for another £8m. In the end, Bovis actually had the first flats ready before their target of 1975, but it had been a nightmare project.

Joe Strummer of The Clash used to live here. Problems of vandalism and gangs on the walkways set in, and as late as 2005, the BBC made a documentary about a twenty-five-year-old drug addict on the estate who financed her habit with credit card crime.

The seven towers form a ring around the World's End Estate, enclosing it like a castle wall. The Greaves Tower is slightly different – it has boiler flues rising alongside it. The towers' edges, serrated by balconies,

Shakespeare at night

The Barbican's 2,000 flats were all let quickly, and attracted more families than expected. Residents included powerful socialists, such as militant miners leader Arthur Scargill, and Labour Party figures John Smith and Gwyneth Dunwoody. The big irony is that the Barbican is the socialist Corbusian dream estate that works, but is so middle-class. Nowadays, the Barbican's citadel is under threat – from underneath. The plans for Crossrail involve a huge crossover tunnel underneath the estate, and tunnels dug by the New Austrian Tunnelling Method have a record of collapsing. . .

and their rooflines, broken by chamfers and steps, as well as the brick cladding to 'humanise' the environment, are all in tune with what was happening at the Barbican in the same period. Both estates are ultimately a final attempt to make the ideas of Le Corbusier work for real people.

Parsons House, W2
(Hall Place)
407–409 Edgware Rd

Tube Edgware Road
Height 61m, 20 storeys
Constructed 1969–71
Reclad 1986–88
Architect Peter Bell

Hall Place was a particularly rubbish tower block. The damp riddling its 130 flats was so drastic that, after ten years, wooden window frames were warping out of the brick-clad walls and crashing to the ground. Westminster Council had two options – demolition, or repointing the entire exterior. In 1983 Westminster approached Peter Bell, an architect who knew about damp – he'd sealed the low-rise housing of Pollards Hill Estate in Merton with waterproof white vitreous enamelled steel skins, making them look like fridges. He proposed the same for the tower, at a cost of £2.5m – four times the budget for the work. However, it was still cheaper than demolition and building replacement homes, and the energy consumption of the block would fall by twenty-two per cent. In 1984 the plan was approved. White shiny panels had been used before, on two Harrow Road blocks built by the GLC in 1966 and now demolished, but they were made of fibreglass and plastic, offered poor insulation, and soon weathered.

Bell was also a mountaineer, and in 1986 he scaled the block to get a good look at the brickwork. The work involved gluing mineral wool to the brick surface, then covering all vertical surfaces with white panels, which had to be imported from Switzerland. Red mullions that snappily ran up the sides were extended above the roofline into a crazy shower of designer-punk filaments, supporting a track for the window-cleaning cradle.

Parsons House has emerged as a literally shining demonstration that the most shoddily built towers can be recycled. Bell commented: 'That's what I call high-tech band-aid technology!' It effectively marks the rebirth of the tower block as a viable social housing concept. Knackered tower blocks across the UK would follow its example to re-emerge from cocoons of scaffolding as clean and shiny new objects. And by addressing energy efficiency, Parsons House also pioneered something else – tackling the environmental impact of skyscrapers.

Chapter 4:
Concrete Jungle

In the classic 1971 British gangster movie *Get Carter*, Michael Caine tosses a local villain over the top of a new concrete multi-storey car park rising high over Gateshead, the then decaying town by the Tyne. At about the same time, public opinion was increasingly feeling the same way about architects as Caine's character felt about the villain.

Office developments were now a plague of banal boxes marching from the heart of the capital to the suburbs, and shoddy council estates were becoming the new slums. Although fashion and television had gone colour in the late sixties, a drabness seemed to return to London after the 1971 IRA bombing of the GPO Tower (now *Telecom Tower*), followed by the 1973 oil crisis and the ensuing world recession. The general anxiety and economic gloom were reflected in the greyness of new concrete buildings. New slip-forming techniques in the seventies enabled concrete cores to be built remarkably quickly. On the outside, concrete was again the architect's favourite material as they revived the style called Brutalism. But, to the public, concrete reflected a different description of the urban landscape – the Concrete Jungle. Punk music amplified the bleakness of the concrete jungle, and even made an icon of Ernö Goldfinger's swansong, the *Trellick Tower*. It seemed to symbolise the new combat zones of drug dealers and disenchanted youth. Gradually in this decade, the planners would abandon wholesale renewal schemes, and the conservation movement would cause a massive reassessment of urban strategies. The skyscraper boom faded and the death of the skyscraper seemed to be on the cards.

The Last of the Giant Glass Boxes

After the Brown Ban in 1964, the office skyscraper boom still had some momentum, because many projects had already been approved or were under construction. From 1965, new projects needed an Office Development Permit (ODP). Richard Seifert would became the master of these, continuing to exploit, like nobody else, the small print of tortuous planning legislation to squeeze out every last square foot of floor and vertical foot of height. 'You've got to start with a knowledge of the planning laws', he once explained, 'There's nothing magic about it'.

Seifert continued to work with Harry Hyams, and, after *Centre Point*, their greatest collaboration was a City bank headquarters at *Drapers' Garden*. This was another eye-opener that went beyond the glass box – a gleaming bow-fronted tower striped with green glass. After it was completed in 1967, Hyams and Seifert fell out – another of the mysterious splits that would impact London's skyline so much. It freed up Seifert to widen his client base and, as we shall see, to unleash a second wave of astonishing towers on London. At Seifert's practice in Red Lion Square, clients would be reassured by the formality of period panelling and classical furniture, but the staff environment was very informal by the standards of the time.

This was still the heyday of the International Style, and there was plenty still to come. Felix Fenston had returned from his long wanderings abroad and developed the Britannic Tower (now rebuilt as *CityPoint*) in the City, a handsome green slab that looked like the latest Manhattan behemoths such as the General Motors building on Fifth Avenue (which curiously was co-developed by Max Rayne).

Fenston worked with Seifert again on his last skyscraper scheme, *99 Bishopsgate*, but would never see it. As construction started in 1971, he died. That year, the *New York Times* wrote that Seifert's 'pop-art style (was) making London look like the worst of the United States'. Seifert would later say: 'My regret in the post-war building of London is that we rushed through the fifties and sixties with inferior materials … there was too big a profit motive amongst developers'. The era of the eccentric property tycoon passed with Fenston. Corporations and financial institutions became the dominant developers. One of the few individuals to make a serious effort to cut a name to equal those of earlier speculators was Lord Palumbo.

No van der Rohe slab was ever built in London, but he did develop a design between 1964 and 1968 for an 88-metre, twenty-storey slab and plaza for No. 1 Poultry in the City. Van der Rohe collaborated with town planner Lord Holford, who had a staggering disregard of historic settings, and was behind the original bleak Paternoster Square office development by St Paul's. Palumbo, who actually lived in a City townhouse, was infatuated with the van der Rohe tower, but public opinion was growing cold to it. The government would finally kill the scheme off in the 1980s. The only dark tower/open plaza in London from the sixties was GMW's Commercial Union Tower (now the *Aviva Tower*), finished in 1969, a decade after its inspiration, the Seagram Building. It looks pure van der Rohe but is far better scaled and positioned than the Poultry plan.

In 1970, Joe Levy's massive Euston Centre development had at last risen from his painstakingly accrued site. It had three towers on a long and hideous podium, the tallest one, *Euston Tower*, attracting MI5 as a tenant. The year it was finished, 1970, Edward Heath's incoming government revoked the Brown Ban.

By the 1970s, the International Style was tired. Sometimes, it seemed deliberately ugly. The clearest example was at the Ministry of the Environment on Marsham Street. Although designed by Eric Bedford, who had masterminded the brilliant *Telecom Tower*, the three 66m-high parallel slabs completed in 1971 were universally hated. They were finally demolished in 2003 for a new Home Office building.

Throughout the UK, provincial towns had desperately wanted to affirm that they belonged in the modern world, and that meant they now had to have a city-centre office slab-on-a-podium in the middle of a road scheme. Conversely, London sub-centres such as Elephant & Castle and the southern satellite business zone of Croydon built offices that made them feel like redeveloped provincial cities. There is something almost Soviet in the alienated mood of these post-war environments — go-ahead modern, yet rapidly tired, built for people to circulate and work in, yet cold to the eye and touch.

Attempts were made to make the International Style friendlier. As if to bring warmth to the icy steel and glass, shiny steel columns were being coated in matt finish, and blue or green spandrels were superseded by brown ones, which went well with the dark glass now used against solar gain.

In the meantime, the great socialist building medium was to take its turn on the commercial stage…

Concrete is back

Let's have a quick look at British Brutalism, which in the seventies would exemplify the gap between the ivory-tower ideals of architects and the down-to-earth reaction of the person-in-the-street. Brutalism was all about big chunky concrete shapes. The word Brutalism, although it suggest crude, brutish things, actually comes from the French for raw concrete: *béton brut*. We have already seen that Le Corbusier, fan of concrete, designed social housing in it, and how the post-war British architectural establishment exposed the British public to concrete in public works. A movement called New Brutalism arose, with the ethos of being true to the building materials, concrete or otherwise. It was led by Alison and Peter Smithson, the architects of the *Economist Building*, which is actually a variation on the International Style and not Brutalist at all. Exposed concrete was an important element in the British social housing designed in the sixties. The Smithsons themselves designed medium-rise Robin Hood Gardens, a very Brutalist concrete housing estate in Poplar finished in 1972 that looked like a prison.

The works of two architects stand out as the peaks of British Brutalism in the 1970s – Denys Lasdun and Owen Luder. Lasdun had designed the innovative *Keeling House* tower block in the fifties, but his most famous London building was the bunker-like National Theatre, completed on the South Bank in 1976. The Queen knighted Lasdun that year, but Prince Charles said the NT was 'a clever way of building a nuclear power station in the middle of London without anyone objecting'. Luder's sixties London designs were mainly medium-rise concrete offices in South London suburbs, but it's his work on multi-storey car parks that epitomizes the British Brutalism movement. The Gateshead Car Park featured in *Get Carter*, along with a similar work of his, the Tricorn Centre in Portsmouth (1964), were seen by the architectural establishment as brilliantly bold masterpieces, pushing what concrete and modern British architecture could deliver. Luder would twice become RIBA president. The public, however, thought his work was rubbish. The Tricorn Centre was later voted the ugliest building in Britain, and was demolished in 2004. The Gateshead Car Park faces the same fate.

So, what is there in the way of Brutalist London skyscrapers? Several major concrete landmarks were built, but not all survive. The twentiy-six-storey, 93m-high Limebank House, completed in the City in 1969, was designed not by Seifert, as is often claimed, but by Fairbairn & Partners, who had designed *Portland House*. It was demolished in 1997, making it the tallest UK building then to bite the dust.

We have seen some Brutalist skyscrapers already. *Knightsbridge Barracks*, reflect a seventies fashion to try to soften the hard impact of Brutalism by using glazed brick, but the towers themselves are concrete. Goldfinger made no such compromise at the *Trellick Tower* and celebrated Brutalism's taste for strange concrete shapes in his tower's signature cantilevered head. *Guy's Hospital*, designed by a committee, also has a weird cantilevered head structure, shaped to accommodate a lecture theatre. At 144m, it is probably the highest Brutalist work anywhere. Finally, there was the London *Stock Exchange Tower*, also designed by a committee, this one composed of commercial architects. This grey tower had a particularly grim, fortress-type appearance. Richard Seifert's widow recalls that he did not like it at all.

Booming Beds

In 1969, the Boeing 747 went into commercial operation, and global tourism was set to become a mass market. Just like Macmillan's government in the early sixties, Harold Wilson's government at the end of the sixties fretted about London's limited hotel bed capacity. The Development of Tourism Act (1969) offered grants of £1000 per bedroom to projects begun before April 1971 that would complete no more than two years later. This generated a rush to build massive hotels. In 1970, there was £60m of hotel construction in the UK, and it doubled the next year. Not all the projects got through. In 1970, Eric Miller's Peachey Property Company wanted to build the mother of hotels with 2000 bedrooms on the Edgware Road, which would have been slabs of thirty-six storeys/107m and forty-two storeys/137m joined together, by architects Stone Toms who had recently designed the rather plain low-rise Churchill Hotel at Portman Square. Their megahotel design looked like the RCA Building in New York's Rockefeller Centre, but was refused by the GLC in 1971.

Seifert, too, drew up a plan for a 2000-room hotel on the Cromwell Road, centred on an amazing huge slab with curves and slopes rising 116m. It was not built, but on half of the intended site the 914-room Penta Hotel (now the *Holiday Inn Kensington*) became the biggest post-war hotel anyway. Just up the road from the Peachey hotel site, the 577-room Metropole (now the expanded Metropole Hilton) went up. These were definitely not Seifert's best works, but, over in Knightsbridge, the 289-room Park Tower Hotel (now the *Sheraton Park Tower*) had some Seifert magic – the podium-mounted tower is a cylinder with bay windows, making the building look like a giant corn-on-the-cob.

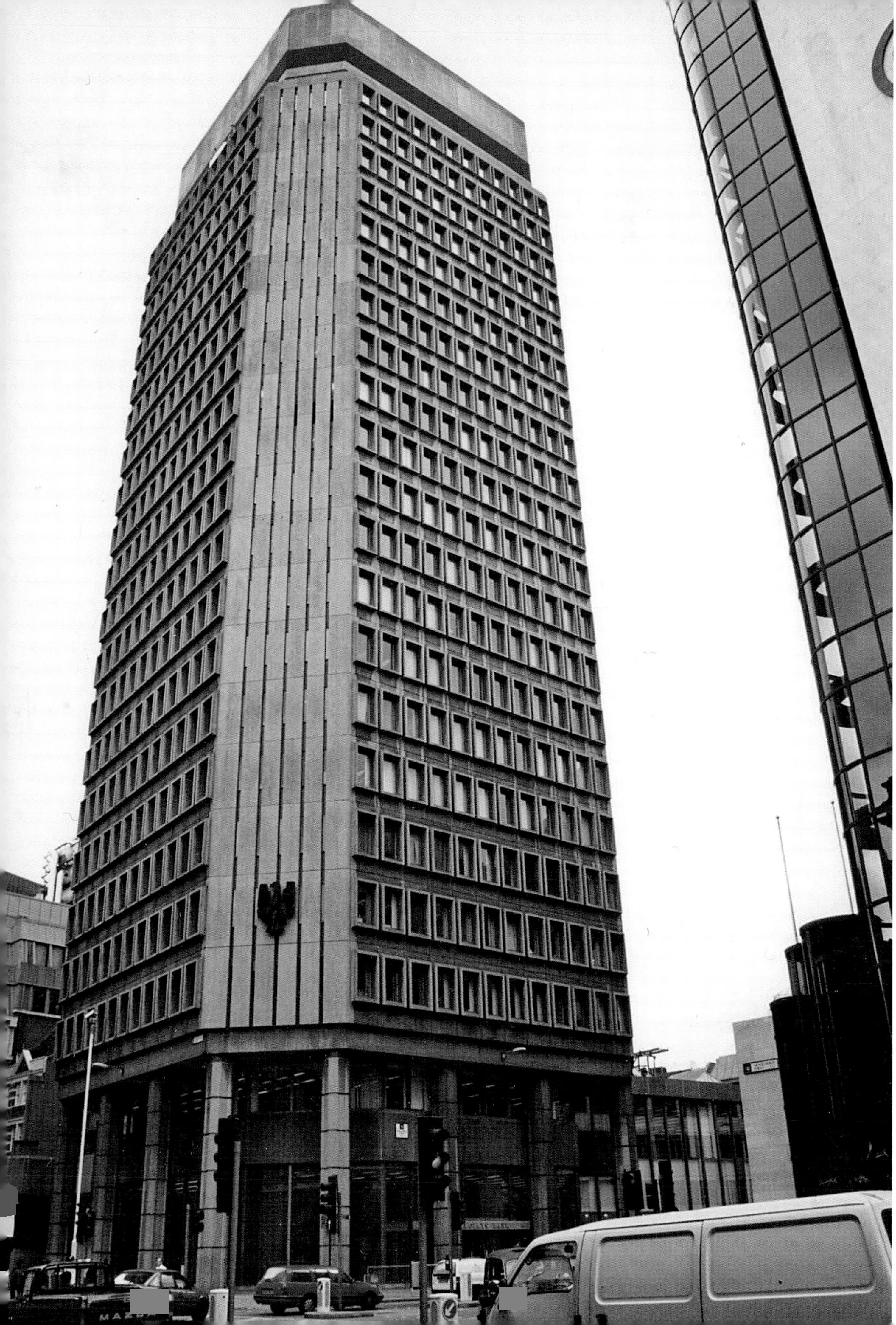

Limebank House, Fenchurch Street

The last of the huge new hotels was also the start of the Docklands revival, which we shall come to later. Howard Ward's *Tower Hotel* was yet another Brutalist exercise in concrete.

By the seventies, architects had realised something that curiously escaped the Brutalists – concrete stains, especially in the English weather. In 1984, Seifert would say that 'we had tried gutters and even gargoyles to throw off the rain, but we realised there was no way to stop it streaking and blotching. The pollution must settle somewhere. The only way to build in London is to use self-cleaning surfaces such as glass and polished stone'.

Indeed, covering the exterior with non-concrete panels gradually became a feature of high-rise blocks. Lightweight polished stone cladding, popular in banks in the fifties, was now covering skyscrapers such as Fitzroy Robinson's *One Angel Court*, as well as Seifert's late designs, *Windsor House* and the mid-rise blocks in front of Euston station. The Post Office's telecommunications arm, unacknowledged patrons of architectural experiment, occupied towers clad in stainless steel (*Keybridge House*) and shiny fridge-like white metal panels (Burne House at Edgware Road, 1979). Covering concrete exteriors with better materials was not just about making buildings look better, but making them weatherproof as well. As we have seen, re-cladding shabby old council tower blocks would start in the 1980s after the pioneering transformation of *Parsons House*; in the 1990s, this would become a key element of recycling old office towers.

What really killed off the concrete tower, however, were the forces that preferred things the way they were before concrete…

Revenge of the Conservationists

London's conservation movement had been kick-started by the destruction of the Euston Arch in 1962. This magnificent early Victorian entrance to the higgledy-piggledy old railway station was swept away to make an open space in front of the redeveloped station, where Seifert blocks would later stand. When news of the arch's impending destruction was announced, it galvanized the Victorian Society, who organized a 'Save the Arch' campaign led by the poet laureate, Sir John Betjeman. During the sixties, the Victorian Society, the Georgian Group and others fought a losing battle against the destruction of old London, but the government was beginning to take notice. The author and broadcaster Ian Nairn pointed out the mundanity of the comprehensive city centre redevelopments. Spike Milligan wrote a piece imagining St Paul's Cathedral entirely surrounded by skyscrapers and no longer visible from afar.

In 1967, the Civic Amenities Act established the first national conservation areas; a year later, the first buildings were officially listed to prevent redevelopment. The art historian Nikolaus Pevsner had already long embarked on a nation-wide comprehensive survey of buildings in a series of books by region, spelling out the heritage to be saved. In 1970, the GLC proposed a High Building Policy, which would protect certain London views from having tall buildings intrude on them. These included the views from the Royal Parks, and St Paul's from Waterloo Bridge. However, even after the government in 1976 approved the GLC's Urban Landscape Diagram, which contained the High Building Policy recommendations, legal enforcement was vague.

Two events made 1973 the turning point for London's conservationists. First, Christopher Booker and Candida Lycett-Green published *Goodbye London, An Illustrated Guide to Threatened Buildings*. Not only did this catalogue list virtually every London building under threat, it also identified the property developers behind the threats, as well as the architects, including Seifert, who won the largest coverage. The book was a surprise bestseller and channelled public protest into the conservation movement. Second, the long-standing plans to redevelop the Covent Garden area, derelict since the fruit and vegetable market was relocated (see *Market Towers*), were dealt a fatal blow by Edward Heath's Environment Secretary Geoffrey Rippon, who listed 200 buildings there in one fell swoop. Terry

Farrell's 1976 restoration of Georgian buildings in Ching Court, Covent Garden, showed that conservation architecture could be cool.

Conservation areas were being officially defined and extended across London. In 1976, a gang of four heritage pressure groups published the Save The City report, and, soon after, the City of London officially abandoned its plan to cover the Square Mile with a network of podium-level walkways, a scheme in which old buildings had only got in the way. In Parliament, the Skyline Bill was introduced in 1977 legally to enforce the protection of historic skylines, but the bill got lost in committees. Nevertheless, the RFAC was taking arms against the sea of distractions to the view of St Paul's from Waterloo Bridge, and that meant the end of plans such as Post Office Communications' projected twenty-storey tower by Cannon Street. Their proposal was to house Europe's biggest international telephone switching centre. It was eventually installed in their Plan B – the bizarre eight-storey stripey 'type-writer' of Mondial House (it now faces demolition).

By the late seventies, modern commercial architecture was exhausted and official support for commercial redevelopment schemes beginning to drain away. The property group Heron's proposal for a 137m-high hotel at the South Bank was rejected at a public inquiry. A glass skyscraper dubbed 'The Green Giant' at Vauxhall was an early case in the in-tray of Mrs Thatcher's Environment Minister Michael Heseltine, and he killed it in 1980. The post-war formula of demolition, road 'improvement' and tower was dead. Prince Charles would later declare, 'planning turned out to be a continuation of war by other means', and the public agreed with him.

Engineers Tube towards the Sky

In America, the late 1960s and 1970s had seen buildings in the modern styles reach mind-numbing heights. These were the result of engineering breakthroughs down to two men both associated with SOM. We have seen how Fazlur Khan's techniques enabled open-plan floors to expand and make buildings more rigid against the wind. Another SOM engineer, Myron Goldsmith, who had worked with Mies van der Rohe, had taken a mathematical approach to the problem of carrying their weight within their dimensions, and one of his solutions was cross-bracing – putting huge cross-girders in an exterior megaframe for rigidity. This solution characterises Chicago's 344m John Hancock Center, designed by Bruce Graham of SOM, and engineered by Khan. When it was finished in 1969, it was the second-tallest building in the world.

The old Chicago/New York rivalry was back on, and, in 1972, the twin towers of New York's World Trade Center, designed by Minoru Yamasaki and engineered by Leslie Robertson, became the world's tallest buildings at 412m. The twin towers were tubes-in-tubes, stacking 110 floors on trusses between the central core and an outer tube of steel columns. Two years later, SOM's Sears Tower in Chicago, engineered by Khan, reached 452m by bundling nine tower frames together for rigidity.

Skyscrapers on such a scale were way beyond the modest projects of European cities, although the fifty nine-storey Tour de Montparnasse in Paris did reach 209m in 1973 to become Europe's tallest. All the high-rise engineering breakthroughs seemed to be coming from America.

All, that is, except Seifert's. Like most high-rise, Seifert's buildings usually carried most of their load in the central concrete core, and he would take that idea to extremes. In his tallest tower completed in the 1970s, *Kings Reach*, the concrete core becomes a roofline asset. Kings Reach Tower in some ways looks like a trial run for his final world-class masterpiece, begun in 1970: the NatWest Tower (now *Tower42*). Here, Seifert actually hangs all the offices off the central core, like branches on a trunk of a tree, and there are no outer columns to take the load into the earth. It's an astonishing synthesis of engineering and aesthetics, and still stands as the world's tallest cantilevered building.

Seifert's staff had grown from twelve in 1955 to 300 in 1980, and he had over 600 projects under his belt – he had become the Norman Foster of his day. His impact on London had been compared to Christopher Wren's, to which the modest Seifert would say that the only thing they shared was ill-informed critics. Did Richard Seifert have a favourite building? Although he once suggested *Drapers' Garden*, it is not clear. In 2005, his widow Josephine Seifert said: 'It was always the next one, he always wanted to do something better. He wasn't interested in money, you know. Ever. He came to me one day. "Do you know?" he said, "we've made some money!" What he was interested in was doing the buildings. It never entered his mind that there was something attached to it other than the buildings'.

Seifert had planned to top even the Americans with a 150-storey project for Liverpool, where as early as 1966 Hyams had had a vision of developing the docks into a 10 million square feet mini-Manhattan, decades before Canary Wharf. Later, the listing of Albert Dock would consign such plans to history. The NatWest Tower was Seifert's only successful attempt to build really high. When it was finally finished in 1981, high-rise was in decline. The planning authorities that Seifert had worked with symbiotically in the sixties had turned on him in the seventies. Not only were they constantly trying to reduce the height of his plans, but Seifert became convinced that the RFAC was advising developers not to give him commissions. After the NatWest Tower was complete, he would hand the practice over to his son John, and become a consultant.

Lord Palumbo was still pushing the Mies van der Rohe slab for Mansion House. Following in the plot-accumulation steps of the 1960s tycoons, by 1982 he had acquired twelve of the thirteen freeholds and 345 of the 348 leaseholds to give him total control of the site. In 1984, the militant pressure group SAVE Britain's Heritage finally killed the plan in order to save the site's Victorian buildings (subsequently replaced anyway). Architects CZWG proposed splitting the office slab into two wedges for a laugh, but the whole idea of a skyscraper there had been put out of its misery. After NatWest, there were only two London skyscrapers left under construction – GMW's sleek van der Rohe-style block at *6-8 Bishopsgate*, and a modest brick-clad skyscraper misleadingly called Westminster House even though it's on the other side of the river. After that, three decades of skyline activity would fall still. By 1984, with a recession biting, construction generally in the City reached a thirty-year low.

The International Style would make a comeback, rebranded as one of the strands of Post-Modernism, but we have to wait until the new century until American corporate architects with global portfolios would bring that to London. In the mid-1980s, the very shape of offices that companies needed would change, and quite different architectural 'languages', along with new star architects, were waiting in the wings…

The Point, HA9
(Wembley Point)
1 Harrow Road

Tube, rail Stonebridge Park
Height 80m, 21 storeys
Designed 1963
Completed 1965
Architect Covell, Matthews & Partners

Covell Matthews have a place in British skyscraper history for their massive Piccadilly Gardens project in Manchester, which includes a huge office slab on a podium called Sunley Tower, rising 107m. But they had another, virtually unknown, massive skyscraper project at the same time – in the suburbs of South Wembley.

Wembley Point, as it was then known, was London's sixth-highest office skyscraper when completed in 1965. It was an unusual tower for the time. In plan, it's basically a triangle; but each façade has a shallow fold, so the building is actually hexagonal. Concrete columns act as mullions on some façades, but the windows between them are angled to the outer perimeter made by the columns, creating a serrated building edge and strange, displaced rhythms across the surface. A big concrete core emerges undisguised over the roofline. At its base, the River Brent flows through a concrete channel.

This century, the building has been refurbished and rebranded as serviced offices, with a health club and even trees in the reception. The top floor is a restaurant with remarkable views – not just the new Wembley Stadium 1.5km to the north, but also the Euston railway line, and, directly below, over the North Circular, the abandoned curved glass boxes by Seifert of Sperry-Univac House (1975).

It may be a coincidence, but there are strong similarities in the angles, façades and sheer heaviness of the *Stock Exchange Tower* before refurbishment. This remote, obscure skyscraper may well have cast a forgotten influence on the City skyline.

Looming over the suburbs

Westminster City Hall, SW1
Victoria Street

Tube Victoria, St James Park
Height 76m, 20 storeys
Area 16,150m²
Constructed 1962–65
Architect Sir John Burnet, Tait & Partners

The City of Westminster, one of London's most anti-skyscraper boroughs, operate from this bland International Style slab in Harold Samuels' massive Stag Place development, dominated by the massive *Portland House*. The council rent the second-tallest block, which juts out over the pavement of Victoria Street. It is clad in Portland stone, with aluminium strips running up at every fourth window to guide the window-cleaning cradle.

Contractors Taylor Woodrow started work in 1962. They floated a 130cm-thick concrete raft on top of bored piles 21m deep. Originally, the building was due for completion in July 1965, but in 1963 this was brought forward in time for the incorporation of the old boroughs of Paddington and St Marylebone into Westminster. When the building was topped out in August 1964, all three mayors – B Fitzgerald-Moore of Westminster, J Gillet of Paddington and Derek Simon of St Marylebone – drank a toast on the roof. The council moved in May 1965, occupying the whole building from the third floor. On the twelfth floor was their restaurant.

On 15 April 1971, when a security truck drew up round the back with £27,277 in cash for the council payroll, a van pulled up behind it, blocking the exit. A man later identified as David George Herrick brandished a shotgun and shouted: 'Don't move or I'll fire!' Herrick was the leader of a gang of six. The others wore balaclavas as they loaded the cash in and made a clean getaway. The guns they used were entrusted to gang member John Hyland, who worked at the '141' disco in Putney. When an irate father came into the disco looking for his teenage daughter, he threatened to call the police. Hyland decided to get the guns off the premises and put them in a zipped-up bag, which he handed to a priest he knew in Wandsworth for safekeeping. The priest couldn't help peeking in the bag and, when he saw guns, he went to the police about it. The gang was busted.

Apart from *Portland House*, the whole Stag Place development was the sixties at their worst. Some of it is coming down now, but City Hall is here to stay.

One Kemble Street, WC2
(Space House)

Tube Holborn
Height 52m, 16 storeys
Designed 1962
Completed 1966
Architect Richard Seifert & Partners

This drum-shaped tower is another project developed by Harry Hyams and designed by Seifert. It is connected to a more conventional block on Kingsway by a two-storey bridge. The cylinder is an efficient shape for a high-rise because it reduces lateral wind pressure, and this follows its use in the *Telecom Tower* and Birmingham's famous Rotunda, both finished a year earlier. What's also special about this building is Seifert's use of pre-cast concrete T-bars on the exterior, just as at *Centre Point*. The original design was far taller, but Seifert was forced to cut it down.

Developer Harry Hyams was keen on using Space Age names for his developments, such as Telstar House in Paddington (see *30 Eastbourne Terrace*), Early Bird House (these named after satellites), Orbit House, Planet House and Astronaut House. This tower was originally called Space House. For most of its life it has housed aviation-related tenants, British Aerospace and the CAA.

The block was refurbished in 2004, its exterior faithfully retained. It was re-named One Kemble Street and now houses CABE, the style police who give random verdicts on proposed developments. CABE chose a rather safe interior design by MoreySmith, but it's good that they chose a Seifert masterpiece to lodge in.

Centre: Westminster City Hall
Right: Lurking off Drury Lane

Marble Arch Tower, W1
Bryanston Street

Tube Marble Arch
Height 82m, 23 storeys
Area 12,500m² of offices
Completed 1966
Architect TP Bennett & Son

This tower on a podium was the eighth-tallest in London when completed in 1966. It overlooks the spot where for centuries rogues were hanged at Tyburn, and where John Nash's Marble Arch (1827) was stranded in a huge roundabout in 1958.

TP Bennett were not only major office architects, but also specialised in cinemas and theatres. The podium houses the Odeon Marble Arch, which replaced the Regal, where in 1928 the first UK screening of a talkie, *The Singing Fool*, took place (it was actually Al Jolson's second talkie after *The Jazz Singer*). The new Odeon had the largest screen in the UK, a giant 23 × 9m, and opened in February 1967.

The office tower gained a new two-storey marbled entrance in 2000 by architects Trehearne & Norman. It changed hands in 2004 for £73.5m, and, nowadays, tenants include Nokia.

The southern end of Central Park presents a sweep of New York commercial skyscrapers, but London's equivalent is this single, rather stumpy looking, square-planned tower. It looks shorter than it is because the floorplates are so wide. White vertical beams on the exterior, which make the windows look tiny, do, nevertheless, stress the vertical. This and the simplicity of the shape make it a classic International Style skyscraper.

New Scotland Yard, SW1
Victoria Street

Tube St James's Park
Height 67m, 20 storeys
Area 37,000m² office space
Designed 1962
Completed 1966
Architect Chapman Taylor & Partners

This International Style slab, and an eight-storey long block next to it, were built speculatively and replaced Victorian offices. It is headquarters of the Metropolitan Police, who put a £6m deposit down to rent the development by Harold Samuel in 1966, and moved in the following March. Their previous HQ, also called New Scotland Yard, was the Dutch-style building by Norman Shaw (1891) on Westminster's Embankment, made famous in newsreels, classic detective stories and films.

New Scotland Yard

Marble Arch Tower, soaring over Hyde Park

The triangular grey 'New Scotland Yard' prism on a stick outside the building opposite *55 Broadway* turns 200 times an hour. In the seventies, Shaw Taylor stood in front of it to present the pioneering television crime update programme *Police 5*, and since then its appearances in the news have made it an icon.

Inside the building, the Met mastermind and co-ordinate the policing of the metropolis. In 1984, the old Information Room, full of pin-board maps, was replaced with the Central Communications Complex, which handles all London's 999 calls to the police – 1.5 million every year. In the Special Operations Room, the Met control major events including demonstrations, terror alerts, processions and accidents. It is said they can track an individual over most of London Transport's Zone 1. The roof has two UHF radio aerial masts on it, each about 15m high.

In 2003, *Police Review* reported that New Scotland Yard was infested with mice. Since 2005, the Met have deployed a visible armed police presence outside it.

New Scotland Yard is bland, anodyne and anonymous, lacking any of the romantic associations of the old Norman Shaw building. It is incredibly shiny because of aluminium in the glass of its curtain-walls. At night, however, its floor-to-ceiling windows expose a lot of activity, and there's a feeling of a watchful Big Brother floating above his vast manor.

Wood Street Police Station, EC2

Tube St Pauls, Moorgate, Barbican
Height 41m, 12 storeys
Constructed 1962–66
Architect Donald McMorran & George Whitby

The slim little tower that is part of Wood Street Police station barely qualifies as a skyscraper by height, but does by its odd design. Like the *Shell Centre*, it resolutely defies the modern architecture of its time. With its pitched roof and stone façade, it looks as it was built in an earlier age. Architects McMorran and Whitby's style was 'progressive classicism', and they specialised in public buildings. McMorran committed suicide the year this was finished. The tower's arched punched windows suggest a building in a de Chirico painting, and indeed the influence was probably the Palazzo della Civilia Italia (1942) near Rome.

Wood Street Police Station was built on the site of a Roman fort. The tower originally provided beds for single police officers of the City of London Police, which is a separate force to the Metropolitan Police. Since 1983, the station houses units such as the Fraud Squad, Scientific Support Unit and the Traffic Patrol Section.

Even when it was being built, the police tower was overshadowed by the new glass boxes of *London Wall*. Nowadays, it's hemmed in by even bigger ones, including *Alban Gate*.

Royal Lancaster Hotel, W2
Westbourne Street

Tube Lancaster Gate
Height 65m, 20 storeys
Completed 1967
Architect TP Bennett & Partners

This leaden slab was adapted by Bennett from a concept for offices originally by Seifert. Pre-cast concrete frames covering the façades look similar to those at *Centre Point*, but are flat, so fail to animate the huge bland sidewalls, made worse with beige spandrels. A spiral ramp accesses a car park in the podium.

The Rank Organisation took over the project in 1966 just as the building was being finished, and opened the hotel in 1967. The Looking Glass Restaurant was at the top. High window-sills made it difficult to exploit the views over Kensington Gardens and Hyde Park, but interior designer Leonard Manesseh tackled the problem by placing the bar on a platform. With its low ceilings, covered with acoustic tiles from which prism lights hung, it was a rather tight space.

In *The Italian Job* (1969), the sociable villain played by Michael Caine has a big party after release from jail. This was shot in the Nine Kings Suite, which is huge – it can seat 1150 diners. Wall panels slide up to open up yet more space, and 89 chandeliers installed in 1989 come down on pulleys for cleaning. In the seventies, Rank turned the restaurant into apartments, and the designer

The Royal Lancaster Hotel

The Presidential Suite

décor was replaced with seventies hotel kitsch. In 1994, the 416-room hotel was purchased by a Thai hotelier, Mr Jatuporn.

In 2004, a £16m refurb by Eric Parry transformed the dull podium with a clean white Mediterranean look, more in keeping with the creamy Victorian terraces of Bayswater around it. A little chink of the original exterior was left over Lancaster Gate station. Interior design by Stiff + Trevillion has made the Forest Suite an airy, minimalist private dining space on the first floor. The smart designer Island Restaurant, serving new British cuisine, is entered from the street.

Mr Jatuporn himself sometimes stays in room 1820 at the top – the Presidential Suite. With its dreamy views over the park, it competes with the five-star hotels on Park Lane. The Royal Lancaster may be dreary outside, but it's classy inside.

Drapers' Garden, EC2
12 Throgmorton Avenue

Tube Bank
Height 99m, 30 storeys
Commissioned 1962
Completed 1967
Architect R Seifert & Partners and F Norman Jones

The magnificent bow-fronted skyscraper Drapers' Garden is the frontline in the struggle to preserve London's skyscraper heritage. By the time these words are published, this dreamy masterpiece by Richard Seifert may already be dismantled. If so, its redevelopment will irretrievably reduce the City's aesthetic and historic capital by eliminating the best sixties element of its skyline.

Swanky
Drapers' Garden rises above a two-storey podium whose attempts to relate to the narrow alleyways around it are, admittedly, a bit lame. However, the lower parts of the scheme have a period charm – a few steps rise from Throgmorton Avenue into an enclosed courtyard, containing a small paved garden with a concrete water feature of fountain and waterfall. Above this, the cantilevered slab floats, with two symmetrical halves curving out from the central core, and each further supported by four interior columns. Above the twenty-six floors of office is a trademark Seifert viewing gallery, and, above that, a concrete crown enclosing plant machinery. This tower is quite different from the contemporary International Style boxes, not just because of its curves, but also because of how the floors are presented.

While *Centre Point* subverts its horizontal repetition of floors with a hypnotic grid, Drapers' Garden accentuates it with wide bands of green-tinted reflective glass and narrow sills covered in white mosaic. Before it became stained by air pollution, this white and green exterior positively gleamed. The whole building has a radiance about it. The curvature exudes swank and class, evoking sunny 1920s architecture as if it were in Miami or Bexhill-on-Sea. It has been compared to great ocean liners. Seifert himself claimed he preferred Drapers' Garden to *Centre Point*.

Lost Banks
Why is Drapers' Garden important historically? First, like *Centre Point*, it was at the forefront of construction techniques in its day, in this case with its deep concrete piling, its flat concrete slab floors, and even the construction cranes used. It was also another collaboration between developer Harry Hyams and Richard Seifert. The Drapers' Guild, ancient owners of land, had offered the site to the highest bidder, specifying a plot ratio of 4:1. Hyams had trumped an alternative bid for four blocks designed by Milton Cashmore (see *CityPoint*) because Seifert, by deftly exploiting the 'Third Schedule' planning provision, managed to get the ratio

Drapers' Graden

Groovy curves

National Westminster's owners, the Royal Bank of Scotland, decided to tear it down (which makes it the tallest skyscraper in the UK to bite the dust), and build a cascade of new slabs designed by Foggo Associates, rising to a stumpy 75m. The planned replacement will offer the huge trading floors big companies demand. It is Drapers' Garden's bad luck that it doesn't fall within the sectors marked out to protect the views of St Paul's, so when Ken Livingstone considered it in 2002, he raised no objection, and the City Corporation granted planning consent to the new building. The tower and the planning consent with it was sold to Morgan Stanley in late 2005. The Twentieth Century Society had recommended listing, but was turned down, and a Certificate of Immunity is in place blocking any listing until June 2007. It's strange that the nearby brutal *Stock Exchange Tower* will get a new life, yet graceful Drapers' Garden is coming down.

But had anyone considered an alternative use for Drapers' Garden? The City has small tenants as well as big institutions, which is why *Tower42* is so successful. But here also is potentially the UK's most elegant retro-chic designer hotel, in the epicentre of the planet's financial powerhouse. Such a conversion would not only bring more life to the City outside of office hours, but would also cap an emerging trend to convert sixties towers to accommodation, which started with *Marathon House*, now flats.

The loss of Drapers' Garden is a mindless act of destruction.

up to 5:1. The Lord Mayor of London, Sir Robert Bellinger, formally opened the building on 15 June 1967. Finally, it was the headquarters of a lost British bank that was one of the major players of its time.

Until the 1960s, the National Provincial was a high-street bank, but then it began acquiring other banks and entered into merchant and off-shore banking. Now a force in the City, it rented the new Drapers' Garden tower at a record rent of £5/sq.foot, which netted Hyams a profit of about £7.3m. The bank's in-house architect, F Norman Jones, worked with Seifert to complete the building just as they wanted it. For a while, this was the most prestigious bank building in the country, after the Bank of England itself. The National Provincial merged with Westminster Bank to create National Westminster Bank in 1970, and the new giant would commission Seifert to design a giant new headquarters – *Tower42*, just a block away. While Drapers' Garden was occupied, it was popular with those who worked there. One can imagine go-ahead sixties public schoolboys in sharp Savile Row suits and groovy sideburns dashing past the bowler-hatted gents to exercise power high above the Square Mile.

20 Fenchurch Street, EC3

Tube Monument
Height 91m, 25 storeys
Commissioned 1963
Completed 1968
Architect CLRP Architects & Wallace F Smith

This nondescript square-planned City tower on a bog-standard podium has only two special features, and one is invisible. To create open-plan offices with no interior obstructions, the floors are hung from steel girders radiating from the central core. This pioneering technique was simultaneously being used in the nearby *Aviva Tower*. At 20 Fenchurch Street there were structural problems using long high-tension steel sections.

The other feature is the 'hat' on the roof, floating clear above the office floors. This houses plant machinery. In fact, 20 Fenchurch Street used to have a neighbour with a similar hat, and similar height and plan as well. That was Limebank House, demolished in 1997, which was wrapped in concrete. However, 20 Fenchurch Street uses glass, which is silvered to reduce solar gain. The tower was occupied by bankers Kleinwort Benson, now Dresdner Kleinwort Wasserstein.

In 2005, Land Securities approached American-Uruguayan architect Rafael Viñoly to design a replacement. His original design, was 192m high and lugubriously curves outwards from the middle, as if Dali had painted a 'soft' office tower. This, however, would have risen behind St Pauls seen from Ludgate Circus, so in 2006, it was reduced by about 40m, and a huge enclosed skygarden put at the top.

Aviva Tower, EC3
(CGU Tower, Commercial Union Tower)
Undershaft, City

Tube Bank
Height 118m, 28 storeys
Constructed 1964 69
Architect GMW

The Aviva Tower is the skyscraper that Mies van der Rohe might have left in London. This almost featureless black glass box rises straight from a plaza to a height that was the second tallest in the City when completed. Its internal structure brought to the UK unprecedentedly deep, open floorplans.

The area between Bishopsgate and St Mary Axe, once a warren of alleys, has long been where the City's insurance business is concentrated. Here in 1961, Commercial Union Assurance acquired the Great St Helens site, adjacent to shipping company P&O's land, and they decided jointly to develop their combined patch. This created a new plaza opposite Lloyd's of London (then still in its 1920s building) between P&O's thirteen-storey block and the Aviva Tower. Just as with van der Rohe's Seagram Building in New York, the creation of a plaza allowed a taller building with a smaller footprint, initially called the Commercial Union Tower, then later the CGU Tower. The Aviva Tower is now occupied by the insurer of the same name, and clusters with skyscrapers all occupied by the insurance sector — *Lloyd's*, Swiss Re in *30 St Mary Axe*, and Willis in the new *Willis Building*. The P&O building is set to be replaced by Richard Roger's *Leadenhall Building*.

20 Fenchurch Street

Miesian night

Aviva Tower

becoming a greenhouse furnace. Double-glazing was considered, but as GMW notes, 'the payback time did not justify the capital cost'. The combination of deep floors and dark glass suggests natural light would have been insufficient, and indeed many lower buildings in the City's tight fabric of ancient lanes were dim places by day unless the lights were on. Terry Brown observes that 'with windows floor to ceiling, there was more than enough natural light. It was only on the north and south that the depth was enough to justify a central zone of lighting'. Thus all the office floors were bathed in permanent fluorescent light. The enhancing effect of internal lighting on external appearance was something that GMW had pulled off before, in London's first glass office slab, Castrol House (which became *Marathon House*).

This dark 26,000m² tower expresses corporate cool at its most severe. Not everyone likes such stuff – Renzo Piano, addressing *The Shard*'s Public Enquiry in 2003, had towers like it in mind when he expressed disdain for 'normal' towers. Because they have to defend the interior space from solar gain, he argued, 'they are quite black. Like those people who wear sunglasses, they have become mysterious'. Yet this mystery at the Aviva Tower evaporates at night when the office lights shine, creating perhaps the best sixties London example of the Manhattanesque box of light. More remarkable still, the Aviva Tower by day hasn't dated like other sixties blocks – it remains timeless, like a pure, simple mathematical form.

Euston Tower, NW1
Euston Road

Tube Warren Street
Height 124m, 36 storeys
Developed 1963–70
Architect Sidney Kaye, Eric Firmin & Partners

This giant Modernist skyscraper was the highpoint of the five-hectare Euston Centre. From 1956, Joe Levy acquired over 300 leases along the Euston Road. Here a motorway style cloverleaf junction of flyovers and sliproads was originally envisioned. As with *Centre Point*, another secret deal was reached with the LCC – they got a strip of land to widen the road and build the Euston Underpass, while Levy got permission to develop adjacent to it. Levy proposed building three identical huge blocks, but the LCC insisted that the blocks get lower towards Regent's Park. Site clearance began at the end of 1963. The following year, the lease collection at last complete, the masterplan was unveiled. One of its architects, Sidney Kaye, had worked on the *Park Lane Hilton*.

The plan was for a complex of long plain office blocks and towers, the tallest audaciously challenging the height of the just topped-out *Centre Point* at the other end of Tottenham Court Road. The smaller tower was finished first (see *338 Euston Road*). The Euston Centre project emerging from the great excavation covering the site cost £3.5m to build but was valued at £17m in 1968, with the

GMW pioneered the design of floors hung from cantilevered beams coming out of the central core. By the time of construction, the Kleinwort Benson tower at *20 Fenchurch Street* and the CU Tower were simultaneously using this technique, creating large floorplates with no interior columns between the curtain wall and the core. The open-plan offices were a change from the compartmentalised offices of the time.

The Aviva Tower has two plant floors, one at mid height. The boilers were placed on the top floor, so skipping the need for flues running up the building, and also allowing 128 basement car park spaces. After the City of London abandoned its vision of a network of high-level walkways in the seventies, the tower's second floor, which could be walked around and was connected to the walkway system, was reclaimed for offices. When the IRA bombed Bishopsgate in April 1993, all of the towers' windows were blown out, leading to a refurbishment. In 2003, Simon Halabi, the property magnate who is now a partner in *The Shard*'s development, brought the Aviva Tower for £238m.

The Aviva Tower's glass, held in aluminium mullions, may look black, but is actually a shade called Parallel-o-Gray, and is there to stop the sealed building

LCC's strip valued at £2m. Euston Tower, with over 35,000m^2 of space, was the last major element to be finished. Stock Conversion was to make £22m from the Euston Centre, making Levy the most successful London skyscraper speculator after Harry Hyams.

Construction had included building larger-than-average cable ducts under the Euston Road, with access from the huge underground car parks. These ducts were used by MI5, whose job is countering all inland threats to national security. MI5's headquarters were nearby at 140 Gower Street, and they installed their Communications Control Centre on the middle floors, probably from the fourteenth upwards. From there, they ran an 0800 (toll-free) number for agents to call in, as well as their telephone-tapping operations. In 1978, surveillance operations, including the A4 'Watchers' department. moved in. MI5's operations were later centralised in Thames House, a refurbished thirties block by Lambeth Bridge, and the Communications Control team left for there in 1994. The fate of the Watchers, however, is not known.

Civil servants from government agencies such as the Inland Revenue also took space, sometimes as a cover for MI5. Another tenant was Capital Radio, London's first commercial music radio station, on the first floor. They started broadcasting in October 1973. Many famous DJs and broadcasters have worked in Euston Tower's studios, including Tony Blackburn, Dave Cash, Garry Crowley, Kenny Everett, Alan 'Fluff' Freeman, Gerald Harper, Chris Tarrant and James Whale. Capital relocated to Leicester Square in 1996.

This century, the current owners British Land embarked on a massive redevelopment of the Euston Centre, demolishing the hideous long blocks along the Euston Road, recycling the smaller tower, erecting new buildings and public spaces, and generally making the whole place a cool urban setting. Euston Tower is the only part of it that has not been refashioned. It had a big internal refit to accommodate modern plant and information services, and secondary glazing was put in. The only

visible change, apart from new Sainsbury, Starbucks and Prêt-a-Manger outlets, is the bright reception and lobby by refurbishment specialists Hawkins/Brown, completed in 2003. The style is white minimalist, electrified by splashes of vivid colour.

Euston Tower is now London's highest example of the glass curtain-walled rectilinear block set on a podium, following Manhattan's Lever House. However, it is not in fact a slab but has a square plan with a small wing on each corner. Euston Tower still has its original exterior – blue glass and dark blue spandrels behind rows of thin vertical stainless steel mullions. Now, nearly four decades later, it's possible to look at this building as a period piece. It is good news for London that British Land have left an outstanding example of a pure sixties International Style landmark.

NLA Tower
Addiscombe Road

Rail East Croydon
Height 82m, 24 storeys
Completed 1971
Architect R Seifert & Partners

Probably the worst cluster of sixties high-rise offices in Europe lies in Croydon. Encouraged by the Location of Offices Bureau, set up to disperse offices from central London, Croydon's zealous head of planning Sir James Marshall put through five million square feet of offices in the 1960s, creating a collection of ugly concrete stumps. Croydon had to wait for Seifert's tower, which was characteristically different. George Marsh executed the project.

Development plans were frustrated from 1964 by a Miss Harding, a solicitor who refused to sell her 1890s offices next door, and brought a Bible to meetings about the plans. In the end, the tower was built on a traffic island without disturbing her house. The tower gets its name from its original occupant, Noble Lowndes Annuities. Locals now call the tower the '50p Building', but when it was under construction it was known as the 'Wedding Cake Building', then the 'Threepenny Bit Building', after a pre-decimalisation twelve-sided coin.

The NLA Tower's floors are squares, alternately twisted forty-five degrees, and then cut at the corners to create octagons. The resulting bay window corners are vaguely reminiscent of Seifert's *Sheraton Park Tower*, but the overall effect is quite different – a rhythmic succession of protruding floors and recesses, all covered in mosaics. It's zany and unrepeated elsewhere.

The NLA Tower is Croydon's tallest building, by just three metres. One day it may be dwarfed by Croydon Gateway, where a thirty-five-storey office tower is planned, but plans have long been bogged down in a dispute about land ownership.

Euston Tower

Stock Exchange Tower, EC2
Old Broad Street

Tube Bank
Height 99m, 26 storeys
Commissioned 1964
Completed 1972
Architect Llewelyn Davies, Weeks, Forestier-Walker &
Bor, Fitzroy Robinson & Partners

Remodelling 2005–07
Architect Nicholas Grimshaw & Partners

This dark, concrete block was a grim presence on the
City skyline but is now being reborn as a bright,
modern glass skyscraper.

London's Stock Exchange had occupied this half-
hectare site since 1802. In 1964, planning permission was
granted to redevelop at a plot ratio of 5.8:1. The new
buildings would link into the City's podium-level
walkway scheme, which was then envisioned to come

even here, within a block of the Bank of England. A
bewildering constellation of architects worked on the
scheme, which included a three-storey building and an
open public area at the podium level above the trading
floors. The tower itself was seven-sided, basically a
hexagon stretched along the axis of the tower's twin
cores, but with a sharp corner cut off. It contained
21,000m² of offices. The tower was topped out in 1969 and
opened by the Queen in 1972. Like contemporaries such
as New York's World Trade Center, the tower had narrow
windows and thick ribs running up the entire height, but
here the material is concrete. This was a Brutalist tower.
Its shape and windows are strangely similar to *The Point*
in distant Wembley, another heavy, forbidding stump of
a building. There was a medieval robustness about the
Stock Exchange Tower.

The IRA left a bomb in a toilet, which exploded early
on a July morning in 1990. Coded warnings came shortly
before, and 300 traders, dressed in their traditional
colourful blazers, were evacuated, so no-one was hurt.
The concrete was sturdy but a 3m hole was blown in it.

For a while this century, it was called the 'exchange
tower' (which got it confused with an 'Exchange Tower'
in Docklands), and a designer reception was installed to
lure in new tenants, but the offices were out of date. In
2003, the Stock Exchange got planning permission for a
refurbishment by Nicholas Grimshaw. The tower will
gain a floor, be re-clad in glass to 101m, and with two new
satellite buildings, one with stepped roof gardens, the
space will double. A new ground-level passage will cross
the site. With the permit in the bag, it was sold to
developer Hammerson in 2004 for £67m, and the Stock
Exchange relocated to Paternoster Square. Hammerson,
after commissioning architect-planners Fletcher Priest
to look at all options, started clearing the site for the
Grimshaw makeover in late 2005.

Hilton London Metropole, W2
(The Metropole Hotel)
225 Edgware Rd

Tube Edgware Road
Height 91m, 24 storeys
Completed 1973 (Phase 1)
Architect R Seifert & Partners

This major four-star hotel has grown in stages, but the
heart of it is still the original concrete slab tower
designed quickly by Seifert in the seventies hotel boom,
and executed by Dick Morris. It stands opposite Seifert's
first skyscraper, remodelled as *Capital House*. Originally,
the hotel was to be called The Plaza, but developers AVP
Industries also owned the grand Victorian Metropole
Hotel in Brighton, and decided to name their London
showpiece after it.

The construction of the tower was an antisocial
nightmare. Continuous slip-forming of the two concrete
cores meant twenty-four-hour working, which was very
noisy and kept students and nurses at nearby St Mary's

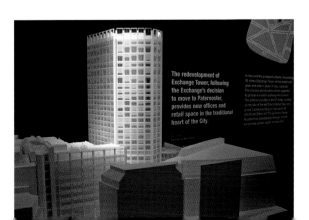

The redevelopment of
Exchange Tower, following
the Exchange's decision
to move to Paternoster,
provides new offices and
retail space in the traditional
heart of the City.

Stock Exchange Tower

The Grimshaw Treatment

Holiday Inn London Kensington Forum, SW7
(Penta then Forum Hotel)
100 Cromwell Road, Kensington

Tube Gloucester Road
Height 84m, 27 storeys
Commissioned 1968
Constructed 1971–73
Architect R Seifert & Partners

Perhaps the worst skyscraper to come off the Seifert drawing boards, this monster hotel also vanquished a Victorian Kensington garden square. Curiously, this could have been one of London's most exciting skyscrapers, albeit in the wrong place.

The Cromwell Road became a major hotel zone in the 1960s, especially after 1963, when BEA (British European Airways) opened their massive new West London Air Terminal, connected by coach to Heathrow. (This has since become the Point West luxury flats.) As the government's grant of £1,000 per hotel bedroom built by 1973 created a rush of giant hotels, Lord Mancroft of the London Tourist Board said the Cromwell Road would soon be the 'Costa Cromwellia'.

When Maxwell Joseph's Grand Metropolitan Hotels commissioned Seifert, they planned Europe's biggest hotel with 2000 rooms, covering two blocks. The design was stunning. A huge slab was designed with a curved sloping profile, which above thirty storeys sloped more gently to a peak at 116m, and plunged at its leading edge at a steep incline. There were three wings on either side, of about twenty, sixteen and twelve storeys, and at the back, an eleven-storey semi-circular structure housing a conference centre. A bridge would have spanned the Cromwell Road to the Air Terminal. The design was a futurist fantasy on a huge scale – brilliant, but totally out of character with Kensington's genteel terraces.

In the end, Grand Metropolitan gained consent for only half their site – Ashburn Gardens. This block had a garden between two Victorian terraces, and planning consent required that the same area of garden be retained. All that remains now are a few mature trees around the hotel. The new hotel was still a whopper and had to be knocked up quickly, and Seifert put Jack Clowes in charge of the job. The height compromise meant that the shorter slab now sprouted three bulky full-height extensions to pack in some of the lost rooms – there are 914. These crude bolt-on boxes are plain bad architecture. The long slab, however, angled at forty-five degrees to the Cromwell Road, still gives some

Medical College awake. By day, workmen wolf-whistled at female students. At one point in 1971, a fire broke out in a work shed. Two workers were injured by falling scaffolding, and cars and buses were damaged by objects falling from the site. The finished hotel contained 577 rooms and nine suites, and was London's tallest hotel after the *Park Lane Hilton*.

In the nineties, cascading terraces marked by globe lamps were added, rising 52m up the side of the Seifert tower. This softens the hotel's appearance from the Edgware Road's southern stretch, where it had looked a bit like a huge tombstone. A massive 356-room sixteen-storey West Wing extension, designed by HOK International, was added in 2000. Hilton put the hotel up for sale in 2005.

Other seventies hotel boom buildings, including Seifert's own Penta Hotel (now the *Holiday Inn Kensington*), were characterised by bland exteriors and upmarket interiors. Although refurbished, the Metropole's lobby still evokes the contract-décor feel of the seventies. In 2004, however, the Aspects of London restaurant at the top was given a cool designer overhaul, including a fairytale silvery spiral staircase.

impression of movement with an angled end and pitched roofs. Another element from the first scheme is the strong horizontal stratification of window-lines. Strangely, the plant machinery's housing there has since become bright white.

In 1986, a £7m refurbishment of the lobby with a glass lift marked an upmarket shift in the hotel, which is now four-star and busy with conference and banqueting facilities, bar and restaurants. The luxury within is a big contrast to the shoddiness outside.

Sheraton Park Tower Hotel, SW1
101 Knightsbridge

Tube Knightsbridge
Height 55m, 17 storeys
Commissioned 1968
Constructed 1971–73
Architect R Seifert & Partners

In the early 1970s rush to cash in on government grants for new hotel beds, some fine locations suddenly found themselves with bulky new neighbours. One such place was Lowndes Square, where from 1839 Thomas Cubitt built his classy trademark white stucco terraces.

The Park Tower Hotel replaced a department store called Woodlands, which was acquired by Maxwell Joseph's Grand Metropolitan Hotels. Prime Minister Edward Heath officially opened the hotel in late 1973. After the design mess of the Forum Hotel, opened earlier that year (see *Holiday Inn Kensington Forum*), this work went some way to restoring Seifert's reputation…

The design, executed by George Marsh, was a change from the usual boxy hotels going up elsewhere. Rising from a podium is a cylindrical tower, which prompted the *Architectural Review* to describe it as 'gasometric'. With protruding window bays for each of the 289 rooms, the visual effect is a bit like an ear of corn on the cob. Seifert

wanted to build a taller, thinner hotel, but was thwarted. He later commented: 'As you push these things down, inevitably they get squatter. Pity'.

Nowadays, the hotel is a five-star Sheraton, and the extended podium houses a casino and the One-O-One restaurant, which has won awards this century as London's best fish restaurant.

The London Studios, SE1
**(London Weekend Television House
then Kent House)**
Upper Ground

Tube Waterloo
Height 82m, 25 storeys
Designed 1968
Completed 1973
Architect Elsom Pack & Roberts (EPR)

This major South Bank tower was originally the headquarters and studios of London Weekend Television (LWT), and is now occupied by ITV.

The riverside area between the Oxo Building and the site of the National Theatre was cleared in the sixties of warehouses and wharves. LWT House rose from the site of paper traders Bowater, and now sits between a Brutalist concrete structure housing IBM and Gabriel's Wharf, vibrant with food and slightly chaotic crafts businesses.

LWT was franchised in 1967 for commercial broadcasting across London on weekends. The plans kept altering even during construction as television operational requirements changed. The first shows were broadcast from the new studios in April 1972. In the nineties, new ITV franchises GMTV and Carlton took up residence, and ITV1 transmission was centralised there. In 2004 the 14,000m² complex was renamed The London Studios. The three studios and supporting facilities are

Kensington and its Holiday Inn

Sheraton Park Tower and The London Studios

in a three-storey podium building, and studio audiences queue at the side of it.

The architects have a long history of commercial architecture in London, dating back to the fifties when founding partner Cecil Elsom designed the *Eastbourne Terrace* offices. From the seventies, the practice transformed Victoria Street from its grim heritage of sixties developments (two of their latest buildings snuggle up to *Portland House*), and was also responsible for the glass wedge of the ABN Amro Bank (1999) on Bishopsgate.

The London Studios tower is basically a square plan stack of nineteen office floors, but what's special is the strong horizontal strata of white mosaic and dark windows (double-glazed anodised aluminium), all cut by vertical columns. The black and white layering gives the tower the look of a huge Licorice Allsort, very different from the seventies taste for brown exteriors. When the exterior columns end, their lines continue upwards as gaps in a wall around the rooftop plant, like open slits in a castle wall.

Recently, on the northeast corner half way up the tower, someone installed a continuous blue glass panoramic window, breaking the building's meticulous exterior patterning. Despite this, the tower rises as crisply and cleanly after thirty years as when it was completed.

The International Press centre, the original scheme

International Press Centre, EC4
Shoe Lane

Rail, tube Farringdon
Height 60m, 18 storeys
Commissioned 1968
Completed 1975
Architect R Seifert & Partners

Fleet Street used to be the world's most famous street for the press, but when Rupert Murdoch moved to Wapping in the 1980s, and *One Canada Square* started to attract newspapers in the 1990s, its ancient print and distribution industry just drained away. In the 1960s, however, Fleet Street was going strong, and a Tory MP and journalist, William Deedes, had the idea to build a Press Centre. Today, few foreign newspaper correspondents are left in the International Press Centre, and the occupants come from all sorts of business.

Seifert's original idea in 1968 was to build a white sliver, shaped like a quill. It would have been one of London's most sublime towers – cantilevered out from its core, a slender curved tower would rise 30 storeys, its profile stepped at 20 storeys, with bands of windows suggesting feathers. *Tower42*'s form would later draw on the concept.

Like many Seifert ideas, it was cut down by the RFAC, but the revised design, executed by Dick Morris, is still unusual. The building is composed of four bundled towers rising above a recessed lobby behind trademark Seifert dinosaur legs. The corners are rounded and slightly shallower than a right angle, making the building an octagon with grooves. The rounded airliner-style windows are huge, dominating the façades. Looking up at the building can feel like confronting a huge creature with polycellular bug eyes. The topping-out ceremony was attended by Environment Minister Peter Walker.

This is another Seifert skyscraper under threat. It should be listed immediately.

International Press Centre

Beds by the Tower

The Tower Hotel, E1
(Tower Thistle Hotel)
St Katherine's Dock

Tube, DLR Tower Hill, Tower Gateway
Height 48m, 15 storeys
Constructed 1970–74
Architect Howard Ward Partners (RHWL)

This bizarre ziggurat marks the first step in the redevelopment of Docklands that would initially peak in Canary Wharf and which continues today. Within months of St Katherine's Dock closing to ships in 1969, contractor Taylor Woodrow won the bid to build a new sort of urban space, mixing historic warehouses with modern buildings and transforming the quaysides to public realm. This is the formula of most future Docklands regeneration. TW paid £1.5m to the GLC for the site, and next to Tower Bridge they built the Tower Hotel.

The 853-room hotel has a long cross plan, with the wings stepping up from the ends to the centre. The shape is unique, with the window lines emphasising the horizontal. It is clad in concrete. In its previous existence, it was a part of the Thistle hotel chain, but in 2005 new operators Guoman Hotels reverted to the name The Tower.

Not many people like the look of the building, and Ken Shuttleworth has called it 'a real blot on the landscape', but it is a good example of early seventies Brutalism.

140 London Wall, EC2

Tube Barbican, St Pauls
Height 69m, 13 storeys
Completed 1976
Architect Powell, Moya & Partners

140 London Wall is the only skyscraper by the legendary team of Philip Powell and Hidalgo 'Jacko' Moya, who designed the first multi-storey social housing at Churchill Gardens, Pimlico, and the amazing Skylon, the science-fiction 75m aluminium mast that was the centrepiece for the Festival of Britain on the South Bank, which was later recycled as scrap metal.

140 London Wall was originally Bastion House, intended as the sixth of the virtually identical sixties office blocks on *London Wall*. It occupies the same envelope, continuing the repetitious configuration of slabs, but with a typically seventies skin of dark reflective windows and brown spandrels. What is special is the way the block floats a clear two storeys above the Museum of London's roof.

London Wall, humanised block

Access from the podium-level walkway is via one of the concrete cores at either end of the slab. 140 London Wall is the only seventies high-rise on London Wall, so it's like a bridge between the original development and the eighties Post-Modernist *Alban Gate*.

Philip Powell is known as the father of 'Humane Modernism'. A better example that illustrates this is the garden in front of the Museum of London's entrance, which spirals down like a vortex into the round fortress-like construction in the middle of the adjacent traffic roundabout.

Market Towers, SW8
Nine Elms Lane

Tube Vauxhall
Height 75m, 23 storeys
Completed 1975
Architect GMW

When Covent Garden was earmarked for comprehensive redevelopment in the seventies, London's wholesale market for flowers, fruit and vegetables had to move out. It was trading about a million tonnes annually, so a new location needed to be huge. It moved to surplus railway land at Vauxhall, handily opposite the Nine Elms Cold Store, a windowless concrete box built to store food for London in the event of war. GMW designed the whole £40m market complex, with trading unit buildings and masses of space for lorries. For the administration centre, GMW came up with two slabs of twenty-one and sixteen-storeys, curtain-walled in the typically seventies style of bronzed windows and brown spandrels, mounted on a podium.

When work began pouring concrete into the pile-bores for the foundations, it seemed to vanish. Project architect Lyn Edwards found that in fact, the concrete was pouring into the Thames down an abandoned culvert, so

the design was changed and a 2.4m thick raft built. The slabs that rose from this contain 16,440m² of open plan offices. They are connected by a massive concrete service core with the main banks of lifts, and smaller concrete cores carry stairs at the slab ends. In plan, the whole shape is like a slipped H. The podium had banks, shops and a restaurant (which would in the nineties become a notorious garage music club). Vauxhall had plans for a City-like network of high-level walkways, so a link was built, now removed. A ridiculously dainty barrel-roofed glass entrance was installed at Market Towers later.

What's interesting about this skyscraper is that the whole structure is a strong mix of late International Style glass boxes and bulky Brutalist concrete columns. Also, with *Keybridge House* going up nearby, it launched Vauxhall as a potential skyscraper cluster location, which should get serious when *Vauxhall Tower* is built.

Keybridge House, SW8
80 South Lambeth Road

Tube Vauxhall
Height 76m, 15 storeys
Designed 1971
Completed 1976
Architect GW Mills & Associates

Keybridge House was built for the telex boom and almost ate a church.

The site facing Vauxhall's Portuguese community was previously occupied by a grim old Victorian building, Brand's Essence Factory. British Telecom's predecessor, Post Office Communications, commissioned a telecoms centre. It would combine a telex exchange to handle 101,000 telexes an hour, a trunk centre for the South East, switchrooms for 500 telephonists, and a service centre for 350 field engineers and 100 vans. £56m was budgeted, £45m of that for equipment. Keybridge House's very name is linked to telex technology, bridging keyboards to telecommunications.

What exactly is telex? It's rather like big text messages – block capital text is sent down a phone line to a teleprinter somewhere else. Faxes began to supersede telexes after 1984.

The design brief specified that the Romanesque-style St Anne's Church (by R. Parkinson, 1874) should not be overpowered, despite being hemmed in on two sides by the site. However, not only did Keybridge House totally overpower the little church, but during construction almost swallowed it! As a huge hole 12m deep was excavated for a cofferdam, the church foundations started to slide towards it. Church walls cracked, holes appeared in the floor, and stairs became loose. Despite all this, the church stayed in business.

By the time Keybridge House became operational in 1978, automatic dialling was rendering switch-board operators redundant, and the Post Office 1971 predictions about telex were optimistic – outbound international telex traffic volume was 58.7 million in 1978,

Market Towers

Southwark Towers
London Bridge Street

Tube, rail London Bridge
Height 100m, 25 storeys
Completed 1976
Architects T P Bennett & Son

This is the huge tower that faces demolition to make way for *The Shard*, London Bridge, and a lot of people are glad about it. It will be the tallest skyscraper in the UK to bite the dust, beating *Drapers' Garden*.

Southwark Towers was tied in to the reconstruction of London Bridge station underneath it, and the new bus station there. It's an unusual building, basically three slabs radiating from a central core, containing 19,880m^2 of offices. The slabs are of different heights and lengths, and their service ends are typically seventies in their use of brick. The façades are unusual in that gold reflecting glass is used in wide brise-soleils mounted beyond the windows. The international accountancy firm Price Waterhouse moved in when it was completed, and still enjoy the facilities such as a swimming pool and the highest roof garden in London.

PriceWaterhouseCoopers (as they are now called) were not initially keen to be moved on by Sellar Property, *The Shard* developer. They were given a deadline of late 2005 to go. That year, they refurbished lifts and redecorated lavatories, but then again there's a lot of wear and tear with 2,500 workers.

The Times described Southwark Towers as a 'hideous block', and it is widely seen as bad seventies architecture. Certainly, Renzo Piano's replacement tower is in a completely different class to it. Nevertheless, Southwark Towers is not a run-of-the-mill office tower. All that gold glass can make it glow with a radiant warmth when it reflects the low sun in the sky. Such moments transcend architecture... but they are fleeting.

against a forecast 81 million. Keybridge House opened with the UK's first electronic telex exchange, directed by a 'Stored Programme Computer' – a pioneering step in telecommunications switching.

The tower and its adjoining long five-storey podium have tall floor heights because exchange equipment dictates a ceiling height of 4.5m. The equipment needs a constant temperature environment, and this gives rise to Keybridge House's two distinguishing architectural features. First, a bundle of big flues runs up from the boilers providing heating. Second, the concrete building is clad with remarkably shiny stainless steel strips, which cover ventilation pipes and air-handling units, and help cool the double-glazed floors in summer.

This complex, metallic exterior service structure anticipates Richard Rogers' characteristic ventilation pipes, as in the *Lloyd's Building*. Keybridge House, like the *Telecom Tower* is actually a foretaste of High-Tech Post-Modernism.

Keybridge House

Southwark Towers

Union Jack Club &
91 Waterloo Road, SE1
(ICFIC Building)

Tube Waterloo
Height 79m, 25 storeys high and 69m, 16 storeys
Constructed 1974–76
Architect Fitzroy Robinson & Partners

Since 1907, the Union Jack Club has offered accommodation to the armed forces – it used to have a reputation for 'randy sailors'. The Edwardian building was replaced by a cluster of towers, two of them housing the current club's accommodation. The tallest tower is very slender and was the fourth-highest skyscraper behind the South Bank when built, while the shorter one is just ten storeys high. The club itself has 346 rooms and was opened by the Queen in 1976.

The Union Jack's redevelopment was financed by the fifteen-storey office tower on Waterloo Road. It's a typical seventies glass box with brown panelling, and is now occupied by venture capital agency 3i. Its service core lurks behind it, clad in the same dark brick as the club's accommodation towers.

Brick exteriors were popular in the seventies, and the Union Jack Club uses a particularly dark purple-brown brick that has the effect of suggesting the smoke-stained colours of London before the war. However, rather than humanising the building, the brick makes the Union Jack Club a grim, dour affair.

King's Reach Tower, SE1
Stamford Street, Southwark

Tube Southwark
Height 111m, 30 storeys
Designed 1972
Constructed 1973–78
Architect R Seifert & Partners
Remodelling design Make, 2005

King's Reach Tower is another extraordinary Seifert building, but will be transformed by Ken Shuttleworth into something quite science-fiction.

King's Reach Tower was contemporary with *Tower 42*, and there are many obvious similarities, not least a huge concrete core that emerges at the top, and the exterior vertical fins. The top of the core contains plant machinery and is overlaid with mosaic. The thin exterior concrete ribs start below this head, and are spaced every 2.7m in a ring that encloses the offices, some extending outwards as fins. Most of the floors are quite small, just 900m². Towards the ground, they recess behind the ribs, which become columns, before vanishing entirely just above a podium walkway. Without the columns, the offices would have had to cantilevered, as at Tower42. The tower is not square in plan, but has two opposite curved corners. The podium-level connects to a six-storey satellite building, and also carries a distinctly seventies garden – plants grow in sloping boxes erupting from a courtyard pavement.

Union Jack Club and Kings Reach Tower

Southwark Council initially refused any offices here, because the area was zoned as 'Waterside and Industrial', but the tower went ahead after a public inquiry. Construction was complex and lengthy, another similarity with *Tower42*. Some find King's Reach Tower stolid and overbearing, but actually it reflects the 1970s attempts to 'humanise' modern buildings with brown spandrels and dark glass, warmer than the cold blues and greens of the International Style and the grey of Brutalism. The soft colour, rounded edges, staggered roofline and vertical ribs together make King's Reach Tower a contrast to any other London skyscraper.

King's Reach Tower became the headquarters of the International Publishing Corporation's magazine empire, now ipc media and part of Time Warner. Staff complained that the offices were dingy and poky, although that seemed to suit some – *19 Magazine*, up on the 27th floor, operated in a chaotic mess that probably reflected the state of bedrooms of their teenage audience. In 2004, ipc decided to move to new premises on Southwark Street rather than renew their lease.

The South Bank is set to become a ribbon of spectacular new skyscrapers, and new plans are emerging on King's Reach Tower's doorstep, including an amazing glass *Beetham Tower*. Competing against such eye-candy, owners Capital & Counties had to do something sexy to make tenants look. They commissioned Make.

Make is headed by ex-Foster partner Ken Shuttleworth. Although it had already won a contract to masterplan Elephant & Castle, and published an incredible skyscraper concept called Vortex, this was its first actual London skyscraper project. The £250m plans were submitted in early 2005. This was a remodelling like none before, transforming King's Reach Tower into a dark gothic fantasy.

Colonel Seifert's tower will be remodelled to increase the floorspace by 46 per cent, to 37,200m². Shuttleworth's design will achieve this by building four extra storeys around the old core where Seifert had left space, and building an 'office-village' cluster of four new mini-towers around the base, in the same style and none rising higher than 12 storeys. A public link from Stamford Street will be created, which will still be blocked at the river by Seifert's huge Sea Containers House. The key to the design is how it complies with the new Part L regulations. A bespoke new cladding system will be deployed that attaches curved blue aluminium sections to the existing exterior ribs and fins, while the windows will be narrower, taller and double-glazed, resulting in a 50/50 mix of glass and solid exterior. Natural ventilation will further increase King's Reach Tower's energy efficiency.

Visually, the most stunning aspect of the reborn King's Reach Tower will be its colour scheme. This will be a dark complex, but that distinctive blue ribbing, will electrify the exterior. Since the plan shown here was made the crown has become clear glass. The loss of a good Seifert tower is usually bad news, but his tower will still be recognisable under the surface. The new storeys will make it look narrower and taller – and the Colonel would have been the last to object to that.

The Make-over

Windsor House, SW1
Victoria Street

Tube St James
Height 70m, 18 storeys
Commissioned 1971
Completed 1979
Architect R Seifert & Partners

Windsor House was an imposing Victorian block of flats of with a distinctively tall entrance, in the small stretch of Victoria Street between *New Scotland Yard* and *Westminster City Hall* that remained untouched by post-war redevelopment. When developers UK Provident announced plans for new offices here, campaigners fought hard to save the flats, and the early 1970s property recession looked like killing it anyway. In the end, as the market picked up, only the Windsor pub on the corner, with its sumptuous Victorian glass décor, was saved.

Windsor House is the last major skyscraper to be built in Westminster and one of the last from Richard Seifert. It is a square-planned tower with open, column-free floors. The structural engineers Waterman devised new methods to cast the central core and floors in concrete simultaneously. This saved money and meant the building went up by one storey a week, fast for the time. Seifert once lamented that he had not had better materials to work with in the 1960s. The dream of self-cleaning exteriors, something that had evaded architects since Charles Holden with *Senate House*, was becoming a reality with the use of hard, polished stone. Windsor House has purple granite façades, which hold full-length windows of dark glass in angular bays. The corrugated surface of Windsor House is unusual and a contrast to the usual plane façades, and Seifert may have been influenced by Eero Saarinen's CBS Building in New York. The façade treatments and simplicity of overall shape make Windsor House the most elegant twentieth-century skyscraper on Victoria Street, very different from the earlier concrete and glass structures. The integration of windows flush to the seamless exterior would become standard in London's commercial developments of the next two decades.

Transport for London are now major tenants at Windsor House, just a minute's walk from their head-quarters at nearby *55 Broadway*. Bob Kylie, the ex-CIA agent formerly in charge of London's transport from 2001 at the highest salary of any public official, had his office here.

One Angel Court, EC2
Angel Court

Height 94m, 21 storeys
Commissioned 1974
Completed 1980
Architect Fitzroy Robinson

The ancient Clothworkers' Company's land at the bottom of Throgmorton Avenue lay next to the ancient Drapers' Guild land where *Drapers' Garden* was built. Like the Drapers, the Clothworkers leased the land out for development. Commercial architects Fitzroy Robinson, veterans of the sixties office boom, were commissioned, and found themselves at last with a landmark City tower to deliver. Partner AB Warner led the design.

This slim tower does not sit on a podium, but rises from the ground through a complex of five-storey offices, which incorporates redundant open passages and bridges that were intended to connect into the City's high-level walkways. The tower plan is an elongated octagon, and all the windows are in bays that run up to the rooflines, accentuating the vertical. Like the contemporary *Windsor House*, the entire project is sheathed in a new,

Windsor House

One Angel Court

classy finish of polished stone, and dark glass windows flush to it. The stone used is purple Dakota marble. The effect feels almost contemporary after a quarter century. In the internal courtyard, two plaques marked 'St X B 1796' and '1867 SCS' are mounted on the tower. These relics are parish boundary markers, marking St Stephen Coleman Street and St Bartholomew by the Exchange.

Curiously, the octagon tower furthered a sequence of polygons shaped into City skyscrapers – triangles at the *Barbican*, squares such as the *Aviva Tower*, a hexagon at *Tower 42*, and the heptagon of the *Stock Exchange Tower*. No pentagon, though.

Angel Court was the London headquarters of American bankers JP Morgan. When they moved to *Alban Gate*, the tower became multiple occupancy. This century, it is firmly established at the high end of the market, and changed hands in 2003 for £104m. Over half the space is occupied by mainly American professional services. JP Morgan liked the place so much, they have even moved some staff back in.

Tower42, EC2
(NatWest Tower)
Old Broad Street

Tube Bank, Liverpool Street
Height 183m, 47 storeys
Designed 1969–70, constructed 1971–80
Architect R Seifert & Partners

Before Canary Wharf, the UK's largest bank commissioned the greatest British skyscraper architect to build the tallest building in the country. The National Westminster Tower is now Tower42 and recognised as a design masterpiece with some serious engineering. It's one of the world's most amazing skyscrapers because, after a decade of battling planning authorities for each project, Richard Seifert played a clever trick to make sure that this skyscraper was exactly the uncompromised vision he wanted.

Small Site, Quick Trick, Long Build
The site in the heart of the City was tiny – just 1.075ha. It includes a great banking hall from 1866 on Bishopsgate by John Gibson, which is still there. The National Provincial Bank had been piecing it together for a century, and by 1959 they had enough to start planning redevelopment. In 1963, they applied for outline planning permission to build at a 5.5:1 plot ratio with a 137m tower. After some changes, the go-ahead came in November 1964, but it was just one day after the Brown Ban was announced. This put the whole thing on hold until 1968, when the ministry finally issued an ODP. Basil Spence (see *Knightsbridge Barracks*) and Hugh Casson were interviewed about the project, but Seifert was appointed – the bank had been very pleased with his design for their flagship HQ, *Drapers' Garden*. His long-standing opponents, the RFAC, had actually agreed that a 180m building was fine there, but then questions were

raised in Parliament and by the GLC about views of St Paul's. This is where Seifert played his trick – he put two alternative schemes on show at the Royal Exchange and asked the public to choose. One had the single 183m tower with 410,600m^2 of office floor, the other a 152m tower with a dumpy 56m tower on the side to make up the same area. The single tower won by a landslide.

In 1970, The National Provincial merged with the Westminster Bank. That May, planning permission was granted, demolition started two months later, and construction company Mowlem got to work on the National Westminster Tower in March 1971.

The tower Seifert designed defied any of the architectural conventions of the time. The big idea was to cantilever all the floors out into space. The result is a slender tower with a 'trifoil' design which folds three separate sections or 'leaves' of office wrapped around a massive concrete core, like shin guards around a leg. In plan, it is uncannily like the hexagonal NatWest logo that had been inherited from the Provincial Bank, but the Colonel denied the connection. It's difficult not to think that the logo influenced him subconsciously. The three sections all finish at different heights, making the core the peak of a stepped profile. Seifert had tried this at *King's Reach Tower*, but now it was bigger. The office sections stand on huge concrete cantilevers tapering out from the core, like branches of a tree. Each is set at a different height, and weighs 3,300 tonnes. They carry the tallest twentieth-century cantilevered building anywhere.

The foundations, too, presented major challenges for structural engineers Pell Frischmann. A river was found beneath the site and had to be pumped away. The weight of foundations below ground had to be higher than the building above ground. The site was excavated to a depth of 16m, and 375 thick piles driven 25m below the concrete raft that was laid on it. This raft would have to support 130,000 tonnes of tower, so it was unprecedentedly huge – 56m in diameter and 4.5m thick. On it, a ring plinth 4m wide contained the concrete as it was poured and reinforced.

None of the demands of this construction were normal. The lower length of the concrete core carries the tower's load as well as stresses from the cantilevers, so it had to be strong – its walls are very thick at 1.5m, with 100 tonnes of steel reinforcing every metre of height. Special mixes of concrete were used. A new 'interrupted slide' technique of slip-form concrete construction was devised. The cantilevers start from 30m up, and support steel frames, spanned by concrete floors. Three cranes rose with the building, and pioneering laser technology was used to check the construction was in line. At the top, it was less than a centimetre from the plans. Builders noted that above about the twentieth floor, pigeons no longer tried to roost – the tower was too tall for them.

Seifert's design was tested in the National Physical Laboratory. The slender verticality is emphasised by 13km of stainless steel ribs around the offices, each separated by 1.5m. These alternate between carrying air

ducts and connecting to core via the steel frames. The internal climate control alone was of unrivalled complexity, and a computerised control room was installed below ground to manage it. Later, it was decorated with a mural of the view from the top. There are plant floors on the thirteenth, twenty-second and thirty-first floors, and the top of the core is a cooling head as well as containing water tanks and machinery. It rises four storeys above the highest occupied floors. The 12,000m² of windows are bronze and the spandrels brown, in typically seventies style. Cleaning would be a big job, and a state-of-the-art automatic system was devised that used re-cycled water.

The tower accommodates 2,500 office workers. Despite its height, there's not that much office space, because the tremendously thick core makes floor depths shallow. There are twenty-one lifts, five of which are double deckers heading straight up to sky lobbies on the twenty-third and twenty-forth floors, where people change for local lifts. A vertical mail distribution system was installed. The core also contains two fire escapes with their own air systems – in a fire, they would be pumping fresh air so fast, smoke would be driven out. The fire safety measures were the most advanced anywhere, and three decades ahead of similar ideas proposed after 9/11.

At the time, the City was still pursuing its podium-level walkway plan, and connecting footbridges were built at the foot of the tower.

Big Bangs

On 14 March 1977, the core was topped out. By this time, tower construction costs had risen from 1971's estimate of £33m to £75m, and when the tower was finally fitted out in 1980, it would reach £82m. Nevertheless, the tower's rentable value already exceeded its cost. The Queen opened the building in 1981, when the bank moved in its International Banking Division.

The project won the European Steel Award in 1981, and in 1983 RIBA, which had always suspected Seifert as crudely commercial, finally gave him a Commendation for the tower. They admitted: 'The architects have created a design of individual character on the London skyline with slim proportions and an envelope of lasting quality.' However, even then, and despite its advanced technologies, there was a feeling that the offices might become obsolete as computers entered the workspace. In 1986, the Big Bang deregulated City trading, and businesses now needed huge trading floors. Suddenly the tower's narrow offices were totally inappropriate. Then the early 1990s recession started bringing lay-offs to the banking sector.

In 1992, the IRA bombed the Baltic Exchange, causing superficial damage to the tower. Its last active day as the NatWest Tower was 24 April 1993, a Saturday, so it was almost deserted. The IRA parked a tonne of home-made explosives in a truck near *99 Bishopsgate*. The explosion killed a *News of the World* photographer and wrecked the area. At NatWest, 3000 window panes were destroyed, and the podium building was shattered.

In May, the City's planning supremo Peter Rees was quoted by the *Evening Standard* as saying the tower 'was not a good building, only kept as a status symbol'. He wanted it pulled down and mused that the world's tallest building could replace it. NatWest announced they would not move back, and in 1997 they renamed it the International Finance Centre. GMW won the £75m contract to refurbish the tower. Their brief was to restore Seifert's design, and build a new podium. They brought the Colonel out of retirement as a consultant, and, pipe in hand, he amiably approved the new works. The tower was stripped back to core and frame, but the exterior was rebuilt as it was. What was gained was a bright, airy new glass entrance pavilion with a glass roof to show off the tower from below. With its jauntily sloping entrance canopy and crisp, clean post-modernist steel and glass construction, it set the tone for later showcase City entrances.

The work was completed in 1998, just as NatWest sold the tower to property company Greycoats for £226m. That price was higher than expected, but what it bought was a modern tower for a market ignored by big City developments like Broadgate – the multiple tenancy market. In height, profile and prestige, it could uniquely compete with *One Canada Square*, but the difference was that it was in the City, not Docklands.

The tower is now rebranded as Tower42, and it's back in fashion – a thriving business owned by Merrill Lynch and Hermes, letting to about 35 tenants mainly in the financial sector, and offering the ubiquitous run of fitness club-to-conference facilities. How wrong Peter Rees had been about it! Some had asked if anyone really wanted to be in a skyscraper, but research in 2002 by the British Council for Offices into four multi-occupant City skyscrapers revealed they did, and would pay for it. In Tower42, the rent premium above 100m is 15 per cent.

In 2001, the building's environmental contractor Inspace installed blue strip lighting along the roofline and floodlit the core head. Architects Fletcher Priest drew up the plan to draw people into the concourse space, and left a selection of slick designer restaurant spaces. By the podium, the Wagamama is an architectural talking point in its own right. On the twenty-forth floor, master chef Gary Rhodes has won a Michelin star for the British fare served in his Rhodes Twentyfour. On the forty-second floor, the Vertigo champagne bar with its sixties/minimalist decor is now the highest restaurant in London, with views to the west and a lunch deal that makes it accessible to everyone, not just City slickers.

Abstract Sculpture

The idea that major landmark buildings should take on entirely new shapes is now part of the cutting edge of architecture, enabled by the massive processing power of computers. In the City, the best example of this is *30 St Mary Axe*, which honoured Tower42 by being designed a little shorter. Back in the 1970s, Seifert's team and engineers Pell Frischmann had no access to the electronic power that makes such designs possible. Yet they too created a new building form, in effect a massive abstract sculpture, now emphasised by the crown lighting. Seifert liked the idea of shapes – early designs for the *Holiday Inn Forum* and *International Press Centre* were quite lyrical in form.

Tower42 has become the perfect City skyscraper, offering lifestyle as well as floorspace. And it all rests on the original, and astonishing, Seifert design.

6-8 Bishopsgate

Tube Liverpool Street, Bank
Height 88m, 24 storeys
Designed 1971
Constructed 1974–81
Architect GMW

This tower was the last Modernist office skyscraper built in London, and along with *Tower42*, it marked the end of the City's first flirtation with high-rise. As with the *Aviva Tower* behind it, architects GMW have created a cool, anonymous curtain-walled van der Rohe-style block, this time in an almost black shade of brown. Seen from afar, it is the lowest step in a chain which rises through the Aviva Tower to *30 St Mary Axe*.

The purity of the featureless façades and shape was exactly what was intended. It was originally designed in 1971 for Banque Belge under Edmund Ward of GMW. He and the other founding partners Gollins and Melvin retired in 1974, about the time construction began. When two outcrops of plant machinery were added later, GMW were not happy – they ruin the building's shape. In 2000, American power-architect Helmut Jahn came up with a 250m, 63-storey cylindrical tower to replace it, but the City wasn't quite ready for such bold plans.

Like the monolith in 2001: *A Space Odyssey*, 6-8 Bishopsgate has a timeless aspect. That may be why it remains one of the best City skyscrapers in the rental market.

A new reception for Tower42

Chapter 5:
Post-Modernism

In 1979, the UK's economy and architecture were both wheezing under the weight of fossilised ideals that didn't work any more. Things had to change. In that year, Mrs Thatcher won the election, and planning permission was granted for a stunningly new sort of skyscraper – Richard Rogers' *Lloyd's Building* in the City.

Richard Rogers

6–8 Bishopsgate

In the eighties, architects were looking for new styles, and two front-runners emerged: High Tech (increasingly abbreviated to Hi-Tech) and historicist. Both are Post-Modernist, although architecturally the label is more associated with the latter, which reflects a return to classical ideas about form and surface. With the deregulation of city trading in the Big Bang in 1986, money would be on the table to back Post-Modern ideas, and a new generation of London skyscrapers would tentatively emerge. Fast-track construction methods would replace the 'I'm alright, Jack' unionised construction culture of the past, and American corporate architects with global portfolios

would shake up the British monopoly on architectural commissions. Finally, after centuries of London's business zones spreading to the west, the approval of Canary Wharf would mean a sudden lurch eastwards, and by far the biggest tower yet.

Inside-out History

What is Hi-Tech architecture? Buildings in this style look inside out. Service structures like pipes and lifts are on the outside, and load-carrying frames are exposed for all to see. This liberates the maximum space for floors and internal circulation. Hi-Tech exploits technology and puts it on show. Such ideas have a long past, a lot of it in London.

Joseph Paxton's Crystal Palace, a great glass and cast-iron structure which used to sit in Hyde Park, was built for the 1851 Great Exhibition. It was a Victorian version of Hi-Tech. The frame, filled in with sheet glass, was the exterior of the building, while, inside, huge open spaces were spanned in a matrix of ironwork assembled from pre-fabricated parts. The metal and glass exterior anticipated the curtain walls of the International Style, but that style placed service structure behind walls or in outcrops on the roof.

A Philadelphia architect, Louis Kahn, wanted buildings to express the process of their construction. In 1952, he teamed up (intimately as well professionally) with Anne Tyng, a follower of the radical architect-engineer Buckminster Fuller who exploited the rigidity of pure mathematical shapes such as tetrahedrons, and was to invent the geodesic dome. Kahn & Tyng's unbuilt Philadelphia Town Hall was a mad-looking zigzag tower of tetrahedronal units secured by massive joints on the outside. At this time, Kahn wrote 'design habits leading to the concealment of structure have no place', and that if buildings were designed with an appreciation of the methods used to build

John Hancock Center, Chicago

services. Perhaps their most comprehensive concept was Plug-In City by Peter Cook; this was an urban plan designed as a state of flux, in which houses and shops were hung from huge frames, and cranes mounted on them were constantly at work building more elements, or moving goods between suspended storehouses and railways connected to the outside world. Warren Chalk, however, focused on a particular structure, a core tower again topped with a crane

them, then ' … the burying of tortured unwanted ducts, conduits and pipe lines would become intolerable.' He talked of building zones serviced by other infrastructures that were 'servants'. Although no Khan building actually put service structure on show, he had pretty well suggested the philosophy of Hi-Tech.

The John Hancock Center in Chicago, designed by SOM's Bruce Graham, is worth mentioning again because it anticipated some Hi-Tech features. When it was finished in 1969, it broke the van der Rohe paradigm that modern slabs should be rectilinear – this one gets thinner as it gets higher. Its façades are dominated by huge diagonal crosses, which are cross-bracing support trusses first visualised by SOM engineer Myron Goldsmith, who had worked with Mies van der Rohe. Here was a clear example of not only revealing structure on the outside, but also giving it a technological feel.

We now move back to the avant-garde of England in the 1960s, where we have already seen how the collective Archigram came up with bizarre sci-fi designs, which were temporary and interchangeable in function, and defiantly exposed mechanical

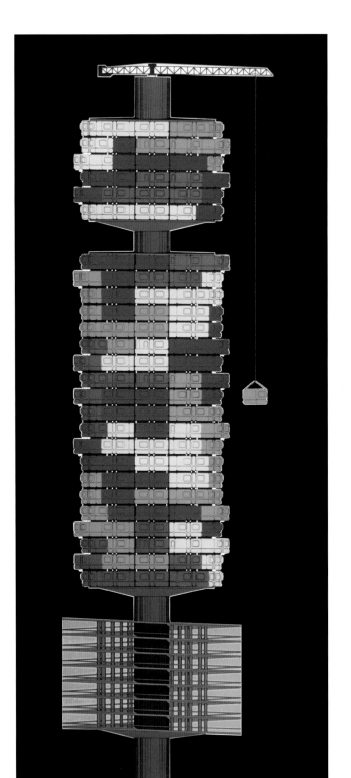

Archigram's Capsule Tower

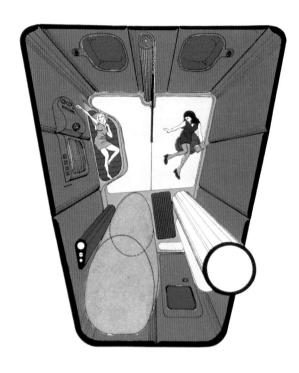

Reclining in a Capsule

for lifting capsules up to create stacked rings of living space. Chalk's drawings were a lot more fun than the drab greys and blues of contemporary designs – they are full of colour, and even have mini-skirted Swinging Sixties women reclining in the living capsules.

Contemporary with Archigram was another visionary, Cedric Price. He set up practice in London in 1960, and his significant London building was a huge Aviary in Regents Park Zoo. Most of his ideas, however, remained on paper, from whence they had an uncanny record of becoming reality a decade or two later. For example, his proposal for a network of technological establishments in Staffordshire antici-pated science parks such as Cambridge Science Park, established in 1971, and his plans for redeveloping the South Bank included a giant Ferris wheel long before the London Eye was built. In 1961, he proposed a Fun Palace, a structure of adjustable spaces that could be adapted to the needs of different cultural event. This concept is precisely that which won the French competition in 1971 for the *grand projet* of a modern cultural centre in Paris, the Palais de Beaubourg. The architectural partnership behind

it was headed by Richard Rogers and Renzo Piano.

The Beaubourg palace is now called the Pompidou Centre after the French President who was keen to leave a Paris legacy with some modern va-va-voom. The Pompidou Centre certainly had that – when it opened in 1977, people gasped at what looked like a technicolour oil refinery, shoe-horned into the tight historic urban fabric of Les Halles. The refinery aspect came from the masses of pipes on the outside of the building. Escalators enclosed in transparent tubes climbed across the façade of the building towards the upper exhibition floors, giving stunning views above the old Paris skyline.

Piano was to surface in London in the new century as designer of Europe's tallest building, *The Shard*, but in the meantime Rogers had set up his own architec-tural practice. In 1978, he won the competition to design a new headquarters for *Lloyd's of London*, beating, amongst others, Norman Foster. As if in parallel, Foster won a competition to design a new headquarters for another venerable British financial sector powerhouse, the Hongkong and Shanghai Bank (now HSBC) – but this HQ was in Hong Kong. Foster and Rogers had both studied at Yale together, and on their return to England in 1962 had founded a practice called Team 4, which pioneered Hi-Tech aspects such as the use of lightweight materials and colour, but in

Post-Modernsim in Paris: Pompidou wall

Hongkong & Shanhghai Banking Corporation

quite small projects. When Team 4 split up in 1967, an unspoken, ambiguous rivalry between the two would emerge, which is still playing out in the twenty-first century on London's skyline. Both would work with other geniuses – Rogers with Piano, and Foster with Buckminster Fuller. As the eighties began, their approach to their prestigious high-rise commissions was quite similar. Both wanted to rethink the skyscraper. Foster's criticism of modern high-rise offices was: 'First a complete absence of variety, inside and out; second, poor technical performance; and third, an almost complete indifference to the public or semi-public, domain at street level.'

Foster's 179m, fifty-seven-storey Hong Kong building and Rogers' 84m, fourteen-storey Lloyds Building were both finished in 1986 and have much in common. Rogers' building cost a whacking great £163m to build, while the construction costs of Foster's tower were the most expensive ever at $670m. Both created new sorts of public space at their base, along with open floors stacked around deep, multi-storey atria full of natural light and accessed by escalators. Both also put on show Hi-Tech hallmarks such as roof-level cranes. Externally, however, Foster shows off the exoskeleton of structural support, with elements such

as cross-bracing, while Rogers almost hides his block behind six surrounding service towers that give the building its extraordinary extraterrestrial appearance.

London would have to wait till to the new century to get its own Foster skyscrapers, but Rogers went on to other tall offices – the Reuters Building (1992) in Docklands, *88 Wood Street* (1999) and Lloyd's Register of Shipping (2000) in the City. Both he and Foster have increasingly put sustainability – the environmentally friendly qualities of a building, to which we shall return – at the centre of their architecture, but Rogers has also stayed true to his distinctive Hi-Tech look, which, apart from the Lloyd's Building, incorporates bright, cheerful colours. Only on the Lloyd's Building do we find him looking romantically over his shoulder. High up, there is a graceful rounded steel and glass skylight structure, an early example of the barrel-vaulted roof sections that would become almost standard in 1990s offices. In this case, though, it looks Victorian... as if William Caxton had been there.

Romantic Americans

While Hi-Tech Europeans had reacted to modernism by being radical and rational, over in America architects were getting romantic and retro. They were saying, how come old buildings could look great while International Style boxes are so cold? This gave rise to a Post-Modernism that is sometimes called Historicism, drawing on architectural elements previously consigned to history. The American name for this sort of Post-Modernism is simply PoMo. The big PoMo eyebrow raisers were fancy skyscrapers with an almost comic-strip retro feel, from two architectural practices.

In 1980, a civic headquarters for Portland, Oregon, designed by a Princeton professor called Michael Graves, was opened. This fifteen-storey cube has façades painted boldly with warm brown symmetrical sections and festooned with a huge blue concrete ribbon. It instantly became a symbol of Post-Modernism, stirring controversy over its frivolous and

Humana Building, Louisville, Kentucky

superficial disguising of a modern block behind a mask. The appearance also attempted to distinguish the base, middle and top, whereas (podium bases aside), the International Style had minimised such distinctions. Graves really went to town on vertical zoning with the twenty-six-storey Humana Building in Louisville, Kentucky, completed in 1985. This pink-marble clad building is an almost random mixture of architectural elements, such as a huge curving bay mounted in a recessed three-storey glass 'window' drawing a line above the middle of the tower, and a ziggurat-stepped tapering peak. Graves likes to play with the architecture, especially at the top. The Humana Building is ludicrous but brilliant.

In 1984, something very odd had appeared on Manhattan's skyline – a neo-Georgian pediment rising to a cut-out circular void, serving no functional purpose. The whole AT&T Building (now the Sony Building) looked like a 197-metre-high

Post-Modernism arrives in Manhattan

Chippendale wardrobe clad in marble. The architects were Philip Johnson and John Burgee. We have met Johnson before, as one of the most celebrated American followers of Mies van der Rohe, working with van der Rohe on the Seagram Building, but he seems to have realised that Midtown Manhattan was losing its identity to the endlessly cloned glass boxes for which he was partially responsible. Two great Johnson/Burgee skyscrapers, already finished in 1983 in Houston, Texas, showed that Johnson had changed his spots. The sixty-four-storey Williams Tower looks exactly like a Manhattan tower from the twenties, but in glass rather than stone (the same effect Cesar Pelli used in London's later *Citigroup Centre*), while the upper floors of the fifty-six-storey RepublicBank Center (now the Bank of America Center) slope steeply like the pitched roofs of Dutch houses. Still, it was the New York effort that caught the world's eye, and in one fell swoop the AT&T Building ushered in big-scale commercial Post-Modernism. Johnson would go on to replicate the shape of the Houses of Parliament's Victoria Tower in glass in an office tower in Pittsburgh for the Pittsburgh Plate Glass Corporation.

London goes Retro

Would either Hi-Tech or historicist Post-Modernism come out on top? Prince Charles made a big impact on the issue in 1984, when he waded into the debate about an extension for the National Gallery. He denounced the Hi-Tech competition-winning design by architects ABK as 'a carbuncle', and that forced another competition, won by American Venturi Rauch Scott-Brown Architects. Their building paid loads of homage to the past, from its unobtrusive stone-faced front to its grand staircases and arches within. Prince Charles had set the agenda: classical was the new modern.

In March 1986, Mrs Thatcher abolished the GLC, and the go-ahead for tall buildings passed to borough councils. Some councils such as Kensington & Chelsea, Islington and Westminster, effectively banned local skyscrapers. Hammersmith & Fulham however, were quick off the mark to approve a luxury block of flats at Chelsea Harbour called *The Belvedere Tower*. This slender tower by Ray Moxley, ready just a year later, is topped with a pointy pyramid roof. It could have come from a vision of a French chateau or a pagoda or maybe just a wizard's hat made square, but the important thing is that it made *The Belvedere* London's first romantic high-rise. Chelsea Harbour is also significant for having pioneered the American-style fast-track construction methods that would shake up construction in the nineties, and the luxury apartment tower was the first of countless others that would emerge along the river.

London's only skyscraper cluster was in the City, but here business was due for the biggest shake-up of the century. The London Stock Exchange had been losing ground internationally, trading a fraction of the volumes of its New York and Tokyo counterparts. In October 1986, it deregulated the trading of stocks and shares. This 'Big Bang' was a complete revolution in how the financial services sector operated. Henceforth, banks could trade directly rather than through brokers, and trading no longer needed to be face to face. The new market place was electronic, and the new need was for huge trading floors, with floors separated by four metres rather than the normal three, so that all the services, including the cabling that would feed the trading screens, could be accommodated. Steel frames had replaced the concrete frames of the sixties, and the steel decking that replaced concrete floors was good for accommodating all these services. Towers such as *Tower42*, with their narrow floors and low ceilings, were rendered virtually redundant overnight.

The floor-space per City worker had already doubled between 1960 and 1980 – now the Big Bang's trading floors needed to be wall-free as well. The new office-block model would be the groundscraper – big bulky medium-rise blocks that maximised their plot ratio by stacking floors across virtually the whole site

area. This was a problem for the City, because there wasn't much site available.

Nevertheless, the City responded. In 1986, Michael Cassidy, chairman of the Corporation's Planning Committee, took the brakes off new developments. The annual planning permissions it granted for new offices increased six-fold between 1985 and 1987, to 1.18 million square metres. Work started on the first phase of a vast new office city, Broadgate, with literally millions of square feet of floor for the electronic age. In the early nineties, the largest part of it rose up like a cliff along Bishopsgate – a long, broad thirteen-storey groundscraper by the American masters, SOM. With its marble cladding, long neoclassical arcades, and vast glass neo-Victorian atrium façades with curving tops, this was a prime example of the now-typical Post-Modernist style going up in American cities – a mish-mash of historical influences, melded into a timeless, location-neutral world that spelt out big money. Sometimes the style is called Beaux-Art.

Some Post-Modernist skyscrapers did go up in the City. None reached 100m, but they weren't relying on height to stand out. Work started on *Minster Court* on Fenchurch Street at the time of the Big Bang, and its historical influence seemed to be fairytale gothic castles. Not everyone liked it, but it was a refreshing break from modernism, and quite surprising considering that the architects GMW had been the leading English exponents of Mies van der Rohe, with buildings such as the *Aviva Tower*. GMW followed it up with *54 Lombard Street*, whose barrel-vaulted glass roofs, echoing the Lloyd's skylight, create the most elegant of all 1990s additions to the City skyline.

In 1990, London's first skyscraper to straddle a railway station was topped out: *One America Square*, designed by RHWL and inspired by the 1920s Art Deco 'modernisme' of Manhattan skyscrapers. The biggest Post-Modernist City skyscraper straddled a road rather than a railway – Terry Farrell's *Alban Gate*. This was the Post-Modernism that Michael Graves had initiated, horizontally banded and with lots of playful structure at the top, including the by-now-ubiquitous barrel-vaulted rooflines.

Like Rogers and Foster, Terry Farrell is another of the sixties Hi-Tech pioneers who became a superstar architect in the Thatcher years. In partnership with Nicholas Grimshaw, he had designed a revolutionary Hi-Tech external staircase in Paddington as early as 1967, and then an eleven-storey apartment block at Regents Park clad in aluminium that was known as 'The Washing Machine'. In the eighties, Farrell combined both historicist and Hi-Tech elements. His massive mid-rise Embankment Place, suspended over Charing Cross station in 1991, is one of London's great riverside blocks.

London Lurches East

Huge new blocks outside the City such as Embankment Place aren't just a response to the need for electronic trading floors. They also result from the Big Bang's other effect – if you didn't need to be near your broker, you didn't need to be in the City. This is the main reason for Canary Wharf, where London's biggest skyscraper cluster now stands.

London's existence springs from the river Thames, and, starting from just by Tower Bridge, a huge swathe of docks and warehouses stretched east along it towards the wide, muddy estuary. This was collectively called Docklands, and, along with Liverpool and Bristol, had been one of the great clearing-houses of goods for the British Empire. The volume of cargo handled didn't actually peak until 1961, but thereafter the Docklands started a long decline, accelerated in the 1970s by containerisation and the migration of shipping to the deep-water docks elsewhere. Between 1967 and 1981, the Port of London Authority closed all of their London docks, so that when the Thatcher government came in, Docklands was a vast area without jobs and investment. Her Environment Minister Michael Heseltine said that Docklands 'displays more acutely and extensively than any area in England the physical decline of the urban city and

the need for urban regeneration'. The Local Government Planning and Land Act of 1980 laid out a new sort of authority for blighted areas that would lift planning controls and back private investment with public money for infrastructure. The most important of these was the London Docklands Development Corporation (LDDC), established in 1981. Initially, development interest was at the western end of its patch. The first off the blocks was London Bridge City in Southwark, just a few minutes walk from the City. Combining refurbishment of the nineteenth-century Hay's Wharf with new offices, this was completed in 1987. The new eleven-storey, 51m signature corner cube by John Bonnington has a spectacular cut-away edge, like a new take on Cubism.

Canary Wharf lies a lot further east, 5km away from the Bank of England, in the Isle of Dogs' West India Docks. It is a myth that it was a brownfield site, an empty finger of land in the echoing desolation of London's abandoned docks. The West India Docks closed in 1980, but the very next year, colourful, angular offices by Nicholas Lacey Jobst & Partners sprung up on Heron Quays, the adjacent strip of land. Canary Wharf housed a line of fifties warehouses and Limehouse Television Studios, an eye-catching deep blue Post-Modernist building by Terry Farrell where series such as *Spitting Image* were made. In the film *The Long Good Friday*, Bob Hoskins' cockney gangster and his classy moll (played by Helen Mirren) operate from a luxury yacht moored at Canary Wharf, and scheme to cash in on the redevelopment of Docklands by attracting the American Mafia to invest there. Spookily, in 1982, an American businessman called Gooch Ware Travelstead (who had nothing to do with the Mafia) rode a taxi out to Canary Wharf and saw precisely the same opportunity. He liked the location not that far from the City, and realised that the optic fibre ring laid out there by telecoms company Mercury would enable state-of-the-art electronic communications. The fact that it had just been declared an Enterprise Zone, offering a ten-year tax holiday to developers, helped. Travelstead proposed an incredible 10m square feet of offices on the 29-hectare site. No less than SOM masterplanned the development in 1985. They laid out a 'Wall Street on Water', rich in public spaces yet with an overall plot ratio of 12:1, a density higher than anywhere in the City. The offices would accommodate massive trading floors, and include three giant skyscrapers, the tallest in the centre rising over 200m.

Ultimately, Travelstead failed to find the funding for Canary Wharf, and in 1987 it was taken over by Canadian Paul Reichmann's company Olympia & York, who committed to developing 12m square feet there. Reichmann was one of North America's great developers. Born in Vienna in 1930, he and his brothers had moved from country to country, but settled in Toronto in 1956. There, Olympia & York had started in tiles and flooring, but gained a reputation for building faster and cheaper than its rivals, despite banning on-site work on the Jewish Sabbath and holidays. In the seventies, Reichmann developed Canada's tallest offices at First Canadian Place, and in the early nineties he snapped up nine New York skyscrapers for $300m at the bottom of the market. All this made the Reichmanns worth billions.

Olympia & York's most significant project was the 6m-square-feet World Financial Center (WFC) on Battery Park City, a patch of land reclaimed from the Hudson River adjacent to New York's World Trade Center. Not unlike Canary Wharf, this was a new waterside city district. Reichmann's architect there was Cesar Pelli, a Connecticut-based titan of corporate architecture who would later design the Petronas Towers in Kuala Lumpur (which overtook Chicago's Sears Tower in structural height but not in office height). WFC construction started in 1980, and four thick square Post-Modernist towers with grids of 'punched' or separated windows like those in twenties skyscrapers, began to emerge. The tallest at 225m, WFC Three, was topped out with a pyramid in 1985. Pelli largely recycled *One Canada Square*, which was topped

out in 1990. The sheerscale was stupefying. London's first tower over 200m high, with over a million square feet of space! It felt like a leap into the twenty-first century, but ten years early. Pelli boasted that it was 'the first skyscraper in England' – rather a slap in the face for London's sixty-year skyscraper legacy and for architects such as Holden, Goldfinger, GMW and Seifert.

The rest of Canary Wharf's first phase is by various American architects, including SOM, ranging in style from kitschy Beaux Art historicism to chunky marble-clad blocks that looked straight out of contemporary Chicago. Three of them rise above 75m, including the only British design, a smooth marble split slab by Troughton McAslan at *25 North Colonnade*. One complaint about Canary Wharf was that visiting it was like entering a lifeless computer simulation. In fact, computer power in the nineties was increasingly offering architects something new beyond the calculations of structural engineering: computer-aided design, or CAD-CAM. By 1993, megapixel images in thirty-six-bit colour generated with half a million triangles per second allowed 3-D walkthroughs of designs. The ultra-clean virtual reality of the computer was eerily like the final product, such as Canary Wharf.

As it attracted major banks and legal firms, Canary Wharf signalled the end of the City's monopoly as the UK's financial services hub, but simultaneously set London up to retain its position as the world's leading financial centre. Just as all that looked to be in the bag, it came under threat. Property prices crashed, and, in 1991, Olympia & York went into liquidation, the world's largest bankruptcy to date. Just as the Empire State Building had drawn a line under the Manhattan skyscraper boom of the 1920s, *One Canada Square* arrived as London had too much new office space. In 1992, less than 160,000m^2 of office was under construction in the City itself, the lowest figure in eight years. Paul Reichmann would refinance with Saudi money and take his estate back in 1995 under Canary Wharf Group plc (CWG), but it would not be until 1999 that the Jubilee Line Extension would reach there. Only then had Canary Wharf really arrived.

Bombs and Refurbs

Now that architecture had found the new language of Post-Modernism, the obvious thing to do was to apply it to some of the older, unfashionable and inefficient post-war skyscrapers. Their cramped, unhealthy, pre-electronic interiors were expensive to refurbish on a floor-by-floor basis, but their skeleton frames were worth recycling. The first office tower to get updated was *City Tower*, sexed up with new cladding by GMW. In 1990, the Thorn-EMI building became a new building entirely – RHWL architects gave the fifties slab the 'Fridge' look, with shiny white panels. Reborn skyscrapers tended to get new names, and this became *Orion House*. Other office refurbs followed, but the slow nineties office market sometimes made it better business to convert offices to residential use. A spate of conversions followed: Century House become *Perspective*, the RHM Tower became *The Panoramic*, Goldfinger's old DHSS headquarters became *Metro Central Heights*, and GMW's pioneering Castrol House became *Marathon House*. Although few commented at the time, these projects were quietly proving that high-rise living was trendy, and not just the privilege of council tenants.

The biggest threat to London's commercial position was that it was becoming a theatre of war. The IRA originally brought its campaign to 'the mainland' in the 1970s, but it hadn't brought the British to the negotiation table, so it decided to target the UK's financial centre. A bomb exploded at the *Stock Exchange Tower* in 1990, another destroyed the Baltic Exchange (now site of *30 St Mary Axe*) in April 1992, and Bishopsgate was bombed in April 1993. The Bishopsgate bomb killed a man, injured forty-four others, and completely destroyed the medieval church of St Ethelburga's (now reconstructed). Five hundred

tonnes of steel and glass rained down on the City streets. The damage wreaked was originally estimated at £350m, but was probably nearer a billion. The IRA struck again in February 1996, killing a newsvendor and destroying the only Isle of Dogs office skyscraper not actually on Canary Wharf – a black-glass tower at South Quay (see *Discovery Dock*).

The IRA attacks gave the City further opportunity to recycle some of its skyscrapers. The leading practice in this was GMW. They transformed the bomb-damaged *99 Bishopsgate* into a gleaming glass-curtained tower rising from a bigger trading-floor-friendly podium in 1995, and then tackled the damage at Seifert's NatWest Tower, soon to become *Tower42*. Strangely, they lost the bid to restore their own CGU Tower (now the *Aviva Tower*). At *Tower42*, GMW's work was approved by Colonel Seifert himself, whose practice was now in the hands of his son John. GMW retained the external look of Seifert's tower, but a new airy glass pavilion entrance was just the right confidence-boosting measure to attract tenants willing to pay premium rents.

It was said that the Japanese government threatened to relocate its banks and trading houses elsewhere in Europe unless the Northern Ireland problem was solved. If the IRA had scared away foreign money, what future would London have had? The British Government eventually came to terms with the IRA and signed the Good Friday agreement in 1998.

The end of the threat from the IRA and the approach of the millennium would bring a new generation of skyscrapers to London, and, as we shall see, the arrival of Norman Foster on the skyline. But this would have to wait till the office market digested all the big build of the 1980s and early 1990s. However, in the meantime, the renaissance of high-rise living was bringing a string of new high-rise projects to the river...

Lloyd's of London, EC1
Leadenhall Street

Tube Bank
Designed from 1978
Completed 1986
Height 84m, 14 storeys
Architect RRP

Hi-Tech arrived in London with a bang when this revolutionary building was completed. Lloyd's, of course, is the most famous insurance business in the world, and the prestige of Richard Rogers' competition-winning design virtually guaranteed it would stay that way. That alone may justify the £225m development, the most expensive of its time.

The trade in maritime insurance underwriting started in the City's coffee houses, and the business takes its name from Edward Lloyd's establishment, more a club than a precursor of Starbucks. Lloyd's didn't actually have their own premises until 1928, when they moved into a neoclassical building designed by Sir Edwin Cooper. This was demolished for Rogers' building, but an old façade has been retained on Leadenhall Street, and its doorway opens into the new structure like a time portal. Through it, we glimpse the futuristic configurations of steel, concrete and light, the tools that Rogers uses to such effect.

In April 1978, Rogers won an international competition to design the new Lloyd's building, against competition from Arup (who would engineer Rogers' design), Foster and IM Pei, as well as Canadian and French architects. A scheme Rogers designed for a controversial site on the South Bank at the time had a similar exterior look, but would be turned down in 1980. Planning permission for Lloyd's was granted in 1979. Courtenay Blackmore of Lloyd's worked in the design team, to help make the design meet the needs of the client. The design was pretty well set by 1980 and, in November 1981, the Queen Mother unveiled a section of column at the entrance.

Lloyd's is surrounded by six bizarre service towers, which look like Archigram concepts of the sixties. They are in stainless steel rather than aluminium, because of its higher melting point in case of fire. Thirty-three stainless steel boxes are stacked on the towers – these are actually loo pods with porthole windows, manufactured especially in Bristol by Jordan Engineering, whose other clients included the nuclear industry. Plant machinery and tanks are contained in three-storey plant houses at the top. Above these are blue cranes, Rogers' only concession to his usual playfulness with colour. These are not for window cleaning – they await the day when Lloyd's may require disassembly. Rogers has the strange conviction that when a building – even his own – has outlived its usefulness, it can go (see *Montevetro*). The lifts are on the outside, giving the building a kinetic dimension. The client had to be taken to the US for a demonstration that this solution worked.

Lurking behind the service towers and linked by glazed bridges is the office building, a 67 × 45.5m rectangular-plan block whose exterior on three sides would be a plain affair by itself. It has a total floor area of about 50,000m². Beneath it, open space skirts the building and connects to a new public area with coffee and wine bars, and a passage from the 1928 doorway through to Leadenhall Market. Here, the building steps down to just six storeys. Inside is a huge open trading area called The Room, which contains the Lutine Bell. This 48kg bell was recovered from the French vessel *La Lutine*, which was insured by Lloyd's when it sank with a cargo of gold and silver in 1799. The bell used to be rung for big insurance news – once if it was bad and twice if it was good.

Above The Room, escalators rise into underwriting floors and, above those, into flexible office space that can switch function. The floors are on galleries around the atrium, spreading out from interior concrete columns. Initially, the whole frame was to be steel, but fire constraints made it necessary to use concrete. The galleries are stacked on three sides around a huge 60m-high atrium, as big as a cathedral. The south-facing skylight is a great Victorian-looking semi-circular-topped structure. This fantastic, romantic crystal-sided element is crucial to the whole design, and fills the place with light.

The highest business level is the eleventh floor, from where the interior atrium void plunges vertiginously down past all the busy offices and floors. Turning away from this we find something as remarkable as the new structures: the Committee Room, also known as the Adam Room, a place usually seen only by Lloyd's committee, distinguished guests and the liveried serving staff. It is a sumptuous banqueting salon originally built by Robert Adam in Bowood House, Wiltshire (which still has a library by him), and re-assembled precisely. Thirty people can sit around a vast table beneath massive chandeliers, golden-framed baroque mirrors and exquisite painted plasterwork in the quintessential Adam style. Between the grand heavy curtains is a breathtaking view over the City at just the right height, reinforcing the sense of power concentrated here. Foster's *Willis Building* will block the view.

The building is a pioneering example of green internal climatic engineering. Light fixtures draw in stale air, which is passed into gaps in the external triple-layer glazing, which in turn diffuses light and sparkles at night. Tanks in the basement collect heat, for recycling. Fresh air is distributed from systems under the floors. The concrete structure also acts as a heat sink, absorbing heat by day and radiating it away by night. All this makes Lloyd's energy-efficient.

Lloyd's Building

Such a complex structure has had its problems. Within eighteen months of opening, corrosion was attacking the building, and it struck again in 1995. Less damaging was Alain 'Spiderman' Robert, who scaled the exterior in May 2003 to protest at the second Gulf War. Lloyd's don't actually own the building but have a lease on it until 2013, and in 2004 the building changed hands for about £240m. In 2006, Gensler, who did the interiors at *10 Upper Bank Street*, refurbished the interior, upgrading the reception and underwriting floors.

At night, Lloyd's is magically illuminated and manages to hold its own with taller buildings around it such as *30 St Mary Axe*. The strategically placed blue spotlights on the service towers make them look as if they belong to a Klingon spaceship. It's just a hint of the amazing sci-fi interior, only open to the public one day each September. Inside and out, the amazing Lloyd's is still thrillingly futuristic, even after twenty years.

One Canada Square, E14

Tube, DLR Canary Wharf
Designed 1986
Completed 1991
Height 235m, 50 storeys
Architect Cesar Pelli & Associates

Just suppose either New York or Chicago was going to get a new skyscraper from one of the world's top architects, and it would be the tallest in the city. What a letdown if it turned out to be a virtual clone of one of the architect's buildings somewhere else. This is what London got with One Canada Square, but few Londoners realise it...

Authentic Manhattan

One Canada Square is the showpiece of Canary Wharf. It is massive, London's first million-square-foot-plus tower with 114,751m² of office and retail space, and over fifty metres higher than *Tower42*. That tower took a

decade to build, but One Canada Square happened fast – starting with the design. Asked by developers Olympia & York to create London's tallest building, Pelli seemed to take a here's-one-I-prepared-earlier approach, creating a building remarkably similar to his 225m-high WFC Three in New York, a thick square tower with grids of punched windows completed in 1986. That year, Pelli started work on One Canada Square. He did at least strip away the extra massing that WFC Three has around its base to create an unstepped, sheer tower for London, and he chose a different cladding.

Construction began in April 1988, when the first of 222 piles was driven 23m deep to create a huge cofferdam of mind-boggling size – big enough to swallow an entire block of the West End below water level. A 4m-thick concrete raft was sunk on which the 27,500 tonnes of the tower's steel framework would be anchored. The Thames, where water-borne trade had been suffering a long, lingering death, was suddenly alive again as 300 bargeloads of construction material floated in every month. Despite the explosion of activity, though, old British work habits surfaced in late 1989. An unofficial strike by steelworkers left the tower just twelve storeys high, and got contractor Ellis-Don MacAlpine fired in March 1990. The resolution of the strike got things moving, and London was soon marvelling at a rapidly rising tower, which appeared to be curiously blue, the colour of plastic laundry bags. In fact, this was blue plastic covering for the 'Patten Hyclad Cambric finish' stainless-steel cladding that gives the building a clinical feel, but at the same time reflects the ambient light, changing moods with weather. In November, Environment Minister Michael Portillo was at the topping-out ceremony. Soon afterwards, 700 local residents sued because the tower had trashed their TV reception.

One Canada Square may be a recycled concept, but it is an impressive building. Most floors are on massive 58 × 58m squares. Thirty-two passenger lifts are fitted with video displays, and there are a further two freight lifts and two fireman's lifts, and four staircases. The tower has 3,960 windows. One Canada Square is iconic because of its pyramid roof, where louvres direct rainwater across it. Up there, where the building is designed to sway 32cm in freak winds, wisps of cloud condensation blow off it in less breezy weather, and a white aircraft warning light blinks forty times a minute.

There are almost thirty different tenants occupying offices in the tower, not all in financial services. The *Daily Telegraph* was an early occupant (now moving to Victoria), followed in December 1994 by *The Independent*. The tower was one of the final nails in the coffin of Fleet Street as the traditional centre for British newspapers. Local newspaper *The Wharf* is also there. London's Olympic bid for 2012 was masterminded here.

The 14m-high lobby uses almost 8,400m² of Italian and Guatemalan marble – more than enough to cover an entire face of *Centre Point*. It is home to contemporary art. In Keith Milow's *Twentieth Century Thames* (1998), the names of twentieth-century artists and architects

Let there be light

Lloyd's Building at night

run in concentric circles around four rusting iron discs. William Turnball's *Blade of Venus* (1985) is a bronze sculpture evoking Japanese swords and Chinese chopping knives, reminding traders that their highly paid jobs upstairs depend on results.

Pelli had proclaimed that One Canada Square was 'for the people of London, and should suit their need', yet there is no public access beyond the lobby. Pelli arrogantly dismisses architects such as Holden, Goldfinger and Seifert, along with all of London's diverse high-rise heritage, by blithely declaring that One Canada Square was 'the first skyscraper in England'.

High Stunts

One Canada Square has attracted stunts since even before the topping-out. Australian base jumper Mark Scott entered it dressed as a courier, changed in the loo, and stepped off a corner at the top, letting out his parachute some seconds later. He landed in a car park where he was scooped up by a getaway motorbike. In 1995, Frenchman Alain 'Spiderman' Robert climbed the outside of the tower without ropes or equipment. Robert has scaled thirty skyscrapers worldwide, including a Petronas Tower, the Empire State Building and Chicago's Sears Tower, but his second attempt in Canary Wharf was defeated by lousy weather in October 2002. When it comes to official stunts, Canary Wharf and the City co-operate on abseiling events for charity. At the British-French Summit of 1997, Tony Blair hosted French prime minister Lionel Jospin and President Chirac on the thirty-eighth floor. Blair may have been showing off – the tallest skyscraper in Paris, at Montparnasse, is 26m lower.

In May 2005, a pipe on the 37th floor burst, causing electrical systems to fail and flooding floors. Six floors were temporarily without power and computer systems were knocked out, but the building remained intact. The next month, London's 2012 Olympic Bid Committee, housed on the fiftieth floor, got the news it had worked for – London had won!

In 2006, Dr Who (played by David Tennant) is captured by the sinister Torchwood Institute, now located at the top of the tower, where Cybermen and Daleks at last meet. Not only is Torchwood still stuck in the imperial measurement system, they don't even have the tower's height right – it's 800ft, not 600ft!

Just a year after One Canada Square, Frankfurt's Messeturm became Europe's tallest skyscraper at 256m. In London, One Canada Square's height record is likely to be usurped by taller skyscrapers, the tallest being *The Shard*. London will then have an original tallest building again.

One Cabot Square, E14

Tube, DLR Canary Wharf
Height 89m, 21 storeys
Area 46,500m² of offices
Constructed 1988–91
Architect Pei Cobb Freed & Partners

This oddly shaped building was the second-highest and third-largest built in Canary Wharf's first phase. It makes an L shape around a corner of Cabot Square, and has façades 30 degrees from the right-angled plan. Topping it is a big plant floor containing back-up power supplies. Portuguese workers installed pinkish-grey German limestone cladding, marked by horizontal granite stripes.

Global bankers Credit Suisse First Boston took residence in 1993, attracted by its vast 7,000m² trading floors. At that time Canary Wharf had few facilities, so the 1994 arrival of the Canary Wharf Health Club in the building, overlooking waterside terraces, was good news for many.

The New York-based architects are home to the famous Chinese-American IM Pei, but One Cabot Square is the work of Henry N Cobb, who has an amazing track record of elegant skyscrapers, from the John Hancock Tower in Boston (1976), an ultra-cool sixty-storey mirror-glassed rhomboid office slab, to the curved mirror slab of the Tour ELF (2001) in la Défense, Paris. One Cabot Square is entirely different from these. Effectively a groundscraper, it's about mass rather than height. Despite its jazzy steps and faceting, this bulky building feels like a lumpy figure in an ill-fitting outfit.

One Canada Square and World Finance Centre, New York

One Cabot Square

25 North Colonnade, E14

Tube, DLR Canary Wharf
Height 80m, 17 storeys
Area 33,425m² offices
Designed 1989
Completed 1991
Architect Troughton McAslan

Canary Wharf's Phase One is American designed, except for 25 North Colonnade, which is by John McAslan of Troughton McAslan. He worked with Richard Rogers in the early eighties, and his practice has major historical restoration commissions from the *Trellick Tower* to Frank Lloyd Wright buildings in Florida. McAslan also designed the twelve-storey Vitro building at Fenchurch Street (2003).

25 North Colonnade was built in just sixteen months. It is basically two connected stepped slabs clad in a restrained grey Canadian granite and glazed with an Italian structural silicon system which makes the façades like mirrors. The smooth skin and rounded edges anticipate by eight years the finish of the nearby *HSBC* tower. The lower floors have angled façades, breaking the rectilinear plan of most of the estate's buildings.

Inside is a screen of translucent blue enamel called *Moving On* (1999) by Kate Blee. A *Sex In The City* sort of bar called Brodie's sits at the back. In 2005, CWG sold the building for £125m.

The Financial Services Authority, a quango that regulates the financial services industry, has its headquarters here. The FSA's move from the City to this building in 1998 not only gave it distance from big institutions it keeps an eye on, but quietly confirmed that Canary Wharf had become the UK's established second financial services centre. The building's anodyne, anonymous character seems just right for the FSA.

25 Cabot Square, E14

Tube, DLR Canary Wharf
Height 81m, 15 storeys
Constructed 1988–91
Architect SOM

Like its sister, *One Cabot Square*, no. 25 is more ground-scraper than skyscraper, and it, too, has an L-shaped footprint. It was the third-highest building in the first phase of Canary Wharf, and its 41,666m² of office is home to Morgan Dean Witter Stanley, the American dynastic financial services company. They also occupy offices at 20 Cabot Square, which is linked to no. 25 by a high-level bridge, as well as the Terry Farrell-designed 15 Westferry Circus, completed in 2001 and clad in the same marbles, giving a corporate consistency with 25 Cabot Square.

25 Cabot Square is more attractive and less bulky than *One Cabot Square*, and is typical of the eighties-style power architecture of the Wharf. Its standout feature is an open plant floor at the top set behind classical loggias, which makes it look remarkably like Germany's first skyscraper, the 1924 Wilhelm-Marx-Hochhaus in Düsseldorf. This is the first London skyscraper by Chicago-based global architects SOM. They have designed so many seminal skyscrapers around the world that this effort is quite modest by their standards.

25 North Collonade

Wilhem-Marx-Haus, Düsseldorf

One America Square, EC3
Crosswall, City

Tube, DLR, rail Tower Hill/Tower Gateway/
Fenchurch Street
Height 65m, 15 storeys
Constructed 1989–91
Architect RHWL

One America Square is a fantastic, indulgent feast of eighties-version Art Deco.

Railway termini are obvious places for office development because they are central and connected. In the eighties, offices were built over a number of stations, including Fenchurch Street itself, where a sloping office block hides discreetly behind the early Victorian station façade. One America Square stands further down the platforms, the first London skyscraper to exploit air rights over open rail tracks. A new, secondary, station entrance was part of the development.

This building is mainly a huge ten-storey podium block, topped by roof gardens and terraces, with a narrow slab rising from its middle. It is clad in granite and the slab carries massive barrel-vaulted glazed arches on either side. Architects Renton Howard Wood Levin went for a full retro feel, directly inspired by 1920s Art Deco 'modernisme'. The entrance, with its jazzy curving chrome canopy and vertical centrepiece, would not look out of place on the Chrysler Building. The reception is dominated by a backlit stained-glass wall by Brian Clarke. At the top, where plant machinery is covered in curving stainless-steel panels, the slab's shoulders jut out into sharp fins which look just like the signature towers of the great 1933 department store Barkers of Kensington (designed by Bernard George). Were it not for the dignified cladding, this development would be outrageously kitsch!

One America Square was bought by the Qatari government in April 2004 for £110m. What they acquired was not just a substantial block of prime City office space, but the best Art Deco design since Barbara Hulanicki revived the style in her Biba fashion shops in the late 1960s.

25 Cabot Square

One American Square and Barkers of Kensington

designed a system of spokes, like spokes of an umbrella, which cantilevered out from the core to carry open-plan office floors.

Only *Euston Tower* remains of the original development, which is now called Regent's Place and is full of smart Post-Modernist blocks and snazzy artworks. These include a naked man by Anthony Gormley. This tower was recycled by Sheppard Robson, who got rid of the podium, replaced the curtain walls, and installed pipes and new lift shafts on the outside. These Hi-Tech elements give a crisp, businesslike feel. Later, Sheppard Robson would take this further at *CityPoint*. Meanwhile, 338 Euston Road is now a popular multi-occupancy block.

Minster Court, EC3
Minster Lane

Tube Monument
Height 74m, 14 storeys and 65m, 11 storeys
Completed 1991
Architect GMW

Minster Court is a mad faux-gothic complex that people either love or hate. Disney thought it was suitably sinister to make it one of the stars in its 1996 remake of *101 Dalmatians*, where it is the headquarters of the villainess Cruella de Ville, played by Glenn Close.

GMW started designing Minster Court in 1986, just as Post-Modernism had arrived in the City with the *Lloyd's Building*. However, the design is not Hi-Tech, but historicist. Apart from Broadgate, this was the largest City office development of the time, with 83,610 m^2 of space aimed by developers Prudential at the insurance sector. Three buildings are grouped around a glass-covered courtyard, which is behind three horse statues by Althea Wynne nicknamed Sterling, Dollar and Yen. The buildings are clad in Torcicoda marble and Brazilian marble. Shortly after it was finished in 1991, a fire broke out in the lowest block, which is topped with a conical glass roof. The interior was fitted out by Anthony Hunt of the YRM Partnership, who installed the tallest centrally suspended bank of escalators in the world, 40m high. The London Underwriting Centre was established there.

The other two blocks have the steeply pitched roofs that make Minster Court so controversial. They're a whimsical take on Victorian high-gothic and even have gold-coloured squares stuck on to corners, references to the fancy gold embellishments of, say, the Albert Memorial. The verticality is subliminally enhanced by making the window heights smaller on upper floors, which also means that lower floors get bigger windows where there's less light in the narrow EC3 streets.

Some people call the place Monster Court, and amongst those who hate it are style entrepreneur Terence Conran and *30 St Mary Axe* designer Ken Shuttleworth, who compared it to Hogwarts or Batman's castle. What is wrong with these people? Minster Court gives respect to older buildings in this tight City quarter yet manages to be fun as well!

338 Euston Road, E14
(Hardy House)

Tube Warren St, Great Portland Street
Height 65m, 18 storeys
Originally developed 1963–69
Architect Sidney Kaye, Eric Firmin & Partners
Refurbishment Sheppard Robson in 1989–91

This was the second-tallest tower in Joe Levy's massive Euston Centre development, dominated by the *Euston Tower*. The curtain-walled International Style slab rose from a two-storey podium and jutted over the Euston Road pavement. Initially called Hardy House, it was renamed by the tenant, the Hearts of Oak Building Society. A building less evocative of hearts of oak would have been difficult to imagine.

However, this plain building did conceal some interesting engineering. It was only the third London skyscraper to have suspended floors, and lessons were learned from the other two, *20 Fenchurch St* and the *Aviva Tower*. At the top of the concrete core sat a concrete 'top hat' structure, strengthened by post-tensioning rods and cables, and from this the steelwork frame was connected, defining the building envelope. Structural contractors Waterman

Alban Gate, EC2
125 London Wall

Tube Moorgate
Height 82m, 18 storeys
Construction 1990–92
Architect Terry Farrell & Partners

In the Druid calendar, the Alban gates mark the seasons at the year's equinoxes and solstices. This Alban Gate marks the season of romantic Post-Modernism, and the passing of the post-war planned vision of the City. It takes its name from Christopher Wren's St Alban church, and spans *London Wall* next to its surviving tower.

Alban Gate replaced Lee House, one of the original London Wall towers. Terry Farrell had already established himself as the UK's star of the romantic school of Post-Modernism, with works like the TVAM Studios in Camden (now MTV) and the (now-demolished) Limehouse Studios at Canary Wharf. Farrell had just designed the huge One Embankment Place at Charing Cross, and at Alban Gate he came up with another stylish giant. With 34,200m² of offices, it was to offer almost three times more space than the building it replaced. And by straddling London Wall, it obliterated at last the spine of the dreary London Wall corridor of sixties glass boxes.

Alban Gate basically comprises two slabs joined at a few degrees off a right angle, each topped with a great arched glass structure, a flourish that was becoming a standard feature of the times. It shares this feature with the *Lloyd's Building*, but otherwise Alban Gate's Post-Modernism is in marked contrast to Richard Rogers' Hi-Tech. It is clad in polished granite, hides its service structures, and revels in the architectural play of arches, stepped roof-lines, curved bays and barrel-vaulting. As we have seen, this playfulness and distinct horizontal banding owes a lot to Michael Graves' Humana Building in Kentucky. Elsewhere, in Broadgate and Canary Wharf, these 'PoMo' ideas were

already drifting towards a detached corporate style, but here they are rendered quite faithfully. Strangely, however, the building lacks the vivacity of the American inspirations, and feels quite stolid and safe.

Alban Gate actually preserves the sixties high-level walkway scheme, drawing people up by escalator towards *The Barbican* from Wood Street, which Farrell had wanted pedestrianised. The bridge across *London Wall* exposes structural steel elements, a small concession to Hi-Tech, and houses a Pizza Express either side, which splash colourful light around.

Initially, the block was multi-occupancy, but bankers JP Morgan, who had been in *One Angel Court*, gradually occupied the whole building. It changed hands in 2003 for £240m, then again for £315m in late 2005. Property investors like safe buildings.

200 Aldersgate Street, EC1
Little Britain

Tube Barbican
Height 91m, 21 storeys
Area 46,000m² offices
Completed 1992
Architect Fitzroy Robinson

1982 plans for the 76m-high block here were revised as the Big Bang approached – the building became bigger and taller, and got the nod from the RFAC. Architects Fitzroy Robinson, with a City landmark tower at *One Angel Court*, now had a chance to deliver another. This £160 million project would sit at the end of the 1960s axis of *London Wall*'s glass boxes.

The design was odd. It's based on square plan sections that are three windows wide but of different heights, all clad in pink marble. The façades make a right angle facing the roundabout that is also the Museum of London's spiral garden (see *140 London Wall*), and an incongruous sloped atrium stretches across the corner like one side of a glass pyramid. The atrium's base is at the podium walkway level, and bridges the street of Little Britain. Above Aldersgate, the building rises to its full height. The two highest sections, however, are not clad in marble, but are black, and the top three storeys are plant floors. The stepping profile may be reminiscent of 1920s Manhattan, but there is also something mediaeval about the black tower. Globe lamps on the roof corners of each building step help that impression. In damp weather at night, they glow like magical torches on an ancient castle.

200 Aldersgate was the headquarters of legal giant Clifford Chance, who moved to *10 Upper Bank Street* in 2003. Two years later, CWG purchased it for £209 million – an unprecedented foray away from their patch in Canary Wharf. They have commissioned John McAslan to come up with redevelopment proposals, with more space and retail and restaurants at the base. The idea is to build out to make two intersecting sloping glass slabs. It will be a pity to lose the romance of this dark, flawed tower.

Alban Gate and St Alban's churchtower

54 Lombard Street, EC3

Tube Monument, Bank
Height 87m, 19 storeys
Area 29,200m² net offices
Constructed 1990–93
Architect GMW

This distinctive Post-Modernist skyscraper, although not as high as neighbours in the City's cluster, makes a subliminally powerful contribution to the skyline with its barrel-vaulted slender tower. Readers of the *Daily Mail* see three towers in the banner of the City page – this is one of them.

Barclays Bank has been headquartered in three London skyscrapers at various times. Their first was just a block up the road, in the 93m-high Limebank House, demolished in 1997. Barclays commissioned a new HQ in 1983, and specified that it should be a signature building for 2,500 workers that not only related in height and mass to Limebank House, but acknowledged the scale and complexity of the Victorian and Edward buildings adjacent to the site, on Gracechurch Street and Lombard Street. The new building would have the same floor space as the ones it replaced, but the space would be flexible as well as modern.

GMW came up with what was perhaps the most context-considered design of any London skyscraper. The four-storey podium is clad in light grey, granite-faced concrete panels sympathetic to the buildings around, and is embellished with cornices, columns and semi-circular windows. Crucially, it preserves the building line on the street and the heights along it. However, above this, the building rises in sections, with a stepped set of no fewer than five barrel-vaulted roofs. The highest, housing plant machinery, echoes the great crystal arch of the Lloyd's Building, but is topped with a discreet pyramid-frame

structure. The upper floors sit behind metal-faced curtain walling, giving a lighter feel. This transition in appearance with height is something GMW had tackled in a different way with *Minster Court*; ten years later, Arup would use similar thinking about weight at street level and lightness on the skyline with *Plantation Place*.

Planning approval came in 1987, and construction started three years later. The building was ready in April 1993, but works on George Yard behind it, where York stone paving and a water feature were installed, took a bit longer. This was a classy HQ for a global bank. The toilets, for example, were lined in simulated oak panelling. On Lombard Street there is an ancient tradition of hanging metalwork shields with company symbols, originally these were a sort of commercial coat-of-arms, the roots of the modern corporate logo – there, in line with tradition, Barclays hung their shield picturing their 'bird' logo.

Barclays have moved on to a new building at *One Churchill Place*. 54 Lombard Street is now occupied by multiple tenants. Massive new neighbours such as the *Bishopsgate Tower* may eventually dwarf it, but 54 Lombard Street will still make a unique and elegant contribution to the skyline.

99 Bishopsgate

99 Bishopsgate, EC2

Tube Liverpool Street, Bank
Height 104m, 26 storeys
Built 1971–76
Architect Richard Seifert and Ley Colbeck
Reconstructed 1994–95 by GMW Partnership

99 Bishopsgate has had two lives. Initially, it was a bank headquarters, but, after having been wrecked by the IRA's Bishopsgate bomb, it was transformed into one of London's sleekest new multi-occupancy glass towers, setting a standard for later reconstructions such as *CityPoint*.

After Seifert stopped working for Hyams, Felix Fenston felt free to commission him for a City site he had built up. The tower's shape, split by a recessed ridge up the middle, was very similar to that of the *International Press Centre*. However, a leaseholder had been blocking Hyams unless he used another architect, Ley Colbeck. The practice was previously known for suburban house design, but took on the Seifert concept. The building was faced with green glass and exterior steel columns. It became the home of the Hong Kong Bank, an ancestor of *HSBC*. Fenston never lived to see his final skyscraper – he died when site-work had just begun.

After the 1993 bombing, GMW completely re-designed the building around the old steel frame. The work took a mere fourteen months. They greatly expanded the podium into a four-storey space suitable for trading floors, and sheathed the twenty-two-storeys above in a reflecting glass wall which rises a full six metres above the top floor, neatly disguising plant machinery, and bringing the sky into the building's profile. Space was expanded to 31,000m². There is also a small and secret pebbled sculpture garden, which can be glimpsed from the remnants of the City's podium-level walkway scheme behind the tower.

Today, 99 Bishopsgate is still four-fifths occupied by bankers, with Deutsche Bank taking the largest part. As we shall see with the *Bishopsgate Tower*, German money likes this part of the City.

88 Wood Street, EC2
London Wall

Tube St Pauls, Moorgate
Height 75m, 18 storeys
Commisioned 1990
Constructed 1995–99
Architect RRP

Along with *Lloyd's* of London and Lloyd's Register of Shipping on Fenchurch Street, this is one of Richard Rogers' three twentieth-century City creations.

The site was once a Roman military parade ground. Richard Rogers won the competition to design a European HQ for Japanese securities house Daiwa here in 1990. Planning permission was granted in 1992, but the site remained empty for three years until the office market picked up. A British Telecom exchange in the basement had to stay operational during the £52m construction, which was contracted to an Anglo-Japanese joint venture and, as at Lloyd's, engineered by Arup. When finished, it won several awards, including a Stirling Prize nomination. Daiwa, however, decided not to move in, and the 33,073m² building became multiple-occupancy. In 2004, it was sold for £160m.

The building comprises three parallel, connected slabs, respectively of eighteen, fourteen and ten storeys. The lowest is the same height as the adjacent St Alban church tower on Wood Street. Although younger partners led the design, the building has all the Richard Rogers Hi-Tech hallmarks, which are especially obvious on the side facing London Wall. This is the 'active façade', clad in 3 × 4m units of double-glazed laminated glass (the biggest ever at the time), and animated by glass lifts in transparent service towers. These towers are highlighted by bright yellow internal steelwork, and are topped by lift-equipment boxes. An 8m-high atrium runs through the building. Giving light so much access makes for massive solar gain, but the façade is vented, and includes blinds controlled by rooftop solar sensors. Huge funnels rise out of the ground, looking very *Yellow Submarine* – the blue ones take in fresh air and the red ones discharge exhausted air.

88 Wood Street is at once similar to but different from *Lloyd's of London*. The latter is closed to the outside and looks inwards, whereas 88 Wood St is about maximum transparency. It's almost as if the building were trying to compensate for the lack of public access. Another difference is the use of colour, which gives the building a kindergarten playfulness – no need here for coloured floodlighting at night. 88 Wood Street is probably Rogers' brightest big building since the Pompidou Centre.

University College Hospital
235 Euston Road

Tube Euston Square, Warren Street
Height 78m, 18 storeys
Construction 2000–05
Architect Llewelyn-Davies

London' first twenty-first century flagship hospital has already been embroiled in three controversies – about beds, a giant pebble, and terrorists.

This is the first London public-sector skyscraper since 1977. Chancellor Gordon Brown's cunning plan for funding big public works, PFI (Private Finance Initiative), gets other people to pay – in this case, £422m. The replacement for two outdated local hospitals, approved in 2000, would be state of the art, with online medical diagnostics, beds with Internet access, and the UK's largest cancer centre. There was talk about not calling the thirteenth floor Floor 13, but that idea was dropped. In summer 2004, Tony Blair stood on the roof to talk up the NHS.

Most of the site is taken up with a five-storey podium. An almost Hi-Tech suspended bridge at the back reaches to an older building, and curvy reception canopies are skewered on exclamatory columns. The pale green banded curtain walling is as smooth as the fridge look of, say, *Orion House*. The roof slopes languidly across the thick tower, which has convex curving façades. The *Evening Standard* described the appearance as having 'the air of a Taiwanese domestic appliance'. Maybe so, but Taiwan makes pretty nifty things. This is more like an iMac, rather than the clunky old tower PCs of other post-war hospitals. It looks modern, clean and efficient, as hospitals should.

The bed controversy started before the hospital opened. In 2002, to tackle the MRSA bug, which was killing an alarming number of hospital patients, the NHS set a minimum distance between beds of 360cm. UCH's 650 beds already failed the guidelines, some by a whole metre. Then, within months of the hospital opening in June 2005, overworked doctors were napping on trolleys in corridors, for lack of beds. Strangest of all, UCH has fewer beds than the Middlesex Hospital's 715 when it opened in 1935, just one of the two hospitals it replaces.

The pebble controversy stemmed from the University College London Hospital Trust's requirement to spend £340,000 on public art, to lift the spirit of patients, aiding recovery. UCH appointed an Arts Curator who installed several big artworks. These include a giant polished Brazilian marble pebble 270cm long, by the main entrance. This is the Monolith in John Aiken's £70,000 work *Monolith & Shadow* (the Shadow is a dark patch on the stairs). Predictably, some people thought the money should be spent on staff and equipment (they probably wouldn't be happy until every person in the country has a hospital bed). Here, however, both art and curator cost the UCH budget nothing – they are covered by donations.

This new hospital has accrued history in a hurry. Two of the four Islamist 7/7 bombings in London in 2005 were local – the tube and bus explosions at Russell and Tavistock Squares. UCH handled the casualties. Two weeks later, when a second bombing wave failed, an e-mail warned UCH that a man was wandering the hospital with wires protruding from his clothes. Police searched the building in vain.

When the Queen opened UCH officially in October, the West End's only twenty-first century skyscraper had already done a lot of business.

Chapter 6:
Water Beds

High-rise living in London has a long history, dating back to 1888 and Queen Anne's Mansions. A century later, when tower blocks had discredited the idea, its revival started along the river.

For most of the twentieth century, affluent Londoners turned their back on the Thames. Trade and industry, of course, needed the river, and before the war, wharves, warehouses and factories were everywhere, even jumbling up the South Bank in London's very centre. Huge power stations loomed at Battersea and *Lots Road*. There was no status to a riverside address, except in a few spots like Chelsea or the Savoy, but there was one extremely significant development.

On the Pimlico riverfront, Europe's biggest block of flats at Dolphin Square was designed by Gordon Jeeves. It had 1,250 flats in ten storeys, its own shopping arcade, swimming pool, and an enclosed landscaped garden. In other words, it offered a complete lifestyle experience in one place – the ethos of so many high-rise river developments today. Developments like Dolphin Square sprang up all over the UK in the 1930s, but this was, uniquely, by the Thames.

We have already scene how *The Barbican* pioneered middle-class high-rise living in the seventies. The first beds above the water with a price attached appeared then as well. Docklands renewal started at St Katherine's Dock, just by Tower Bridge, and, in 1974, *The Tower Hotel* opened for business. As we have seen, this was a massive, bizarre Brutalist construction rising in steps to fifteen storeys.

Downstream from there, the Docklands stretched east to the muddy estuary, and as commerce closed down, it became a vast, silent place, left to wildlife and decay. But there had always been a tiny middle-class enclave of Georgian houses at Limehouse. Around them, following the New York trend, pioneering conversions of old warehouses into trendy loft apartments were underway by the 1980s. These were the first glimmers of what the river would gradually become: a long metropolis-wide canyon of upmarket apartments.

Dolphin Square

The Return of High-Rise Living

Over in the west, ten years after London's last tower blocks were finished on the *World's End Estate*, 1987 saw London's first prestige high-rise apartment riverside block just a few hundred metres upstream. We have already seen that Ray Moxley's *Belvedere Tower* was London's first romantic Post-Modernist skyscraper. The council estate had ignored the water, but the new tower was there precisely because of the water. Its glass penthouse would be repeated endlessly in subsequent riverside developments. By now, a river view commanded a price premium in the estate agents, and so, unexpectedly, did height. A formula combining the two worked.

Back in the East, two other upmarket towers were already underway. Across the water from Wapping, at Jacobs Island, a disused grain silo called *Vogan's Mill* was converted to flats by Squire & Partners. Nearby, architects CZWG squeezed a colourful block of flats with semi-circular windows – China Wharf – into the old riverfront. This was an example of the bright, eye-catching Post-Modernist architecture on a traditional scale that was popping up like unexpected delights in the dull-hued stretches of Docklands, and it put CZWG on the architectural map. They also had ideas about building high-rise. Shortly before Canary Wharf's construction began, they designed *Cascades* for an Isle of Dogs site nearby. The twenty-storey upmarket block brilliantly reflected the nautical heritage of the docks with amusing architectural features. CZWG followed their *Cascades* with a sting of other vibrant riverside apartments that were quite different from the usual riverside stuff. These included the medium-rise yellow spirally Bankside Lofts (1998) by the Tate Modern. Sadly, few later developments would draw on their local past like the warehouse conversions, *Vogan's Mill* and *Cascades*.

During the nineties, new apartments spread east all the way out to Woolwich. Even where wharves had never been, new developments mysteriously became Wharves. Often in deprived or desolate areas, CCTV and 24-hour security made them like little gated estates. In style, they tended to repeat a safe formula of reassuring brick cladding, glass balconies, suburban-style pitched roofs and perhaps some Post-Modernist embellishments such as barrel-vaulted bay windows. They would often include a tower, but usually it was merely a stumpy ten storeys or so. Tallest at the time was the 75-metre high, twenty-two-storey Berkeley Tower in CWG's own high-rise apartments. These were completed in 1998 at the western end of the estate, and are fairly typical – they look almost like brick-clad sixties tower blocks, but with glass penthouses.

While Docklands had become a new home for affluent financial sector types, old money preferred West London, and here too were stretches of brownfield ripe to build on. High-rise living didn't get moving here until the late nineties, when a redundant office tower in Pimlico was recycled and reborn as *The Panoramic*. It still looks rather like an office block, but its extensive glazing was a sign of things to come.

A Bend in the River

A little further upstream, the big names of the British Post-Modernist architectural establishment focused on the bend of the river between Battersea and Chelsea, where in the 1870s James McNeill Whistler had captured the moods of the water in his *Nocturne* paintings. *Lots Road* Power Station used to power the Tube, and in 1996 Terry Farrell started masterplanning here, intending to recycle the power station and put two diamond-roofed apartment towers on either side of Chelsea Creek. Despite Farrell's impeccable credentials, the scheme would take almost a decade to be passed.

Directly across the river, another great piece of London's industrial heritage, an abandoned Hovis flour-mill, was not as lucky as the power station. Its demolition was a tragedy, but the building that replaced it in 1999 was exceptional – Richard Rogers'

Pan Peninsula lifestyle

Montevetro, West London's answer to the *Cascades*. This is another great sundial of flats, but with floor-to-ceiling glass for maximum viewing of the river. Rogers had always wanted to tackle the river – as far back as 1986, he had exhibited a South Bank river plan at the Royal Academy that included a pedestrian bridge and Archigram-like structures rising from the water. Even his practice is on the river, occupying a Post-Modernist barrel-roofed block in Fulham where his wife runs a restaurant. Coincidentally, Norman Foster's practice also faces the river, near *Montevetro*. His response to *Montevetro* would follow in the new century, a massive medium-rise silver doughnut of flats called Albion Riverside, next door to the practice.

Upstream at Vauxhall, big riverside redevelopment plans had come and gone for a quarter or a century, but at last, in 2000, work started on Central London's largest luxury-flat development at the Broadway Malyan-designed *St George Wharf*, where gull-wing roofs bring drama to connected towers. The final tower, however, will be very different: a 180m-high tube called Vauxhall Tower, the tallest block of flats in the UK. The planning hurdles it faced crystallise the new century's issues in high-rise living, from affordable housing to strategic views and sustainable design.

High Style and Affordable Housing

When Ken Livingstone's GLA drew up its London Plan in 2002, with a little help from Richard Rogers, it was the first comprehensive blueprint for the metropolis since Abercrombie's in the 1940s. The plan set out to tackle the massive issues of London's population, which had stopped declining, and from the year 2000's 7.4 million was estimated to reach 8.1 million by 2016. Yet first-time buyers are priced out of London. Ken's policies aim for half of all new homes to be affordable. This is pretty loosely defined, covering social housing and property selling at the low end of the market – theoretically, it means homes where key workers such as nurses or firemen can afford to live. Affordable housing now flows from high-rise developments. Height also fits in neatly with a big London Plan theme, the densification of London. Finally, the London Plan reiterates the need for environmentally friendly buildings.

High-rise living is now firmly re-established, and getting higher. Savills Research's surveys in 2004 and 2005 found that, across the UK, new schemes of twenty storeys or more jumped forty-six per cent over that period, with the average height increasing from twenty-four to twenty-seven storeys. Building above twenty storeys gets expensive because of foundation work, so developers need to raise more from selling to the higher-end market. They rely on getting money in the bag upfront, especially from penthouse sales, which sell for millions. There was a time when flats went on sale when the building was there, but nowadays the luxury towers are launched with fanfare well in advance. The current record is at *Pan Peninsula* on the Isle of Dogs, launched when diggers had barely started on site, over three years before the flats would be ready!

Riverside blocks, Isle of Dogs

New York has led the way with marketing modern prestige high-rise, with Donald Trump's towers the best known. A more recent arrival there is the infamous Michael Shvo, a 'condo broker' who in 2004 started his own development company. Developments such as his forty-three-storey Bryant Park Tower, a slick finger tower in the heart of Midtown, are marketed via websites where moody jazz plays and couples relax above the New York skyline. That sort of style marketing is coming to London. Every development is heralded by marketing suites and glossy brochures, and nowadays it's not just the building and location that you get sold. Ice-cool women may recline dreamily on designer furniture, or share moments on a balcony with groomed thirty-something men, chilling down after the stress of their day on the trading floors of Canary Wharf or the City. In the case of *Pan Peninsula*, an entire magazine has been made, with pages of style shoots and design spreads mixed with interviews and intelligent articles about architecture.

Millennial Designs and Mixed Uses

Architecturally, most of the new century's luxury towers are variations on themes from the 1980s. Gerald Manton's seventeen-storey Barrier Point tower (2001) out in Silvertown was different — a cylinder with a clean white finish evoking the 1920s seaside. In 2004, Patel Taylor's *Putney Wharf* and SOM's New Providence Wharf introduced tiered penthouses. SOM also gave an interesting twist to the sundial form of the *Cascades* by bending it into an arc. This created a very long roof-line to play with, and the penthouse steps, each with a swimming pool, climb it like a long staircase. New Providence Wharf's final element is a twenty-seven-storey lipstick column of flats called the *Ontario Tower*, which introduces the diagonally cut roof-line, although Terry Farrell had already designed chamfers into the frustrated *Lots Road* scheme.

New Providence Wharf and *Pan Peninsula* are from London's leading luxury tower developer Ballymore,

an Irish company which originally invested in Docklands in 1990, and soon commissioned CZWG to design two ten-storey apartment projects. Their plans have become increasingly ambitious. Their developments are becoming self-contained mini-cities, and *Pan Peninsula* will have London's tallest apartment block to date.

The biggest architectural change, introduced at *Montevetro*, is the arrival of fully-glazed façades. As we shall see when looking at offices, glass is a defining characteristic of the greatest new Millennial towers. A key example of the trend in residential is the curved *One West India Quay*, by architects HOK, which is not on the river but a quayside. It also has the first penthouses above 100m to actually hit the market, and, because the block incorporates a Marriott hotel, it is London's first 'mixed

Barrier Point

development' skyscraper. Mixed use tends to generate bigger buildings, but the developer's risk is reduced because it is not reliant on a single market.

In some of the UK's other great cities, mixed-development landmark skyscrapers are major symbols of urban renewal. One Northern practice in particular, Ian Simpson Architects, stands out for world-class designs. In 2005, the Beetham Organisation unveiled plans for an incredible futuristic streamlined Simpson-designed sixty-eight-storey glass *Beetham Tower*, beside Blackfriars Bridge.

The trouble with building high on riverside sites is that there are so many strategic views to protect, and not just those of St Paul's. A challenge faced by Vauxhall Tower was its effects on views of Westminster. When that was cleared, plans for two more towers just behind it, designed by Squires & Partners, stepped forth in early 2006. These Vauxhall Cross apartment towers are lipstick-shaped, like the *Ontario Tower*, and respectively 178m/forty-eight storeys and 144m/twenty-six storeys high. They offer an 'urban forest' of trees under a canopy between them. Another curvy tower on the South Bank, this one 127m and thirty-two storeys high, and designed in 2001 by Kevin Dash & Philip Gumuchdjian, fell foul of objections by local residents, in part because of local, but unprotected, views. The Tate Modern is next door, and its director Sir Nicholas Serota led the 'nimbys', claiming it would dominate his massive art gallery with its 200m-plus façade and 90m

Vauxhall Cross proposal

chimney. On only slightly safer ground, because it sits on a site a block inland at *Doon Street* by Waterloo Bridge, is a forty-eight-storey Lifschutz Davidson Sandilands-designed apartment block. Like the *Beetham Tower*, it would be visible from St James's Park. As with Queen Anne's Mansions almost 120 years earlier, the views from this Royal Park create debate that will doubtless play out during 2006-7.

Luxury living has transformed the entire city's social geography. Whole new residential districts have sprung up along the river, from Wandsworth to the Royal Docks. Incredibly, the dense new developments have helped East London to become a hot property market. At current rates of development, there would be no London riverside left to develop by the next decade. The hunger for waterside development opportunities has taken them inland. North of the river, inner London is ringed with the Regent's and Grand Union Canals, which were transformed in the nineties by British Waterways from a dark linear rubbish tip to post-industrial shangri-las of narrow boat communities. Their chief executive Robin Evans reckons a waterside location adds a twenty to thirty per cent premium to property prices, and he controls a lot of waterside. Already, Paddington Basin is hemmed in by a wall of seventeen-storey apartments. At Islington's City Basin (see *261 City Road*), masterplanned towers of twenty-eight and thirty-five storeys are approved.

We will look at green skyscrapers in the next

Manchester's Beetham Tower

chapter, and particularly at the development of vented façades to regulate internal climate. Residential towers are bringing other environmental features to the architecture of high-rise. Over 70m under central London is the London Aquifer, strata of water-bearing chalk and sands beneath the London clay. The water here is at a more constant temperature than surface water, which means it can cool buildings in summer and warm them in winter, with big savings on energy. The *Vauxhall Tower* will draw on the London Aquifer, and it will also be the first London building to boast a wind turbine.

Sky Communities

RIBA President George Ferguson may have said that apartment blocks of fifty storeys are 'unnecessary', but if there is a demand for them, the market says otherwise. When penthouses sell for millions, it is necessary to get some of that property spend flowing to local communities, and it is necessary to keep pushing the quality of high-rise design up. Luxury towers are beginning to do both. This century has seen a jump in design quality as well as height.

Taller still are the mega-high projects that follow the model set by Chicago's 1969 John Hancock Center, which brought offices into the mix alongside residential accommodation. We shall come to the *Columbus Tower* and *The Shard* in the next chapter.

The London Plan formula of densification, social mix and environmental sustainability doesn't necessarily mean high-rise, but they do all come together in a design that may have a future in London – the Skyhouse. This is the work of David Marks and Julia Barfield, designers of the London Eye. It follows in the tradition of Le Corbusier's idealised community housing characterised by generous measures of air and light, as well as Archigram's capsule-dwelling pod tower dreams of the 1960s, but also tackles those green and social mix issues. Initially, the Skyhouse design was 72 storeys and 305m high, but the refined version is just 50 storeys, and stacks three modular banks of flats around a central core. Wind energy is harvested by turbines at the centre of the three-leaf structure. The design looks good as well – a Hi-Tech glass and steel structure with two levels of skygardens enclosed within. Skyhouse is a project without a site, although the Greenwich Peninsula below the Millennium Dome had been suggested before the 2012 Olympics bid re-zoned the area.

Skyhouse's social mix is already evolving on the London skyline. In some ways, old tower blocks and new luxury high-rise are on a convergence path. We have already seen how the introduction of privately owned flats into tower blocks can help their revival, while new luxury blocks can equally accommodate increasing amounts of affordable housing. One day, the blander luxury blocks could even become the new nightmare tower blocks – ugly, neglected intrusions in the urban landscape. Only time will tell.

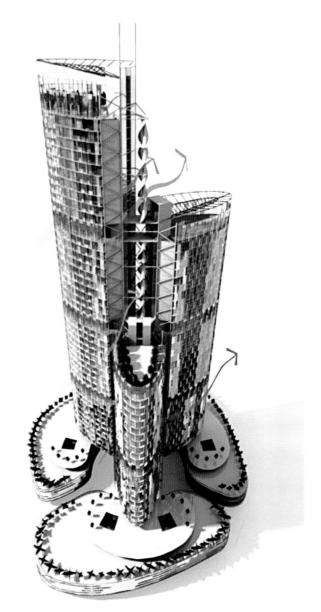

The Skyhouse

The Belvedere, SW10
Chelsea Harbour

Bus C3
Height 77m, 20 storeys
Completed 1987
Architect Ray Moxley

This whimsical landmark is the very first of London's riverside luxury apartment high-rises, and a pioneering Post-Modernist tower.

In March 1986, Mrs Thatcher abolished the GLC, reverting planning applications for tall buildings back to local councils. Local council elections were scheduled for May, and the pro-development Tories in Hammersmith & Fulham expected to lose. They rushed The Belvedere through just in time.

The tower is the centrepiece of Chelsea Harbour, an exclusive residential development on a brownfield site. Architect Ray Moxley won the commission – he understood the water (his hobby was designing catamarans) and, as he said, he enjoyed 'architecture in the context of spaces, avenues, crescents, squares and vistas', exactly the environment West London's rich were used to. Chelsea Harbour has a lot of these elements, but it was there to exploit the water. At its heart is a marina, and The Belvedere lies between it and the river, with overlooking balconies. An external spiral staircase climbs the tower to the glass penthouses. The outstanding feature is a golden pyramid roof, topped with a spire, on which a gold ball rises and falls, indicating the tide.

Moxley was the Chairman of the Society of Advanced Methods of Management, so it's no surprise that The Belvedere is an early example of American fast-track construction. After Chelsea Harbour, he designed the vast ExCel exhibition complex in the Royal Docks.

The tower and marina soon filled up with the elite and their yachts. Michael Caine and Elton John occupied penthouse flats. Chelsea Harbour is not a gated estate but feels like it. There's often an eerily

deserted feeling, like being in an episode of *The Prisoner*. The thin retro-futuristic Belvedere could even be a modern version of an architectural curiosity in PortMeirion, Clough Williams-Ellis' romantic Welsh village in which the iconic TV series was shot. Like the best pre-war Modernist seaside projects such as Bexhill's De La Warr Pavilion, The Belvedere is essentially a waterside romance.

Cascades, E14
2–4 Westferry Road

DLR Heron Quays
Height 64m, 20 storeys
Designed 1986
Completed 1987–88
Architect CZWG

One of the early problems with Canary Wharf was that the only way to get there was via the then-tiny Docklands Light Railway. As City planners had realised with *The Barbican*, one solution was upmarket homes next to offices. Developer Kentish Homes spotted the opportunity and wanted something unusual for a riverside patch just minutes from Canary Wharf. The obvious choice was the Campbell Zogolovitch Wilkinson Gough partnership, which had visions of bringing back high-rise living. Their designs upstream such as China Wharf at Jacobs Island were eccentric buildings with colour and flair.

Dockland's first yuppie flats in a skyscraper happened quickly. The design was ready in January 1986, permission granted in October, and construction took just eighteen months, with the concrete lift core taking less than three weeks to make. The first tenants moved in while the building had just reached the seventeenth floor! The 171 flats sold like hot cakes, surprising considering the barrenness of the area then. As a symbol of the new London rising in the east, a drawing of Cascades featured on the London telephone directory of the time.

The idea of the building was partner Rex Wilkinson's, and the influence is nautical. It has features such as round porthole windows and flues like ship's funnels – there's even a sloping smokestack-shape on the roof. The exterior stairs, wrapped in curvy metal cages, evoke rigging and crow's-nests. The block is finished in light sandy brick, with horizontal bands of darker brown that prevent the wide façades becoming overwhelming. Aligned to the riverwalk, the other side faces Canary Wharf, so everyone gets a spectacular view. The most striking element of the shape is the huge sweeping ramp rising sharply to the main body of the tower. The ramp descends to a residents' swimming pool block. CZWG's Piers Gough once joked that it was the largest slide into a swimming pool anywhere.

Nowadays, Cascades is just one block in the ribbon of luxury flats along the Thames, but is still among the few outstanding riverside developments.

Belvedere Tower

The longest slide

Vogan's Mill, SE1
Mill Street

Tube Bermondsey
Height 55m, 18 storeys
Completed 1989
Architect Squire & Partners

This elegant white structure was only Docklands' second luxury flat tower and recycles a disused grain silo.

Vogan's Mill sits by St Saviour's Dock, a muddy creek that harboured pirates in the eighteenth century. The dense jumble of alleys and haphazard waterside buildings around it was the Jacobs Island where Fagin's lair was sited in Charles Dickens' *Oliver Twist*. When it fell into the LDDC's regeneration remit in the eighties, the creek was full of shopping trolleys and flotsam half-buried in the mud. The Vogan's Mill silo was a blank tower with a line of windows at the top.

Architect Michael Squire's conversion could fit only single flats across the silo, but above it is a three-storey penthouse apartment, with a graceful curved roof. The penthouse apartment sold at a price unprecedented for the then-moribund area, and can claim to be the very first of countless Docklands glass penthouses. Squire also converted the adjacent Victorian warehouse into forty-eight flats. The whole scheme won a Civic Trust Awards commendation in 1993 and kick-started local regeneration.

Nowadays, St Saviour's Dock is completely lined with luxury conversions, boats bob up and down in its dredged waters, and a shiny steel wire bridge spans it. Parallel to the creek, Mill Street is so narrow, it's impossible to get a clear view of the whole tower. Squire retained the original white colour of the tower, which gives it a crisp Mediterranean brightness. Its colour and roofline distinguish it from the waterside high-rise to come.

Montevetro, SW11
Battersea Church Road

Rail Clapham Junction
Height 64m, 20 storeys
Designed 1994
Completed 1999
Architect RRP

Montevetro means 'glass mountain' in Italian, which is a good description of these luxury flats. The building's sharply raked profile is similar to that of *Cascades*, but here there are Hi-Tech elements also found in the *Lloyd's Building*.

This site was previously occupied by an early twentieth-century Hovis flour-mill, similar to the one in Gateshead which was converted to The Baltic art gallery. After Battersea's mill was abandoned in the 1980s, plans were approved to convert it into flats. Richard Rogers himself had little sympathy for obsolete buildings, and building from scratch would yield even more flats. Despite a local campaign to save the mill from 'the Monster Vetro', the Government ruled in favour of redevelopment.

To maximise the views across the river, Montevetro's western side is fully glazed. This does not mean, however, that there's a set of flats at the back with no river views – all the flats face east as well. This is because, rather than access to the flats being provided via corridors along the block's axis, there are four service towers housing lifts and stairs, dividing the building into five sections, the lowest, by St Mary's Church, only four storeys high. The lift towers are transparent and mounted with widow-cleaning cranes. They climb the eastern side, where the building has warm terracotta cladding. There are 103 flats, including penthouses under the sloping roof with high, airy interiors, like artists' studios of a century earlier. In 2005, a three-storey penthouse was on the market for £4.65m – about twice as much as comparable penthouses in Docklands towers.

Vogans Mill and Montevetro

Rogers' previous riverside apartments, Thames Wharf, near his practice in Fulham, were not Hi-Tech, and Montevetro was a unique London experiment – the application of Hi-Tech to flats. The result is a masterpiece, and the price paid for it – the loss of the Hovis mill – will be gradually forgotten.

The Panoramic, SW1
(RHM Centre)
Millbank

Tube Pimlico
Height 73m, 19 storeys
Completed 1971
Architect PJ Mills of Chapman, Taylor & Partners
Converted 1999 by Halpern Partnership

This exclusive luxury-flat tower used to house offices where people managed the UK's supplies of bread and, later, gas.

The tower was built as the headquarters for baking conglomerate Rank Hovis McDougall, on a riverside site just downstream from their London flour-mill (later replaced by the *Montevetro* building). Preliminary excavations uncovered some of the original 1816 Vauxhall Bridge, at the same time as new Victoria Line tunnels were being bored underneath. The narrow office tower was completed in 1971 and tiled in a shade of brown the colour of Hovis loaves. In the 1980s, the tower was the headquarters of British Gas, which had moved from a grim eighteen-storey block in Paternoster Square by St Paul's.

The new owners embarked on a £24m conversion into ninety flats. At each corner, the floors were extended outwards a little, and glazed full-height. The original plant floor became a massive penthouse, capped by a subtly domed roof. Bore holes 120m deep bring up London aquifer water to regulate the building's climate – a technique new towers will use. The Panoramic is a discreet tower, strangely sympathetic to Pimlico's cream terraces below.

Perspective, SE1
(Century House)
100 Westminster Bridge Road

Tube Lambeth North
Height 73m, 22 storeys
Completed 1959
Converted 1999–2002 by Assael Architecture

This chunky apartment tower once had an earlier life as the headquarters of Britain's Cold War spy network and for two years was the tallest skyscraper in London.

Century House was an early post-war office block influenced by the Seagram Building, rising twenty storeys and 67.7m straight up from the ground, with a recessed entrance behind columns. A connected low-rise block was at the side, next to the tube station. Despite its height, its nondescript look and location made it a suitable place for Britain's Secret Intelligence Service (SIS), otherwise known as MI6 or 'The Firm', which moved from St James's Street in 1966.

MI6's purpose is to gather overseas intelligence, as opposed to MI5, whose sphere of operations is within the UK (see *Euston Tower*). From 1956, its director-general or 'C' was Dick White, previously head of MI5, where he is said to have had the Labour Party and trade unions infiltrated by MI5 agents. Nevertheless, at MI6, White got on well with Labour Prime Minister Harold Wilson, and the move to the new offices would have fitted in with Wilson's perspective of a modern, post-colonial state. In the 1970s, a new 'C', Sir Maurice Oldfield, took over in Century House. A long-standing rivalry between MI5 and MI6 resulted in Oldfield being outed as gay by leaks from MI5. In 1995, MI6 moved to the new Post-Modernist riverside HQ they refer to as 'Legoland' at Vauxhall, designed by Terry Farrell (architect of *Alban Gate*).

Century House lay empty until 1999, when Nicholson Estates got permission to convert the building into 236 flats, including fifty-six affordable homes. The project cost £50m.

The Panoramic and Century House before conversion

Perspective after conversion

unhappy about the scheme's felling of three Norway Maple trees. A revised scheme was finally approved in 2000.

The design added two storeys, and sliced back the slab at the top to create a six-storey cascade of stepped balconies below the re-used lift core. Putney Wharf now houses sixty-six flats, and the penthouse on the top three floors sold for £2.7m straight away. The riverside edge was rounded off with great semicircles of glazing and balconies, contrasting with the terra-cotta cladding behind it. The mix of silvery sci-fi curves with warm side-walls has a strangely exciting effect. At night, it tingles with blue point-lights. Transforming one of the worst sixties office slabs into such urban chic is an achievement!

Assael Architecture's design uses the new century's formulas for luxury towers to good effect. The first five floors are clad in red terracotta brickwork. The entrance has a big jaunty canopy. The biggest feature is the addition of two extra floors of glass penthouses underneath fly-away roof wings. The new name, Perspective, is about the views from up there. Just like the spies who used to occupy it, the building seems to be looking out, watching...

Putney Wharf, SW15
(Bridge House then ICL House)
1 Putney High Street

Tube Putney Bridge
Height 54m, 18 stories
Designed 1960, completed 1962
Rebuilt 2001–04
Architect Patel Taylor

A big feature of Bridge House, an office block by the river at Putney Bridge, was its exposed concrete lift column, a forerunner of the separation of floors and service towers in tower blocks such as the *Balfron Tower*. The building overpowered the residential streets behind and loomed uncomfortably close to the Grade II-listed St Mary's Church.

After Harold Wilson backed the creation of a British challenge to IBM's dominance in computing, ICL was set up in 1968, and this became their head-quarters. ICL fared badly in the eighties, and was later taken over by Fujitsu. They left the building in 1997, and Putney was left with an empty eyesore. Developer St George acquired the block, but their initial plans stirred controversy and were raised in Parliament. Locals wanted the block demolished and were also

One West India Quay, E14

DLR West India Quay
Height 111m 34 storeys
Constructed 2001–04
Architect HOK International

Other developers have built high-rise, but the Manhattan Loft Corporation and Marylebone Warwick Balfour were the first to go above 100m. Their sleek, elegant tower presents a wide bow-curved glass façade to the Canary Wharf estate across the water of West India Quay, as if puffing out its chest to it.

It is also the first major UK tower to combine luxury flats and hotel, a formula now shared by Beetham Towers in Birmingham (also with a convex curving façade) and Manchester.

Architects Squires & Partners, who transformed *Vogan's Mill* into flats, prepared a masterplan in the nineties to make West India Quay a leisure and residential zone. They restored the early nineteenth-century listed warehouses (now the Museum of Docklands) and, behind them, designed a cinema complex and the twelve-storey Horizon House block of flats. Squires also envisioned a waterside tower, but that design was by the London office of American-based HOK. Construction started in July 2001 and the concrete core had reached full height in April 2003. The official topping-out was in September, just three weeks after a base jumper was reported jumping off the top. Mysteriously, CCTV cameras saw no intruder.

Unusually, rather than steel decks, the floors are concrete with embedded cables stretched to seriously boost strength. This makes it the highest post-tensioned concrete building in the UK. Glass imported from the Netherlands screens the sun's UV and provides thermal insulation.

One West India Quay has a waterfront restaurant and a colonnade. The lowest twelve floors are a Marriott Hotel, opened in June 2004, with 348 rooms and serviced apartments entered from a seven-storey podium block behind the tower. The Marriott restaurant made the newspapers in September 2004 when it asked customers ordering rare hamburgers to sign a form waiving responsibility if they got food poisoning. The twenty floors above the hotel have 158 flats. The six on the top three floors are two- and three-storey penthouses with glass staircases, walk-in wine cellars and other features. One of them sold for £2.8m in 2004. Before a garden roof terrace was installed, the roof was a location shoot for the British gangster film *Layer Cake* (2004), in which thugs suspend a man over the edge in a plot to do with cocaine. In a 2005 episode of the BBC's police drama *Waking the Dead*, a counterfiet drug racketeer left a corpse on the roof, exposed to nature in the Parsi tradition. In real life, One West India Quay is still about the dizzying heights that money can bring.

SeaCon Wharf, E14

Tube Canary Wharf
DLR South Quay
Height 59m, 21storeys
Constructed 2002–04
Architect CZWG

SeaCon Wharf stands like a book slid into a gap in the Isle of Dogs riverside. It is a little downstream from *Cascades*, CZWG's first distinctive tower.

The original plan was for sixteen storeys, but then it got revised to twenty-three storeys, then back to 21. The striking feature of SeaCon is the iron-red frame that turns into a cantilevered flat roof cover. This is a reminder of the Express Wharf's massive 1960s shed that used to stand on the site, one of the few Isle of Dogs cargo-handling facilities that survived the closure of the docks. It jutted out over the water to cover the hanging cranes which handled containers from ships moored on the river.

Away from the river, the slab widens out into white-faced wings that accommodate the flats at the back, but the alignment means that everyone from the thirteenth floor up gets a river view. Beneath the roof are three storeys of penthouses, including two-bedroom penthouses that went on the market in 2005 for up to £1.8m. SeaCon residents get not just the usual features like designer kitchen and bathroom fittings but also a communal glass-floored mezzanine lounge with a library upstairs. The reception hall has a Japanese-style fireplace and a porcelain work commissioned from Hong Kong artist Fiona Wong. Designer lifestyle features are becoming standard in luxury blocks, but here the bespoke cool takes on a zen-like quality. What really distinguishes SeaCon Wharf from the usual brash or anodyne high-rise design, however, is its slim frontage and industrial frame exterior. That makes it a great skyscraper.

...when it looked like this

Putney Wharf, it used to be an eyesore...

SeaCon Wharf

Discovery Dock East, E14
Marsh Wall

DLR South Quay
Height 78m, 24 storeys
Constructed 2003–05
Architect Chantrey Davis

This development is named after the ship *Discovery*, despatched in 1901 by the Royal Geographical Society from here, with Captain Scott and Ernest Shackleton aboard, to Antarctica, where the two fell out. In the late 1980s, the site saw one of the first major Docklands developments, the distinctive black-glazed medium-rise office space towers with pitched roofs of South Quay Plaza, which had been designed by the Seifert partnership under Richard's son John. It was partially destroyed by the IRA in 1996. Subsequently, London's World Trade Centre was planned here, but with so much office coming onstream in Canary Wharf, just across West India Docks, it failed to attract tenants. Developers Capital & Provident decided to go for the booming residential market instead. Steel frames of the bombed buildings have since been recycled into new flats and a Hilton hotel, but this eastern tower was built around fresh concrete cores. There were problems when finishing the construction work, and some of the 192 flats actually changed size from their specification after they were sold.

This L-shaped edifice is composed of two 16-storey slabs with the tower where they meet. It's a heavy block with punched windows, presenting an overbearing façade to the water, which the sloping roofs of the glass penthouses fail to alleviate. The effect is a little like a grand Tibetan building in Lhasa, but without any mystery.

St George Wharf, SW8

Tube Vauxhall
Height The tallest tower is 72m, 22 storeys
Construction from 2000
Architect Broadway Malyan

The arresting development of St George Wharf rises up into a set of towers topped with distinctive gull-wing roofs.

St George Wharf is not named, as is usual, after some local historical enterprise, but after its developers. The huge Efra site used to house the Nine Elms Cold Store (1961), a big windowless concrete box that was said to store emergency food supplies for London. Broadway Malyan's scheme returns the riverside to the public realm, with a 275m-long stretch of public riverside walkway (raised over car parking). It has 942 apartments, 177 as affordable housing, and behind them, facing Vauxhall's transport interchange, offices. Construction has been in stages. Broadway Malyan won a British Green Apple Award in 2004 for the design's green credentials, and there's even an electric car club based in the development!

Particularly eye-catching is the set of residential towers, which cascade down in steps towards the river from the development's spine. Bridge House, the lowest tower, rises 15 storeys beside Vauxhall Bridge, while Flagstaff House, the tallest with 22 storeys, is the centrepiece of what will eventually be a symmetrical array of five towers. The last, Kestrel House (not to be confused

Discovery Dock East

St George Wharf

with an Islington tower block of the same name), was put on hold awaiting a decision on the estate's controversial *Vauxhall Tower* next door. When that was approved in 2005, it was moved slightly back from the river, to create more public space. These towers are partially clad in stone, but curved glazed sections cut through them like ships breaking through ice, and they are further glazed beneath the gull-wing roofs. The glass is green, echoing Terry Farrell's MI6 building (1993) nearby. The steel roofs are from the Netherlands, and the penthouses beneath them sell for several million pounds.

The suggestion of flying birds has prompted some to call this zoomorphic architecture.

There is something freewheeling about the design, and places Broadway Malyan with CZWG (see *Cascades* and *SeaCon Wharf*) as one of the few UK architectural practices so far who have brought imagination to the frenzied build-up of riverside flats.

Aragon Tower, SE8
Deptford Strand, Lewisham

Rail Deptford
Original Height Originally 78m, 26 storeys high
Constructed 1963–66
Architect LCC Architects under Ted Hollamby
Remodelled 2004–06 by A&Q Partnership
Height 91m, 30 storeys

The residents of Aragon Tower used to complain, not just about the common problems besetting tower blocks, but also about the bleakness of the view across the river to the Isle of Dogs. New residents are paying big money for that view – Canary Wharf now scintillates and dominates it.

This area has a maritime history much older than the surrounding Docklands. Henry VIII established the Deptford Dockyard here in 1513, and it was later in the charge of celebrated seventeenth-century diarist Samuel Pepys. The 1780s Navy Victualling Yard is still there, recently restored. Hitler's Luftwaffe hit this area badly, and in 1959 it was earmarked for four-storey housing. It became the LCC's massive £7m 111ha Pepys Estate, with 1,324 homes, and included three twenty-six-storey tower block slabs with 144 split-level flats, horrendously clad in pebbledash.

These towers were very tall, and separated the lift and stairs from the housing, as Goldfinger would later do at the *Balfron Tower*. Interestingly, the maisonettes were Z-shaped, with central stairs so that they looked out on each side of the slab on a different floor. This meant that the residents in the only tower on the river, Aragon Tower, got river views in both directions.

The Pepys Estate was heated by used water from power stations and won a Civic Trust Award for its

The Pepys Estate got a new look

Aragon House, 2003

Aragon Tower, 2005

enlightened design in 1967, but gradually deteriorated in the classic pattern of many council estates. Vandalism, teenage gangs, and, in later years, crack houses haunted the estate. Refugees, many from Vietnam, were dumped into this alienated environment. The film *Nil by Mouth* (1997), directed by Gary Oldman, about a working-class family, was shot here. After Lewisham Council inherited the estate from the GLC, they worked with residents, and matters improved, but upgrading the tower blocks was beyond their budget. In April 1999, they decided to sell the Aragon Tower to Berkeley Homes for £10.5m. The funds would enable Lewisham to refurbish the Aragon's sister blocks, Daubeny and Eddystart, which would later receive the largest waterproof cladding job in Europe. They got the 'fridge treatment' pioneered at *Parsons House*.

Berkeley Homes got planning permission in 2002 for an audacious plan. They would build five extra storeys containing fourteen penthouses on top, ascending away from the river in steps. This idea, also seen at *Putney Wharf*, not only gives the building an interesting profile, but creates a cascade of wide patio balconies.

Although many residents were happy to quit, moving them out was controversial locally, and even leaseholders were not allowed to stay on. The clearance started in 2002. The last man out, a professional clown with twenty years of fond memories there, hung on until 2004 when the council cut off the water before handing the block over to its new owners.

The new Aragon Tower was going to be blue but is now a golden cream, and the glazing is green-tinted. These colours give the tower a warmth rare in luxury developments. Not only does Aragon Tower now stand tall without looking brash, the whole idea of pumping real money into an estate by selling a part of it and diversifying social mix looks like working. Everyone should benefit.

Ontario Tower, E14
New Providence Wharf

DLR Blackwall
Height 104m, 29 stories
Construction 2004–07
Architect SOM

Unlike, say, *30 St Mary Axe*, the shape of the Ontario Tower, the centrepiece of a Docklands bastion of exclusivity and style, suggests something feminine.

New Providence Wharf is where Charrington Wharf once operated. The 8.25ha brownfield patch is sandwiched between Rogers' 52m-high Reuters Building (1992) and some post-war social housing. In 2002, a vast terracotta-clad cliff started to emerge. Developers Ballymore had turned to architects with more all-round experience than any other – SOM. Like *Cascades*, this was another sloping wedge of flats, but with rounded ends and, crucially, the whole shape bent into a huge U. A chain of seven penthouses, each with a swimming pool, sweeps down from nineteen-storeys in terraced steps. These went for £2m–£3.5m. Just the name of the interior decorator, Carter Tybergheim, suggested class. Below them, water flows and falls in a designer garden. It may be almost claustrophobically dense, but with the approval of its signature building – the Ontario Tower – in 2004, New Providence Wharf became the biggest Docklands residential development so far.

When originally planned in 2002, the Ontario Tower was going to be 89m high, but increasing the height to 29 storeys added another 15m, making it the first purely residential tower in Docklands to break the 100m mark. The core reached its full height in September 2005.. The 260 flats were pretty much sold by the year's end.

The tower is elliptical in plan, with up to eleven flats per floor, from studios to two-bedrooms, looking out either east or west. The great sloping cut across the top houses

another three storeys of penthouses. Unlike the older blocks below, or the 169-bed Radisson Edwardian hotel in a new eight-storey block on the other side, the Ontario Tower is more fully glazed and distinctively clad in aluminium. This is a shiny, futuristic tower.

Ontario Tower marks the arrival of American-style luxury condominium blocks in London. They may lack the Euro-eccentricity of, say, CZWG or Broadway Malyan works, but they are slick and, in this case at least, strikingly glamorous. American corporate architecture in office towers can slide into a New Bland (see *25 Bank Street*), but not so SOM's residential towers. There will be more; in 2005, Ballymore and SOM had already started the next ones – higher, more New York – at *Pan Peninsula*.

Ontario Tower and New Providence Wharf

Pan Peninsula, E14
Millharbour

DLR South Quay
Height 155m, 50 storeys and 122m, 36 storeys
Construction 2005–09
Architect SOM

Mid-decade, Pan Peninsula is the most ambitious residential development underway in London. One of the two towers will have the highest penthouses in the UK. The architects were inspired by Manhattan skyscrapers from the fifties, but the concept is more like this century's exclusive 'condo' towers there.

Back in 2000, the area immediately south of Canary Wharf was masterplanned as a business zone called 'The Millennium Quarter'. Ballymore proposed a focus for it – a thirty-seven-storey tower of office 'villages' like those in the *Heron Tower*. Meanwhile, a wave of massive new offices was coming up in Canary Wharf and the market moved to oversupply. In 2002, the plan was changed to two residential towers of forty and twenty-seven storeys, higher than any before and designed by SOM. Ballymore didn't get consent – the site was still zoned for offices, and in any case there wasn't enough affordable housing in the deal. Ballymore tackled the local issues and came back with a better, taller plan, submitted at the start of 2005. It was approved in March, and in November foundation work and marketing began, with a new name – Pan Peninsula.

Walk around Midtown Manhattan these days, and, in amongst the great office towers, there's a new sort of tower shooting up, like tree saplings trying to break into the sunlight. These are thin finger buildings packed with luxury condominiums and the market for them is hot. Chris Harvey of SOM has come up with an equivalent for London. Pan Peninsula's towers look elegant not just because of their height and styling, but also because they step back at the top, creating an overall impression not unlike New York's McGraw-Hill Building by Raymond Hood. The taller tower's highest floor will be a cocktail bar. The plant levels at the top will be covered in a grid of crown lighting that drops to the ground in strips of light. Ballymore commissioned Maurice Bell Lighting Design, whose designs light up the Burj Hotel in Dubai. Everything has been anticipated: even the balconies have balustrades about 45cm higher than normal, to give a sense of security if you're out there.

Canary Wharf Contractors, the builders with a record of handling serious logistics building CWG's estate, were taken on, and DMWR, authors of the *Columbus Tower*, appointed as executive architects working with SOM. The £300m construction started with the driving of piles 30m deep. It's reckoned the project will need 600 people working 3.5 million man-hours. The planning is so thorough that the cladding for the 756 flats was tested during research by being subjected to blasts from jet engines. Some 40,000m³ of concrete and 17,000m² of glazing will be used. The towers should top out simultaneously in 2008.

Ballymore sorted out the affordable housing with thirty floors of the shorter tower, and further flats in nearby Mastmaker Road, but of course what Pan Peninsula is about is the top end of the market. Launching the marketing over three years before the flats are available is a London record, and there are two special features of this marketing drive. First, at nearby Arrowhead Quay (earmarked for a twenty-five-storey office block), Ballymore have a marketing suite building that actually floats, with a bespoke boat just to reach it. More subtly, there's something quite intriguing in the arty glossy marketing images. Posing sophisticated couples in simulated, stylish Pan Peninsula apartments may be no surprise, but these don't smile glibly. Instead, they seem detached from each other, absorbed in their own worlds, suggesting ambiguous relationships. In the bedroom, for example, the couple may be preparing for bed, but the woman's legs are crossed away from him. Photographs like those Lee Powers shot for Pan Peninsula could have been for *Vogue* or *Harper's* and go far beyond the normal real-estate pitches.

Pan Peninsula

The Pan Peninsula penthouse maisonettes, or 'duplexes', are selling for £10m. The prices reflect not just location or lifestyle, but also design as lean and cool as a catwalk model. There will be more like it – a forty-three-storey SOM-designed condo tower for Ballymore is set to follow at nearby Crossharbour.

Lots Road, SW10

Rail Imperial Wharf opening 2007
Height 122m, 37 storeys and 85m, 25 storeys
Designed 1996–2005
Architect Terry Farrell & Partners

These towers, dubbed 'Romeo and Juliet', have thrice been refused by the Royal Borough of Kensington & Chelsea (RBK&C), which is implacably opposed to high-rise. This is ironic considering that architect Sir Terry Farrell, the celebrated Post-Modernist behind *Alban Gate*, often cites Kensington as proof that you don't need to build high to increase urban density. He likes pointing out that while London's average density of 46 people per hectare is only half of New York's, the highest local density is in Kensington, at 131/ha – and what a pleasant environment the medium-rise borough is.

Lots Road Power Station (1905), behind whose 85m-high chimneys lies Chelsea Creek, was decommissioned in 2002. Farrell's masterplan converted it into apartments, with a seven-storey atrium and an internal street. Two apartment towers of thirty-nine and twenty-five storeys were planned for either side of the creek, one falling in Hammersmith & Fulham, the other in the royal borough, and in 2001 planning permission was sought. With poor transport access, and housing densities three times higher than the boroughs' planning guidelines, there was plenty of ammunition for local opposition, led by a local architect. English Heritage's Sir Neil Casson actually backed these towers, even as he was fighting against *The Shard*, but RBK&C rejected the application. Even when the tallest tower was reduced to thirty storeys and swapped over so that the Royal Borough got the shorter one, they would have none of it. After the third refusal, a public inquiry followed in 2005, and the final plan was approved in February 2006.

The £500m scheme by developers Circadian will provide 821 homes, 46 per cent of which will be affordable housing. Building towers means that 3.3ha of the site's 4.6ha will be open space – after a big decontamination job on the brownfield site. The scheme opens up Chelsea Creek, and extends the riverside walk by 600m. As for the towers themselves, they have balconies facing the river, are trapezoid in plan, and have diagonal cuts across the top eight storeys. This architectural device creates a sloping diamond roof, and follows Chicago's iconic 41-storey A Epstein & Sons-designed Smurfit-Stone Building (1983).

Around 2010, these sharp, chamfered towers will stand like slender sentinels at the resuscitated creek. Their cool glass shapes by the great old power station will be quite a sight.

Lots Road

261 City Road, N1
Islington

Tube Angel
Height 115m, 35 storeys
Designed 2003–06
Architect Squire & Partners

This is the tallest apartment tower to be approved on London's canal network, taller even than the *Trellick Tower* at Grand Union Canal in North Kensington. Still in its early stages, 261 City Road is beside City Road Basin, an offshoot of the Regent's Canal, and low-rise post-war buildings currently block access to the water. Squire has designed a 300-flat scheme in eight-storey waterside blocks, with the tower. Islington Council then commissioned Bennetts Associates to masterplan the area. They incorporated the Squire scheme and envisioned a similar tower of twenty-eight-storeys at 259 City Road. Islington, despite an anti-high-rise past, liked the plan and granted outline planning approval. Now 261 City Road has been taken over by a Boston-based developer, Pembroke Real Estate, whose philosophy is 'to add value by creating

"pieces of communities" not just individual buildings'. With big public-realm gain, including a new towpath, the scheme does that. The development has an 'excellent' EcoHomes rating. The lower blocks have green roofs, everything is serviced by a low-NOx boiler, and there are even power points to recharge electric cars.

Not everyone was happy about a tower here. Some accuse Ken Livingstone, who gave it his support, of betraying the GLA's Blue Ribbon Network plan, drawn up to protect and revive London's canals. Local architect Harley Sherlock said placing a tower here was 'monstrous', because the canal is about small-scale buildings. It may be a fair point, but a host of tower blocks such as *Peregrine House* lie just across the City Road.

The glazed tower is remarkably like Farrell's *Lots Road* – trapezoid in plan, and cut diagonally from its apex to the twenty-eighth floor, creating a south-facing diamond sloping roof. There is just one apartment per floor, but, as with Squire's towers at *22 Marsh Wall*, natural materials will be incorporated. Around 2009, it should show that new, exciting ideas have a place in the idyllic industrial heritage of the canals.

22 Marsh Wall, E14

DLR Heron Quays
Height 140m, 40 storeys and 110m, 28 storeys
Construction planned 2006–09
Architect Squire & Partners

Developer Redwell Investments have been promoting this as 'the gateway to the Isle of Dogs', which of course is dominated by Canary Wharf's glass-box skyscrapers. This residential development contains two more glass boxes, so avoiding the 'New Bland' look has been one of the challenges here. The original plan had been for a 160m-high elliptical building – which swiftly got dubbed 'The Testicle' – but that was thrown out in 2001.

The site, behind *Cascades*, has a few tatty-looking light industrial buildings. Architects Squire have a good record in Docklands, remodelling *Vogan's Mill* and masterplanning the waterside area around *One West India Quay*. Here, they have laid out a public space of cafés and shops around four blocks, two of them eight-storey, containing 691 flats. The plan promises thirty per cent less CO_2 emissions than normal flats, and there's fresh thinking about how to do it. Water will be heated by 740m² of solar panels on the tower roofs, and general heating will be from biomass.

As for the towers, these are completely glazed slabs, but behind the glazing will be masonry panels and timber sliding shutters. The whole effect should feel refreshing: light rather than massive, and warm from its organic layers, rather than clinical.

22 Marsh Wall

Doon Street Tower, SE1
Waterloo

Tube/rail Waterloo
Height 168m, 45 storeys
Designed 2002–05
Architect Lifschutz Davidson Sandilands

Since the 1980s, Coin Street Community Builders (CSCB) has completed the South Bank riverside walkway, converted the derelict landmark Oxo Tower into one of London's most successful buildings, made Gabriel's Wharf into a mini-Covent Garden, and developed a mix of social housing that works. Now, this social enterprise has produced plans for a refreshingly different residential tower.

The Doon Street site is a strip of mainly car park with poor ground access, and CSCB started planning for it in 2002. They wanted to increase the local population, provide a community sports centre, open up public realm and house the Rambert Dance Company. The development would need to generate funds – the leisure centre alone would cost £20m to build and need subsidies thereafter. Apartments with a river view can create vital revenue.

Architects Lifschutz Davidson, who remodelled the Oxo Tower and later designed the wonderful Hungerford Bridge walkways (2003), were the natural choice. Their final plan was to divide the strip into sections – going east from Waterloo Bridge. There is a new public piazza, offices, the Rambert home designed by Allies & Morrison, the leisure centre, the apartment block with river views and, finally, courtyard apartments. All the buildings are joined and share a roof-line 30m high – except the 308-apartment tower.

The tower is not yet another curvy glass-skinned riverside residential project, but a very slender rectilinear slab rising straight up, with flats in two sections 153m and 134m high, sandwiching the full-height service core. The apartments have anodized aluminium window frames, creating a silvery look, and sun-activated blinds. The effect of the core and roof-lines is a little like those of *Tower 42*. The shape also relates to the fly towers of the National Theatre below it, and even makes a balance with the nearby *London Studios* tower: although twice as high, from the river it is just over half as wide.

The Doon Street tower will be visible from St James's Park, which complicates the planning process. It would be a shame if the Royal Park stopped a tower enabling such great facilities for the people.

Vauxhall Tower, SW8
Nine Elms Lane

Tube Vauxhall
Height 180m, 50 storeys
Construction planned 2007–10
Architect Broadway Malyan

Most proposed Millennial towers have been in London's skyscraper clusters, but this residential tower is set to stand alone, a slender glass finger by the river, and also breaks new ground by incorporating a wind turbine. It stands at the end of Nine Elms Lane – no promenade between manicured hedges, but a highway to Central London. Referring to the eighteenth-century English landscape gardener, architect-in-charge Peter Crossley says that, from there, his tower will be 'an object at the end of a long vista ... like an obelisk by Capability Brown'.

Developer St George first applied to build the UK's tallest flats here at the end of 2001, as the final stage of *St George Wharf*. Broadway Malyan's first plan had clear similarities to their London Bridge Tower design – a cylinder with sweeping helical ledges. The official response was mixed, with concerns about the landscaping and affordable housing. The proposal was revised in 2002; the next year, a public enquiry followed, but it still didn't get the approval of Lambeth Council. A third version of the tower followed, and the ODPM finally approved the £100m plan in June 2005.

Essentially, Vauxhall Tower is a cylinder 24m across that, by accident, has the same proportions as a classical column. It rises straight from the ground, has an airy two-storey lobby, and above that, 200 flats. The floor plan is inspired by a Catherine wheel, with edges extending out from the perimeter circle. Each of the five flats per floor has its own conservatory in the exterior corner made at the tower's circumference, and these protruding edges also deflect the wind. The circular core bearing the structure gets further support from radial columns, which separate the flats. The radial support allows the two- and three-bedroom flats to be very uncluttered. Above them, three penthouse storeys are stepped back.

Like Millennial office towers, this has a vented façade of triple glazing, except that a single glass layer is inside and the double layer outside, rather than the other way around. The glazing is floor to ceiling, so the architects thought about the visual clutter that could shine out – televisions, lamps etc. A particular glass manufactured by Saint Gobain provides optimum vision out and limited vision in. There are blinds within the façade, so the whole internal climate is always comfortable. Nevertheless, after a debate, it was decided to let residents open the windows if they really wanted to – they will pop out approximately 20cm.

The London Aquifer's more constant temperature will be harnessed to warm the building in winter and cool it in summer. The newer innovation is more visible – a great 10m-high corkscrew wind turbine. A vertical corkscrew is more efficient than a normal windmill turbine, and produces less vibration. It will generate up to 20kW, at least powering the lighting of the common parts. All of the green measures mean that Vauxhall Tower will produce fifty-six per cent less CO_2 than a block of typical flats, and use sixty-two per cent less energy than electric/gas conventional flats. These ambitious engineering feats will spread to planned towers elsewhere: in 2005, Mutiplex already plan wind turbines at Elephant & Castle.

English Heritage did object to Vauxhall Tower. To be fair, a great tower just 1.4km from Westminster could be a problem, but from Westminster Bridge it will actually appear lower than the *Millbank Tower* and, from Chelsea, it's no higher than the Battersea Power Station chimneys. Another question is the whole idea of stand-alone towers, but some of London's best are just that, notably the *Telecom Tower*, which has a similar envelope. Besides, Vauxhall is already an emerging cluster, although its towers are only forty per cent as high as this. Plans are brewing for more towers of similar height at Vauxhall Bondway and along Nine Elms Lane. With or without them, Vauxhall Tower will be one of London's most elegant landmarks.

Doon Street Tower

Vauxhall Tower

Chapter 7:
Millennial Offices

As the millennium approached, London had firmly re-established its self-confidence as a World City. The City could no longer ignore the question of building more high-rise offices, lest its tenants slip away to Canary Wharf, or even Frankfurt and Paris. When Tony Blair's New Labour won the General Election of 1997 – a victory masterminded by Peter Mandelson in *Millbank Tower* – a bright, modern future seemed just around the corner. New Labour reinstated local government for London, in the form of the Greater London Authority (GLA). The first elected Mayor would soon be Ken Livingstone, someone who found New York's skyline thrilling…

Various corporations tabled their schemes. Meanwhile, two friends, Irvine Sellar and Gerald Ronson, would each emerge with ambitious skyscraper plans. They would both face public inquiries that proved decisive to London's future. This period's landmark skyscraper developments are very big, largely glazed, increasingly sustainable and they play with form and technology. This loose formula can be called Millennial.

Foster Goes Green

An early spin of New Labour's was to promote Cool Britannia, an idea that the UK was a world centre of creative activity, as it had been in the 1960s. For Blair, architects were cool as well, and had to be honoured. His friend Richard Rogers, who had advised Labour during their long exile in opposition, had already became Lord Rogers in 1996, but Blair could still elevate Norman Foster. He became Lord Foster of Thamesbank in 1999.

Foster's prestige was unrivalled in the nineties. His practice had remodelled the Reichstag as Germany's parliament, created the world's largest airport in Hong Kong, transformed the Great Court of the British Museum, and much else. At the

decade's end Foster collected the Pritzker Prize, an American award seen as the architectural equivalent of a Nobel prize. Along with another high-rise visionary in the team, Ken Shuttleworth, Foster had designed a Millennium Tower for Tokyo Bay in 1989. If it had been built, a vertical city 840m high would have risen in an amazing cone criss-crossed with cross-bracing steel, wrapped around five neighbourhood sections, separated like stages of a rocket. In 1991, Foster was commissioned to design Europe's tallest building, the 259m-high Commerzbank headquarters in Frankfurt. When completed in 1997, it was Europe's first green skyscraper.

What are green skyscrapers? Environmentally friendly buildings are low on energy consumption, and energy had been an issue since October 1973, when Arab countries imposed an oil embargo on the West, quadrupling oil prices. Before that, energy was so cheap that some office buildings in the US had been designed without light switches. The reaction there to the oil crisis was to cut by two-thirds the legal requirement for replacing air in air-conditioned offices. However, that blew in another problem – sick building syndrome. Identified in the early 1980s, this makes workers sick because of chemicals produced by

Lord Foster

photocopiers, cleaning agents and other day-to-day office technologies, as well as by biological factors, from fungi to Legionnaire's disease. In the 1980s, the World Health Organisation reckoned that 30 per cent of all new buildings suffered sick building syndrome.

In the 1970s, Buckminster Fuller conceived a building with its own microclimate sealed within a glass space, which he called the Climatroffice. Managing the internal environment, particularly light and air, and reducing energy consumption were key elements of Richard Rogers' 1986 *Lloyd's Building*, and this agenda set the stage for green skyscrapers. In 1990, the UK's Foundation for the Built Environment laid out a set of environmental bench-marks for new buildings, called BREEAM. These covered energy consumption, water use, materials, pollution, and the well-being of workers. They also covered transport connectivity, which has a CO_2 cost.

The first green skyscraper developments were abroad. In Malaysia, the UK-trained architect Ken Yeang tackled air-conditioning, the biggest running energy cost of a tropical office, and developed his concept of 'bio-climatic skyscrapers'. In Germany, Foster's Commerzbank tower channelled natural airflows inside the building, providing all the ventilation for over nine months of the year. This is partially achieved by a sophisticated variation on double-glazing, whereby exterior slots outside can be opened to allow air into the cavity made by the inner glass windows. Vented façades are now common. They draw on the microclimate concept of Buckminster Fuller, with whom Foster had worked. Furthermore, in the Commerzbank's internal atria which separate sections of office, Foster created skygardens for the workers, which were also natural air regulators. Another green German skyscraper was also completed in 1996: this was Ingenhoven Overdiek's twenty-eight-storey cylindrical RWE headquarters in Essen. The green skyscraper had arrived. Sustainability would quickly become a must-have aspect of landmark skyscrapers.

London was well overdue a Foster skyscraper. In 1996, his practice designed what would have been the mother of them all. The Norwegian conglomerate Kvaerner, new owners of the St Mary Axe site where the IRA had destroyed the Baltic Exchange, had seen the approaching bottleneck in City office supply coming, and were ready to do something big. Foster came up with a 'statement of confidence in the City for the next century' – a seventy-two-storey bendy glass slab of offices topped with two great bumps, each a curvy apartment block, one with a roof garden and the other sixteen storeys high. Altogether, the proposed structure reached a phenomenal 385m. The Millennium Tower would have been Europe's highest, as tall as the Empire State Building, and would have brought the new green thinking to the UK. It was an amazing vision, but just too big for the City of London's planning committee under Peter Rees.

Commerzbank, Frankfurt

Three years later, m3 architects went even higher with a similar streamlined concept called the Citygate Ecotower – a 108-storey, 460m sail-shaped multi-use tower with photovoltaic cladding. They won a lot of press, but it was a non-starter.

Beacons of Light

Foster's break on the London skyline finally came in a 1996 commission at Canary Wharf, where his vast tube station was under construction. The American bank Citigroup decided to move there, and their dark glass block was connected to a plant tower that was only the second London skyscraper to reach 100m since Seifert's day. It heralded a wave of Millennial high-rise on CWG's estate.

In 2002, agents Insignia Richard Ellis identified over fifty London organisations with at least 36,000m² of office spread around different locations that could be consolidated into one building. Consolidating operations under one roof would boost efficiency. In the City, the big buildings just weren't there. Canary Wharf was just the answer: not only was it speculatively building massive offices, but the buildings had big floorplates suitable for trading floors. In 1998 HSBC decided to relocate there. They commissioned Foster, as they had nineteen years earlier in Hong Kong. Like Foster's Citigroup centre, the *HSBC* Headquarters is a glass-skinned square tower with rounded corners, but this one reaches up forty-five-storeys. Meanwhile, Citigroup decided they that their new Foster block was not enough. This time, Canary Wharf's favourite architect Cesar Pelli came up with an original design: this was a Philip Johnson-like style of stepped thirties tower expressed in glass, exactly as high as the *HSBC* building. Foster's and Pelli's new towers, simultaneously completed in 2002, are still the UK's joint-second tallest. They are giant buildings, both with over a million square feet of office space. Canary Wharf now had a cluster of skyscrapers that put the City in the shade. Part of the reason for that is the way the three skyscrapers shine at the top like beacons.

Canary Wharf is a feast of 'crown lighting'. *One Canada Square*'s pyramid roof is illuminated on the inside, while on the *HSBC* and CitiGroup towers, lights are installed behind the exterior skin around the plant machinery floors, and neon separately illuminates the banks' logos. Some locals got in a huff about that, outraged at the blatant commercialism of illuminated logos, and there was a half-baked campaign to get CWG to ban them. But the banks were not the first to advertise on a UK skyscraper: the *Telecom Tower* had carried an illuminated British Telecom logo from the 1980s. In any case, with the Millennium Dome across the river providing a spectacular lightshow, and with London trying to outshine any other city for the Millennium, crown lighting was in. In the City, the *Lloyd's Building* had been lit like an alien spaceship since 1989. The lightshow is by Imagination, designers known for blue-sky brainstorming, who subsequently updated the Telecom Tower's crown lighting. Meanwhile. *Tower42*'s core top is floodlit, with neon laid along its roofline, all in blue. Atop Seifert's West End masterpiece, illuminated letters spell out *Centre Point.*

Crown lighting actually dates back to New York's golden skyscraper period. In 1930, lamps showed off the new Craig Severance-designed Bank of Manhattan's pyramid roof high over Wall Street, while, in 1931, the Empire State Building's crown was dazzlingly floodlit. The next year, RCA lit their logo in neon on their 259m-high building in the Rockefeller Centre. In London, *Senate House* was floodlit when finished in 1937.

As the millennium turned, CWG was now the UK's most successful property company, despite being entirely sited on a single tract of land in London Transport's Zone 2. A host of huge global legal firms and finance houses were already reserving the estate's next wave of skyscrapers. Planners from as far as Moscow came to marvel at the emerging city district with virtually no roads, where eighty-four per cent of workers arrived on public transport. Furthermore,

Dusk brings Crown Lighting at Canary Wharf

average CO_2 emissions and water consumption per occupant were falling with every new building. In terms of light flux as well as environmental impact, the estate was a cluster of beacons of light.

In April 2000, developer Irvine Sellar, who had started his fortune selling trendy clothes in the 'Mates' chain in the 1970s, came out of nowhere with an audacious skyscraper proposal. His site was neither in Canary Wharf nor the City, but at London Bridge. His proposed tower was as bold as Foster's Millennium Tower – an eighty-seven-storey, 365m cylindrical office tower with a breathtaking curving spiral. Unlike Foster's Millennium Tower, though, this one was the work of then-obscure architects Broadway Malyan.

The City had to respond. So, who would speak up for skyscrapers there?

Axing the Skyscraper Embargo

In May 2000, Ken Livingstone was elected Mayor of London. Livingstone brought a political argument for skyscrapers to the table. He saw commercial development as a driver to fund the massive upgrade in social infrastructure that the capital would need. In the June 2002 draft of his London Plan, he spelt out how to tackle London's increasing population, and the 600,000 new London jobs, two-thirds of them office-based, anticipated by 2016. The London Plan was largely about promoting housing density. However, his GLA had only limited power and revenue to support the city's expansion. Livingstone's vote had humiliated the Labour candidate Frank Dobson, so he couldn't count on Chancellor Gordon Brown for extra cash. A key element of Livingstone's strategy was to make developers pay, by giving them a part of the increase in land values they generate. The strategy is basically an extension of Section 106 of the 1990 Town & Country Planning Act, which legislated for developers to contribute financially to public improvements. Allowing developers to build big meant skyscrapers, and the London Plan endorsed them.

In July 2000, the Planning Committee of the City of London approved its first skyscraper of the millennium. Swiss Re, a reinsurance giant, was now the owner of the Baltic Exchange site, and not only had they got perhaps the most exciting skyscraper plan in the world, they hinted that they would quit London for the Continent if they weren't allowed to build it. They brought Foster back to the site. The big idea was to model a fantastic shape that immediately earned it a nickname – 'The Gherkin'. Foster's *30 St Mary Axe* was designed with the same sort of environmental ideas as the Commerzbank. Work on it began in December that year, and the tower was completed in 2004. It instantly became the most popular new skyscraper on the planet.

The Swiss Re approval had released the logjam of the City's embargo on high-rise, and within weeks it was followed by a proposal for a second sleek, sexy and green new tower of the same height. This one came from developer Gerald Ronson, who had rebuilt his Heron property empire after the Guinness scandal of the early 1990s. The *Heron Tower*, designed by KPF, was not to going be a shoo-in like the Gherkin. English Heritage's new chairman Sir Neil Cossons was militantly anti-high-rise. English Heritage have a duty to protect distant views of St Paul's Cathedral, and the protected views from Waterloo Bridge effectively limit high-rise in the City to pie-like slices, one east of Bank and the other around *The Barbican*. By objecting to a planning application, English Heritage can initiate a public enquiry, which costs money and time, and can in turn kick the final call to the government. In February 2001 a public enquiry was called into the Heron Tower.

New City skyscraper proposals had been brewing up gradually. Now they were on hold, awaiting the decision on the Heron Tower. A thirty-four-storey, 144m tower by Wilkinson Eyre for Fenchurch Street applied for planning consent in July 2000. In 2001, Sheppard Robinson conceived a design for Ropemaker Street that would have towered over their *City Point* refurb just across the road — each floor would be incrementally displaced sideways, so the whole block would lean from the vertical, with Rogers-style lifts climbing the exterior. For Bishopsgate, American power-tower architect Helmut Jahn designed a cylindrical sixty-three storey tower with two helix ridges twisting around it. (With the *30 St Mary Axe* twisting atriums, the area promised to be busy with giant spirals!) In June 2001, English Heritage released a crude picture in which grey shapes crowded the skyline behind St Paul's, based on a few plans and a lot of rumours. In September 2001, the City's first million-square-footer was proposed — a thirty-six storey, 159m block called St Botolph's House to be built on a site in Aldgate.

In the middle of all this, a skyscraper event happened that would change the world forever. On 11 September 2001, a date that separates the twentieth century from the twenty-first far more than the fall of the millennium, al-Qaeda fanatics piloted wide-bodied jets into the World Trade Center. The Twin Towers collapsed essentially because fire protection on the steel structure was dislodged by the impact of the jetliners, exposing it to temperatures of up to 1100°C sustained by burning jetfuel and paper and fanned by wind blowing through the open-plan floors. The steel trusses supporting the floors melted, and at the weakest points, where they were bolted to vertical columns, they gave, so the floors started slamming down onto those below.

In London, *One Canada Square* was evacuated. For a moment, the entire idea of new skyscrapers became obscene.

Ken defeats the 'Obsure Monastic Order'

In May 2002, the Heron Tower verdict was still a month away. At a property conference that month, Livingstone proclaimed that 'interesting, well-designed and particularly clustered tall buildings will add to London's vitality, enhance London's skyline and contribute to the built environment'. The powerful forces not buying that message included the veteran campaigning journalist Simon Jenkins from London's newspaper the *Evening Standard*. He levelled three charges at Livingstone's vision: that development should be in deprived areas like Inner South London; that Livingstone was uncomfortably chummy with developers, and that skyscrapers over 100m high were ego-trips by developers and architects. In fact, Livingstone's London Plan saw development as a tonic for deprived inner-city areas. As for making pals with developers, surely only unreconstructed Trotskyists could still object to confidence-building relationships with big business if there are social benefits in the 'planning gains' to be secured. The final charge about the skyline was to be the real battleground, and the army that took the field to fight Livingstone was, of course, led by English Heritage. At that conference, Livingstone described EH as 'an obscure monastic order' and that 'a decisive defeat of English Heritage is vital'.

That is precisely what happened in July, when the Heron Tower was finally approved. At the public enquiry, English Heritage presented a poor case; it had cost them vital funds and opened up internal divisions. Nevertheless, EH would decide to take on one more skyscraper…

A fresh London Bridge tune

Irvine Sellar hadn't been put off by the press outrage at his London Bridge Tower proposal. He proceeded to hire an architect considered by some to be the best in the world — Renzo Piano. After designing the Centre Pompidou in the 1970s with Rogers, the bearded Genoa-based Italian, like his Post-Modernist peers Foster and Rogers, had built a global track record of

James and Irvine Sellar with *The Shard*

extraordinary projects, including a cultural centre in New Caledonia, in French Polynesia, the restoration of war-torn Sarajevo, and the creamy curvaceous forty-four-storey Aurora Centre in Sydney. In 1998 he had won a Pritzker Prize. His London Bridge design was unveiled in March 2001, and was instantly dubbed '*The Shard* of Glass': this was a stunning plan for a crystal spire over 300m high incorporating a vertical city of offices, flats and sky piazzas over the railway station, all with impeccable green credentials. English Heritage objected, and another public enquiry saw English Heritage defeated a second time.

After 9/11, Sellar consulted with security specialists Kroll, and the design became stronger as well as more sophisticated. Insurers, rather than new building regulations, would see that skyscrapers were not just sustainable and sexy, but secure as well. The Foster proposal to replace New York's twin towers was a perfect example: 'kissing towers' that touched each other at regular intervals, enabling escape from one to another, and a stacked tetrahedonal structure that maximised rigidity and redundancy.

In London, HOK's *One Churchill Place* was the first post-9/11 skyscraper, and has loads of security features built in. When it was completed in 2004, it joined the three new Heron Quays power towers just finished at Canary Wharf, all million-square-footers. The best is KPF's *10 Upper Bank Street*. It stands in subtle contrast to the increasingly unimaginative design ethos that was in danger of making Canary Wharf look more and more like a sixties comprehensive redevelopment, but on a bigger scale. Meanwhile, *25 Bank Street*, an anodyne, soulless Pelli slab, exemplified the 'New Bland' tendency beginning to make Post-Modernist architecture as dull as the International Style had turned out to be when it, too, had gone fully commercial.

Whatever the aesthetics, Canary Wharf was continuing to win City-type tenants, with a working population reaching 60,000. When a consortium called Songbird, led by Morgan Stanley, took over the CWG estate in May 2004 for £1.7bn, seven of London's tallest

ten skyscrapers were there. Songbird now owned all but three of the estate's towers. In 2005, as the market picked up, they would start selling them off.

Old Stars with Big Plans

English Heritage and al-Qaeda had failed to defeat skyscrapers. Now, a new and subtler battle was brewing: that between the world's best architects for their place on London's skyline.

We have already seen how Rogers and Foster had worked together in Team 4 in the 1960s, and had gone separate ways. In the nineties, from promoting pedestrian precincts and planning policies to picking up prizes, their practices seemed to be running in parallel, although Foster's was almost five times larger than Rogers'. They seemed to hold the key to making the third millennium workable, at least in the environments they created. In their curious rivalry, it was initially Rogers who seemed to be nosing ahead in leaving a mark on London. As we have seen, he followed the *Lloyd's Building* with more Hi-Tech office buildings and the *Montevetro* apartments, but his biggest splash

But the Foster practice had lost a crucial partner. At the end of 2003, after thirty years, Ken Shuttleworth quit the practice, taking eighteen staff with him to set up a new practice called Make. This quiet man, known to insiders as 'Ken the Pen', had already caused a stir by claiming credit for the big ideas that shaped most of the recent blockbuster projects, including the Gherkin. In September 2004, Make released a vision of perhaps the most exciting City project of all – the Vortex. The 300m circular cross-section design, with its colourful cross-bracing, is like a vase that narrows in the middle but widens out to a maximum at the top: a shape called a hyperboloid. This represents a canny move, since rent premiums rise with height, and so do the Vortex's floor areas. The design may have just been a bold PR stroke for the new practice – after all, it didn't actually

was the Millennium Dome on the Greenwich Peninsula, completed just in time for the government's ill-fated Millennium Experience to open in 1999. Despite Canary Wharf, the most eye-catching London skyline action in 2000 was in non-skyscraper structures, led by Marks & Barfield's 135m-diameter London Eye. Rogers' Dome was only 50m high at its centre, but was supported by 12 steel masts 100m high. Both looked like artefacts from a science-fiction film. Foster surely had to compete – and, sure enough, in 2000, his plan for a new Wembley Stadium was approved. It was to be spanned by a 132m-high arc of steel, erected in 2004.

With the *HSBC* tower, the Gherkin, the GLA's new City Hall, the Millennium Bridge and various office projects, Foster was now way ahead of Rogers in the capital. A twenty-six-storey Foster tower looming over Lloyd's, which would become the *Willis Building*, was approved in 2002. His impact on the skyline was being compared to that of Seifert. In 2004, another Foster tower was proposed for Ellerman House on the City's Camomile Street, this one holding a huge skygarden under its 115m-high roofline.

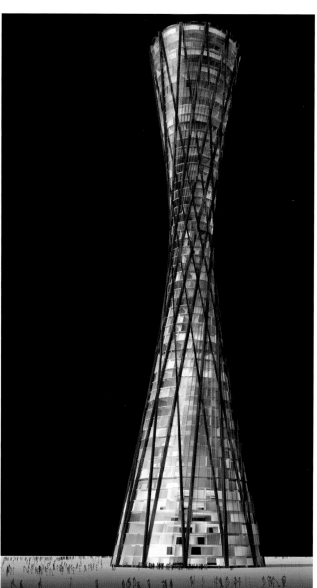

Vortex

have a site. In October, in the official Foster's seventieth-birthday group photograph, Shuttleworth's image was moved by four person-widths from Foster's right-hand side. In July 2005 someone took revenge when a spoof version of the Foster photograph replaced the entire front row with clones of Foster himself.

Meanwhile, the Rogers practice had not been idle in the City. In 2004, approval was granted to their 224m-high *Leadenhall Building*, a great wedge embellished by trademark exterior lifts and colourful pipes. This was almost like a return shot in the ongoing Foster-Rogers match: it would be Rogers' greatest London project since the Dome and might even upstage the Gherkin just across the piazza between them.

Other old sixties-trained colleagues were popping up plans for the City's skyline as well. Sir Nicolas Grimshaw is sometimes referred to as the 'Meccano Man', because his early industrial buildings in the

seventies looked like they'd been assembled with a giant Meccano set. His sinuous glass Waterloo International Terminal (1993) and giant Eden Project biosphere domes in Cornwall (2001) propelled his reputation into the stratosphere. In 2000, he proposed a forty-two-storey, 194m tower above Paddington station, which was thrown out by Westminster Council. In 2002, he unveiled plans for a super-sleek new million-square-foot tower, the Minerva Building, basically two sheer glass-and-aluminium prisms, the taller rising 217m. After the *Heron Tower* inquiry, its approval seemed to be a shoo-in, but in 2006 its future is uncertain.

Over in Canary Wharf, the landlords were giving Cesar Pelli yet more business, on a new patch of land acquired close to West India Quay DLR station. Two more towers about 200m high are promised, but, working with Will Alsop, the safe Pelli corporate style may yet be sexed up a bit. A more exciting proposal popped out of the blue in 2003 – a tower not actually on the Canary Wharf estate, but right next to it. The 61-storey multi-use *Columbus Tower* by architects DMWR, approved in 2004, is not only designed to be taller than *One Canada Square*, but would break the straight lines that rule the local skyline with an elegant, curved sliver of a tower crowned by a horned roofline. Meanwhile, Rogers was at last commissioned to design for Canary Wharf itself. His practice has come up with two gigantic linked stepped slabs for the Canary Riverside site.

Minerva Tower model

With pastmasters Foster, Rogers, Grimshaw and Shuttleworth all in play on the City skyline, the dominance of Pelli's New Bland architecture at last challenged at Canary Wharf, and a Piano structure rising taller than anything else, London in 2004 looked set to have the most exciting skyline in Europe. Yet these new Millennial skyscrapers were on hold. The forces of conservatism had an unexpected ally...

Waiting for the market

Urban property markets tend to suffer booms and busts, and, as we have already seen, such fluctuations have caused London's skyscraper construction to dry up before. During the seventies recession, up to twenty per cent of City offices were empty, and the market collapsed again after the Big Bang boom of the eighties. In 2000, at the height of the dotcom boom, office vacancy rates in the City were only 2.5 per cent. In 2004, they climbed to about forteen per cent and rents dropped a quarter from their peak of £63 per square foot annually. Landowners were so desperate to entice new tenants that three-year rent holidays were on offer for a long-term let, while existing tenants with surplus space replaced property companies as the main landlords on the market. Over in Canary Wharf, tenants were exercising options to hand back space, and vacancies had reached ten per cent. Even as Livingstone had been talking up skyscrapers and some of the best architects in the world were designing them, the millennial office party was dying. Swiss Re

had moved into fifteen floors of their Gherkin, but finding anyone to take the floors above took almost all of 2004.

In 2005, the low-rise West End led the way out from the bottom of the market. The financial sector's hottest growth area, hedge funds, had a taste for small, classy old buildings, and colonised St James's. As for the City, the growth from the nineties that had driven it to employ 300,000 workers was returning. At the year's end, Ken Livingstone proposed narrowing the protected views from Waterloo Bridge as Millennial skyscrapers returned to the news. British Land started work on the SOM-designed *Broadgate Tower*, and the almost-forgotten *Heron Tower* was happening again. Most spectacularly, another KPF-designed tower was unveiled on the Bishopsgate site. The jaw-dropping *Bishopsgate Tower* design, although cut back in height for nudging up to an aircraft corridor, would sweep up in majestic organic curves to create an entirely new central peak in the City cluster.

With projects such as the *Beetham* and *Vauxhall Tower*s and *The Shard*, Graham Morrison of Allies & Morrison scoffed that the South Bank was becoming a self-conscious 'Costa del Icon'. In early 2006, his practice's proposal beat competition from Make, KPF and Foreign Office Architects for a skyscraper project by Waterloo Station, replacing Elizabeth House. The design envisages two tapering office towers and a taller residential tower, dubbed 'The Three Sisters'. They promise to loom behind the *Shell Centre* and the London Eye with robotic menace. It's a strange way to make a point about how the skyline could go wrong.

Which new towers will survive the planning battles and vagaries of property cycles is still not clear. How long they will last into the twenty-first century is another question. Great Seifert skyscrapers face demolition after a mere forty years – might Foster towers face similar oblivion by 2050? And what new ideas will follow? The next chapter will look beyond Millennial towers, and show that the real issues are sustainability and heritage.

CityPoint, EC2

(Britannic Tower)
Moor Lane, City

Tube Moorgate
Height 127m, 36 storeys
Commissioned 1963
Completed 1967
Architect F Milton Cashmore & Niall D Nelson
Re-constructed 2000 by Sheppard Robson International

CityPoint now radiates a sense of bright, modern business, but it came close to being quite madly brilliant, with a giant fin on its roof. Before its makeover, it was the headquarters of British Petroleum, and London's second-highest office skyscraper when built.

Goldfinger had designed a twenty-seven-storey block for Moorgate in 1955, but this was never built. Lord Holford was consulted about the site, and he connected it to the *London Wall* plan and the City's new podium walkways. laying out a plaza in front of what would be the City's biggest skyscraper yet. Curiously, developer Felix Fenston commissioned the skyscraper design from Milton Cashmore, a contemporary of Holden and architect of Shell-Mex House (now *80 Strand*). Milton Cashmore was old school, but his practice had adapted to the International Style demanded by the times.

Britannic House was completed in 1967. It was a rectangular slab in the International Style, relating to the modest boxes on *London Wall*, but on a massive scale. Its façades were green glass and spandrels, set just behind vertical stainless steel-sheathed concrete column ribs that narrowed imperceptibly with height. It rose thirty-five storeys and 122m straight up from the plaza. Built around twin concrete cores, it contained 29,000m^2 of office floor space, which needed plant machinery floors every ten storeys. In appearance it was similar to the latest Manhattan behemoths, particularly Chase Manhattan Bank's new Downtown tower, a 248m slab designed by SOM and completed in 1960 – both

buildings accentuate the vertical with exterior columns. It was the perfect headquarters for British Petroleum, reflecting the corporate culture of a global company, and accommodating the most senior executives at the top of the tower.

Weathering the oil crisis of the early seventies, BP was breaking its dependence on the Middle East by diversifying into Alaska and the North Sea, and a parallel diversification was happening with its corporate hierarchy. In 1975, the company dispersed staff from the Britannic Tower to a new BP House on Victoria Street and elsewhere. By 1996, out-of-date Britannic House was abandoned. BP sold it in 1996 for £300 million to developers Wates City of London Properties. They commissioned Catalan architect Santiago Calatrava, a rising star known for his clean, mathematical style characterised by graceful, curving structures and ribbing, to re-engineer the tower. His design was pure Star Trek. It would get a new spine on its southern end, which would support a restaurant cantilevering into space, and above all that, an enormous fin would reach up to a height of 203m! The plan was rejected – the excuse was that it would spoil views of St Paul's. Westminster Council said it was just too 'aggressive'.

The next set of plans, now called CityPoint, won approval in 1997, this time with architects Sheppard Robson, who had brilliantly refurbished *338 Euston Road*. They retained a lot of Calatrava's ideas, especially the two twelve-storey wings at the base, with their sloping ribs. A new extension now rounded the southern end. Plant machinery floors became offices, and all of this extended the office floor area to 51,520m^2 – a massive seventy-five per cent increase. A curtain wall of green glass with aluminium mullions now provided floor-to-ceiling glazing. The acoustics were tested in Italy, not least because now plant machinery was close up to offices at the top. A roof structure that cantilevers out on ribs sits like a hat. At the base, they drove skylit arcades through the building, and placed a huge entrance canopy swinging out like a bell onto the plaza. The £130m works were completed by contractors John Mowlem in 2000.

Much more than a refurbishment, this was a spectacular new building that ushered the new century's style into the City's skyline. Like the *99 Bishopsgate* refurbishment, it let light pass through the structure, but also defied the constraints of the old tower's rectilinear frame with its new curves and ribs. Like *Tower42*, it's now a successful lifestyle business centre. Upmarket bars, a health club, and food outlets, including a Wagamama, occupy the ground floor, and the offices are let out at premium rates to multiple occupants, mostly professional services such as accountants and lawyers. The developers, since absorbed by British Land, put CityPoint up for sale in late 2005 for over £500m to offshore investors. While New Bland rent-slabs of similar size such as *25 Bank Street* have proved profitable in Canary Wharf, a nine-figure return on the investment in CityPoint proves that more imaginative commercial architecture also pays.

Britannic Tower

Citigroup Centre, E14
Canary Wharf

33 Canada Square
Tube Canary Wharf
Height 105m 24 storeys
Completed 1999
Architect Foster & Partners

25 Canada Square
Tube Canary Wharf
Height 200m, 45 storeys
Completed 2002
Architect Cesar Pelli & Associates/Adamson Associates

Citigroup is the world's largest financial services company, and at Canary Wharf their European headquarters is housed in three skyscrapers, all connected into a single structure containing 170,000m² of offices.

Despite leaving its mark on the skylines of Hong Kong, Tokyo, Frankfurt and elsewhere, the Foster practice had not delivered a single skyscraper in its home city until the Canary Wharf commissioned a headquarters for Citigroup, when it decided to move there in 1996. The go-ahead on site DS5 also triggered the development of Canada Square's park and the shopping mall beneath it. Dockwaters had already been pushed back by cofferdams in 1992. Work on the site started in February 1997. Deep water was pumped out before the foundations were laid so that the building would not rest on soggy ground.

The Foster design is basically in two parts. An eighteen-storey square block of offices rises 76m, containing 52,000m² of offices, including two trading floors. Stepped atria draw light deep into the building, which has a smooth, double-glazed skin with curved corners at its western side. All the plant machinery is in a thin slab to the east, only the second Canary Wharf building over 100m high. It connects to the main block via a cross-braced atrium which now houses a sixteen storey installation of hanging coloured rhomboids by legendary abstract artist Bridget Riley. The building was topped out in May 1998 and finished in 1999, the same year that Foster's vast Canary Wharf station opened. This is connected by Citigroup's own underground entrance, a serene passage of yellow and green light.

Not satisfied with one block, Citigroup leased another, even taller tower next door on site DS6, designed by CWG's favourite architects Cesar Pelli. Construction here ran in parallel with that of the *HSBC* tower, and used a special self-climbing 'jumpform' system to build the core. The new Citigroup tower, with 113,000m² of space, is exactly the same height as *HSBC*, but Pelli designed a completely glazed structure, stepped at the top similarly to *One Canada Square*, but without the pyramid. The style borrows from a 1980s Houston skyscraper designed by Philip Johnson and John Burgee, which evoked the shape of New York's Golden Age skyscrapers in glass rather than stone. Buildings like this are now found in many American downtowns, but this example is unique in London. The tower is conjoined with Foster's part of the complex via another set of glass bridges at a height of twenty-one storeys. It is crown-lit and mounts the Citigroup logo on all four sides of its head.

In March 2001, just before the topping out, two base-jumpers paraglided from the tower and rushed into the tube. The ten-minute wait for their getaway Jubilee Line train must have been excruciating!

The *Citigroup Centre* is one of London's largest office complexes, but ownership is now split. In early 2004 CWG raised £1.1bn by selling 25 Canada Square as well as *5 Canada Square* to the Royal Bank of Scotland. This deal dwarfs the usual hundreds of millions involved in skyscraper sales.

CityPoint

Pelli's Citigroup tower

HSBC, E14
8 Canada Square

Tube/ DLR Canary Wharf
Height 200m, 45 storeys
Constructed 1999–2002
Architects Foster & Partners

The world's third biggest bank by market capitalisation, valued at $200bn in 2006, is headquartered in an ice-cool tower that was the third largest single-occupant building in London when completed.

In the 1990s, HSBC wanted to consolidate twelve different offices into one global headquarters in the City, but finding a site there for the giant of a building required was a tall order. The banking corporation even considered redeveloping its Lower Thames Street HQ, but the location limited height, and even a groundscraper could not pack in enough space. In early 1998, HSBC signed with CWG for a site by *One Canada Square* designated DS2. Here, a new headquarters could accommodate over 8,000 workers, and be built quickly. HSBC would own the building rather than lease it from CWG. The same team was commissioned that had delivered the seminal Hong Kong HSBC flagship in 1986 – architects Foster and engineers Arup.

Foster basically designed a box for 102,190m² of offices, but a very slick one. It had four basement levels and a five-storey podium for trading floors. Above this, a forty storey square tower 56m across would make it London's second tallest building, exactly the same height as Pelli's *Citigroup* tower going up simultaneously, directly across Canada Square. Twelve lifts in four banks would link skylobbies at the fifteenth, twenty-fifth and thirty-fourth floors. Plant equipment was placed on the seventh and forty-third floors, while on the eighth a central equipment nerve-centre would control everything, including two phone exchanges handling 10,000 lines. Some 2,000 km of cabling would be needed to feed the IT and communications! The design, wind-tunnel tested at the University of West Ontario, has its roots in Frank Lloyd Wright's smooth, rounded-corner designs of the 1930s for Johnson Wax. Foster had done round corners in his part of the Citigroup development, but here he also gave the building a millennial version of the shiny fridge finish – a clinically clean skin banded by white.

As at the Citigroup site, a cofferdam built out into the dockwater was already in place, and in 1998 deep aquifer water was pumped out. In November, work began driving 338 1.5m-diameter piles. Making the aquifer dry meant the piles could be shorter and saved money. Construction began in January 1999. A concrete raft was poured, 3.15m thick in the centre to carry the tower's core, but tapering to 1.85m at its edge. The tower's steel frame started rising from the basement.

On 21 May 2000, tragedy struck. The tower had already reached twenty-seven storeys when the crane broke away from it, twisted, and crashed to the ground, smashing across Canada Square. Three construction workers were killed. The deaths would almost certainly have been higher had it not been Sunday, and Canary Wharf deserted. After years of investigation, the Health & Safety Executive, police and constructors could still not offer a conclusive explanation, although a similar accident had happened in San Francisco in 1989. A stone memorial to the dead workers now sits in Canada Square.

The tower was topped out in March 2001, simultaneously with the new Citigroup tower. In August, the crown lighting was switched on, neon light diffusing through the walls surrounding the plant machinery, and separately illuminating a storey-high HSBC hexagonal logo. The first staff were installed in September 2002, and 8,500 had moved in by 2003. In April that year, bank chairman Sir John Bond officially opened the building.

This is Foster's tallest London skyscraper to date, and continues the practice's environmental record. The façade is double glazed, with interior blinds against solar gain. The building meets many BREEM standards, and even includes a means of treating grease generated by the 850-seater staff restaurant on the first floor, which incidentally has a remarkably long 17m serving counter.

Outside, two stone lions brought from Hong Kong guard the entrance. The entrance is five storeys high and has a huge wall installation by Thomas Heatherwick, which mounts 3,743 pictures relating to the bank's history from the 1700s: viewed from certain angles, they make the letters HSBC. Up on the forty-first floor is the bank's boardroom. Boardrooms at the top of London skyscrapers date back to 1958 at Thorn House (now *Orion House*), but this is the highest and is in itself double height, its big window clearly visible beneath the crown logo. Inside, a world map on the wall opposite the window is made of extruded aluminium, which also serves to dampen the room's acoustics.

This is one of Europe's great skyscrapers. Its rounded minimalism seems to have influenced the design of Ingenhoven Overdieck's acclaimed 146m-high 55 Georg-Brauckler-Ring, Munich's tallest tower. The HSBC tower is best seen at night, when its crown lighting and stacked floors blaze with the calm confidence of a bank set upon conquering the whole planet.

The History Wall, HSBC

10 Upper Bank Street

10 Upper Bank Street, E14

DLR/ Tube Canary Wharf, Heron Quays
Height 151m, 31 storeys
Constructed 2001–03
Architect KPF

Clifford Chance, the world's largest legal firm, occupies 10 Upper Bank Street. The glass slab was the first of three new skyscrapers completed on the Heron Quays side of the Canary Wharf estate in 2003. This whole building is massive – with 92,903m² of offices, it is the fourth of Canary Wharf's million-square-footers. The tower connects via an eight-storey atrium into a ten-storey block with trading floors, conference facilities and a swimming pool.

Clifford Chance's London offices had been all over the place, including headquarters at *200 Aldersgate* and Litigation and Dispute Resolution in *CityPoint*. To consolidate, they signed up with CWG in November 2000 and waited for what was then called HQ5 to be built. Architects Gensler fitted the interiors, including an in-house client juice bar. In September 2003, Clifford Chance moved in. That December, when a fire broke out in the basement, workers on the twenty-sixth floor took just eight minutes to get out of the place – good news in the post-9/11 world.

Kohn Pedersen Fox are New York-based architects, now with a London office where they have the most detailed 3-D topographical London model in existence. This is their first London skyscraper, but the *Heron Tower* has established them as big local players. KPF's tallest work is Shanghai's 492m-high World Finance Center, a slim, gently twisted tower with a circular void at the top.

Compared to that, 10 Upper Bank Street may seem a rather plain offering. However, KPF have made their rent-slab cool. The narrow side facing west over Jubilee Gardens shows off its vertical stepping, making a slim, elegant profile, and the glass creates a dramatic mirror to the weather on clear days. By evening the whole building exposes the details of stacks of working offices. At night, the top three floors become a box of blue light, as if to attract blue-chip clients like moths to a flame. The slab's sides are set with vertical fins which create a curious diffusion effect from shallow angles, especially when office lights shine out – the sides look fuzzy (see page 11). A confident, bright building with focus-defying walls is exactly the ticket to fill with slick lawyers.

25 Bank Street, E14

Tube Canary Wharf
DLR Canary Wharf, Heron Quays
Height 153m, 33 storeys
Constructed 2001–03
Architect Cesar Pelli & Associates

25 Bank Street, a huge glass rent-slab full of bankers, is the essence of the new century's New Bland commercial architecture. Originally designated HQ2, it is one of the three towers in the Heron Quays group and has 96,693m² of offices, partly housed in a 'backpack'. The tower was topped out in November 2002. Lehman Bros, the New

25 Bank Street

York-based global investment bank which occupies it, set up a London base in 1972, and moved here from Broadgate in 2003. Base-jumping in London was popular that year, and in November two base-jumpers did a midnight jump from 25 Bank Street.

The building is a neighbour to interesting architecture. Will Alsop's colourful, futuristic Heron Quays DLR station (2003) is at its western side, while behind it is a dreamy curving footbridge by Wilkinson Eyre connecting to South Quay. In itself, however, 25 Bank Street is dull – London's least interesting twenty-first century skyscraper. Anodyne and featureless, the tower at 25 Bank Street is the return of the sixties bland box, but on a scale a magnitude bigger, with shinier materials. The vast cliff façade looking down on MacKenzie Walk's bars and restaurants is mind-numbing.

To alleviate the monolithic effect, crown lighting by LightMatters was installed in 2005 in the double-height gallery around the plant machinery, just above Lehman's executive dining rooms. It is a low-energy installation using LEDs which change colour. Every hour, the band shines blue for a minute, then changes to green and a blue patch chases around the building. This is not exactly an exciting visual stimulation – the displays on an unattended pub games machine can provide similar diversion.

40 Bank Street, E14

Tube Canary Wharf
DLR Heron Quays
Height 153m, 33 storeys
Constructed 2000–03
Architect Cesar Pelli &Associates

This is the most slender of CWG's three speculatively built Heron Quay towers. It connects into the Jubilee underground shopping mall, and its 56,225 m^2 of offices is let out to American legal firms such as Allen & Overy and Sladden Arps. Originally a stepped skyscraper by SOM was conceived for the HQ3 site here. Another block, 50 Bank Street, is in the same style as the skyscraper; between them, Pelli has designed aWinter Gardens, enclosed by a graceful parabolic glass arch, that give public passage between Jubilee Park and the waterside-facing South Quay.

Both 40 and 50 Bank Street are clad in a warm Brazilian marble, and the interesting thing about the skyscraper is the way the solid façades with punched windows meet glass curtain walls, as if two different buildings have been fused together. Pelli used this technique extensively in New York's World Financial Center (see *One Canada Square*). The effect is clean, very much like a computer rendition, and the slender shape is a big contrast to its overbearing neighbour, *25 Bank Street*. All this makes 40 Bank Street one of the most elegant and understated towers on the Canary Wharf estate.

5 Canada Square, E14
Canary Wharf

Tube/DLR Canary Wharf
Constructed 1999–2003
Height 88m, 16 storeys
Architect SOM

5 Canada Square, backs on to the water next to the *HSBC* building. SOM's architect behind it, Chicago-based Adrian D. Smith, is a master of super-tall skyscrapers, designing Shanghai's 421m pagoda-shaped Jin Mao tower, China's tallest in 1998, and he has several others on the go. In London his only building had been the ten-storey 10 Fleet Place near St Paul's, covered with granite fins which give the building a dark, menacing sense of power.

His 5 Canada Square is huge, with 46,264m² of offices – more than two *Centre Point*s. It was built speculatively, and the Bank of America made it their European HQ in November 2003. This is basically a U-shaped glass-walled box. The gap facing Canada Square is glass fronted to create a large lobby and two atria stacked above it, similar to *One Churchill Place*'s airy spaces and the *Heron Tower*'s 'office villages'. There's something sci-fi about the hollow metal roof structure, which is now mounted with the bank's logo in neon. Along with 25 Canada Square in the *Citigroup Centre*, it was part of the new century's largest commercial building sale in 2004.

Although 5 Canada Square doesn't look very big against its neighbouring towers, in any other part of town it would be a massive, theatrical corporate landmark.

30 St Mary Axe, EC3

Tube Liverpool Street
Height 180m, 40 storeys
Construction 2000–04
Architect Foster & Partners and Arup

This is the world's most sensational skyscraper of the century so far. It's also at the heart of the century's first great architectural controversy. Originally, it was going to be named after Swiss Re, but the name was changed to 30 St Mary Axe, better to attract tenants. Of course, everyone calls it the Gherkin. Terry Farrell once aired a theory that it 'was quickly nicknamed by the authors in case it got called something else'.

The Swiss Insist
The story starts at one of the City's global trading houses, the Baltic Exchange, which had been at 30 St Mary Axe since 1903. Here, global shipping deals were brokered in a great room known as the Gorgonzola Hall because of the veined marble in its baroque columns and walls. In April 1992, it was obliterated by the IRA.

English Heritage wanted the Baltic Exchange restored, and had the fragments individually numbered for later reconstitution. GMW secured air rights for the block, including the Chamber of Shipping next door, and worked on plans to incorporate the old trading hall. When English Heritage realised that there was not much more than shattered walls to work on, they dropped that plan. In 1995, the Exchange settled at 38 St Mary Axe and no. 30 was sold to developers Trafalgar House, who were then taken over by Norwegian conglomerate Kvaerner. In May 1996, GMW, Michael Hopkins, Foster and the daring *grand projet* French architect Jean Nouvel were invited by Kvaerner to design high for the site. In September, Foster unveiled the winning design. As we have seen, this would have been the mother of skyscrapers – the eighty-four-storey, 385m-high Millennium Tower. It was too much for the City Corporation and they threw it out.

In 1997, reinsurance giant Swiss Re acquired the site, commissioned a new design from Foster, and threatened to quit London if they couldn't build it. The City had changed its mind about skyscrapers but ruled that anything new at St Mary Axe should be no higher than *Tower42*. Foster's design evolved from a bubble covering the whole site to this tower. It was approved by the City's Planning Committee in a vote of fourteen to seven in July 2000. Even English Heritage backed it…

Green Twist

We have already seen how the Foster partnership pioneered the green skyscraper in Frankfurt for Commerzbank. There, they tackled the energy expense of internal climate control by exploiting natural air circulation inside the structure, and drew light into huge skygardens. These ideas would be adapted for Swiss Re, and the same structural engineers, Arup, would make it happen.

The other big idea, of course, is the shape – really, more an upended Zeppelin than a gherkin. Circular cross-sections that deflect wind pressure in London date from the sixties (*Telecom Tower* and *One Kemble Street*), but a shape that curves vertically as well is even more aerodynamic, and can reduce vortices which can generate strong gusts at the base. Packing the required office volume into such a shape was found by 3D 'volumetric' or 'parametric' modelling. This needs big computer-processing power, because the forces on every location are recalculated as the model incrementally homes in on the perfect shape.

This final form bulges gently out from its base to reach a maximum diameter of 57m around the 16th floor, before tapering gently all the way to the top. Once this shape for the outer envelope was fixed, Arup designed the steel structure for it. Their solution was a diagrid of criss-crossing steel bars, holding 24,000m² of glass in 5,500 triangles or diamonds, all flat, a few of which open to connect with the atmosphere outside.

Effectively, another building stands within this envelope, containing 42,000m² of offices. It is built on steel fingers extending out from a circular core, and its outer edge is double-glazed and vertical. The floors are concrete, and share the lateral wind stress with the diagrid. This means that the core only has to handle the vertical load, for which steel would suffice – no need for a huge reinforced concrete shaft like that of *Tower42*. The rings of concrete floors have wedge-gaps at the edge, and are rotated five degrees clockwise with each storey, creating six helical or corkscrew voids. These

twisting atria are sealed at every sixth storey to prevent fire spread. Bands of dark glass in the diagrid mark these atria. Initially, cascading gardens were planned for the atria, but the idea was shelved. The building can rely on natural air ventilation for forty per cent of the year – that helps reduce the building's energy consumption by half. Not least, the atria fill the internal environment with light and create sightlines from outside deep into the open-plan floors. Slots can draw air through the concrete floors into the air-conditioning machinery. A lot of plant machinery was actually placed in a completely separate small building just to the north.

At the top is a restaurant/bar for the building's occupants, actually a few metres higher than *Tower42*'s Vertigo. Above that is a circular platform floor for viewing, accessed by stairs. The only curved component anywhere on the envelope is the lens window that looks straight up at the very top of the apex dome.

A final green twist is that, despite a capacity of about 4,000 workers, a stand was taken against the tyranny of the automobile. The basement was to accommodate 52 motorbikes and 118 bicycles, but just five car parking spaces – and they were designated 'mobility impaired'!

Constructing A Subtly Shifting Structure

Work began in December 2000 with demolition, then 333 piles were driven and the concrete raft laid for the steel structure, which started to rise in October 2001. Construction company Skanska used three cranes around the structure. The steel core led the way, and was never more than 3mm off from the vertical centre, measured by laser. Some 35km of steel bars were used. Interestingly, as the building progressed, the weight of it would compress its height by 12.5cm and increase the maximum bulge by 2.5cm. These shifting dimensions and stresses presented a massive challenge for Arup.

Nineteen lifts were installed, some whisking passengers as far as skylobbies on the twelfth, twenty-second and thirty-fourth floors. Two lifts travel from the

twenty-fourth through three floors of plant machinery to the restaurant at the top. Around the plant floors are two ring rails mounted outside to carry mechanisms holding a platform on an extending arm to reach the upper floors for maintenance, and another for a window-cleaning cradle. When extended, they look rather like weapons mounted on a bloated Dalek.

In November 2003, with just weeks to go before completion, men on safety ropes where clambering around the top like mountaineers. One in 200 of the glass panes had cracked in transit and needed replacement. Finally, in early 2004, the building was ready. It had cost £220m to build – about the same price as *Tower 42* went for five years earlier. The floor space was also about the same, but the difference was that here was a green building for the new century.

The Rift

Swiss Re moved into the first nineteen floors, but with the City office market flat, it wasn't until December that anyone rented another floor. New icons have a tradition of failing to fill, going back to the Empire State Building. Swiss Re was probably not that bothered – the building was global branding that money couldn't buy. Two hundred architects canvassed by *Building Magazine* voted it the best 2005 building in the world. In October, the building won the Stirling Prize, the panel agreeing unanimously for the first time. Totally unrelatedly, the upmarket restaurant opened in the ground floor in April 2005 is called Sterling, and fish on the menu changes everyday, just like the maritime market in the former Baltic Exchange.

Within the architectural world, the building had already produced a second sensation. After thirty years, in November 2003, Foster partner Ken Shuttleworth, known as 'Ken the Pen', declared that he was setting up his own practice, Make. Although he insisted that the Foster partnership's work was a team effort, he quietly insisted that it was his hand that drew the shapes of many Foster icons, including the Gherkin. 'I don't know where they come from really. I sketch them out and they get worked up', he modestly told *Building Magazine* in January 2004. Foster would not be drawn on the subject.

30 St Mary Axe may be the first superstar skyscraper of the century, but is it the future? Being glazed and green isn't easy – glass creates a greenhouse effect in summer and leaves space cold in winter, needing the complicated venting schemes of today. Opaque materials are better insulators. Shuttleworth himself declared the glazed building dead, just as a new icon in Barcelona, the Torre Agbar, was finished, with a 150m-high shape very similar to 30 St Mary Axe. Jean Nouvel designed it with an outer skin of concrete, punched with a random array of rectangular windows. This was a new-look green skyscraper. Meanwhile, there are still plenty of other Millennial glass spectaculars such in the pipeline, not least *The Shard*…

One Churchill Place, E14
Canary Wharf

Tube/DLR Canary Wharf
Height 156m, 32 storeys
Constructed 2002–04
Architect HOK International (UK)

The first London skyscraper to be built after 9/11 was a massive block at Canary Wharf, which is now the global headquarters of Barclays Bank.

Barclays had wanted to consolidate operations at twelve locations into one. They needed space for 5,000 workers, twice as many as their headquarters at *54 Lombard Street* could hold. Like HSBC, they just couldn't find a City site, and Canary Wharf offered a solution. Here, CWG were planning their estate's eastern end, and they envisaged a group of office blocks around a new green space called Churchill Place. The tallest, at thirty-storeys, on a site called BP1, was sketched sometimes as an elliptical-plan slab, and sometimes an east-facing bow-fronted tower, a shape like *One West India Quay*. It became a 92,900m^2 box designed by the latter's architects, HOK International.

The day after the destruction of the World Trade Center, news emerged that Barclays was to lease about 60,000m^2, almost two-thirds, of what would be One Churchill Place. In November, Barclays confirmed the deal. The safety of their workers was clearly paramount, and they asked for design changes. The redesign was quick and soon 215 piles were being driven down to carry the tower.

In July 2002, the London-based Institution of Structural Engineers published their 'Safety In Tall Buildings' report, with recommendations including structural frameworks that have alternative load-bearing paths,

One Churchill Place

Plantation Place, EC3
Fenchurch Street

Tube Monument
Rail Fenchurch Street
Height 68m, 16 storeys
Completed 2004
Architect Arup Associates

This massive 76,000m² office development may not quite be a skyscraper, but its two connected glass towers float like giant ice cubes on the City's skyline. The building is occupied by insurers Royal Sun Alliance.

British Land's redevelopment needed to reflect its old surroundings, characterised by solid 1930s offices. This seems to have been taken literally — the two connected towers reflect the adjacent Wren's St Margaret Patten church in their glass façades, while the first seven storeys, which follow Fenchurch Street's street line, look like a stone building. The illusion of stone is made by fins of Jura limestone, which limit solar gain. They also 'provide privacy in the manner of an Ottoman jalousie' say architects Arup. Above, a stepped-back glazed layer acts like a podium for the six-storey towers. This transition from a stone base acknowledging surrounding buildings to a light structure on high is

Plantation Place

fireproofing materials capable of withstanding 1200°C, and protecting escape routes from smoke. Some of these features could already be seen on the Churchill Place construction site — as well as the massive central core, two pencil-thin satellite cores also rose a scarily sheer 150m, housing two of the four fire escapes, which would have wider stairways with loudspeakers to guide evacuation. The main core contains safety havens, while the concrete used is enhanced against hydrocarbon fire. The core walls are 10cm thicker than normal, and the perimeter frame is designed so that even with the loss of any two adjacent columns, total collapse could not happen.

One Churchill Square is shorter and squatter than its neighbours in Canary Wharf, such as the *HSBC* tower next door, but it was now the most resilient skyscraper in London. In October 2003 it was topped out and the Barclays logos were in place soon after. Workers started moving in late 2004, and it was officially opened in June 2005. After London won the 2012 Olympics bid (masterminded from *One Canada Square*), the Organising Committee took space here.

The building is big on environmental credentials, and won the 2004 Green Apple Award for sustainability. The roof is a stony skygarden, attracting wildlife. The highlight of the building, though, lies behind the huge south-facing glass sheet that separates offices. Here are five stacked atria, filled with installations by Martha Schwarz. She likes playing with space and often uses plant themes. One atrium has giant suspended bamboo models while real bamboos grow from the floor level; another has huge green leaf shapes floating above real growing leaves. The whole building is awash with natural light, and no worker is more than five metres from where it falls. In the lobby is a pure liquid sci-fi sculpture called *Constant Change*, by Tony Cragg.

Frankly, One Churchill Square looks like a big bland box, but inside, workers enjoy inspirational spaces.

In early 2002, the archaeological dig unearthed millennia of artefacts from Neolithic or Bronze Age flints to a nineteenth-century culvert. The site was dug deep, because the work required a 36m-deep ventilation shaft for Crossrail. The developers lobbied Parliament with concerns about subsidence (a worry for the *Barbican* as well). Provisions were made for a new ticket hall, despite Crossrail still evading funding after decades. The building contract with Skansa was worth £85m. In late 2004, Moor House was valued at £156m, even before construction had finished.

The different size of each floor will make it a classy multiple-tenancy block. Foster also designed a friendly public space at the front, with a tree on a patch of undulating grass. Another interesting feature of Moor House is the two giant window-cleaning joists, which extend telescopically like huge guns when they're not at rest in their rooftop bays.

similar to *54 Lombard St*, but handled in a different way.

Plantation Place has an atrium a full 43m high, with an internal glass bridge and further fins around the walls, but in glass. The towers are surrounded by tenth-storey external skygardens, which are still rare in London.

London-based Arup Associates are known more for state-of-the-art structural engineering than architecture, but their 1984 Finsbury Avenue offices in Broadgate's first phase, with its exterior metal frame-work, established their design reputation in the City. Plantation Place's façades continue their interest in layered environmental cladding. In the upper levels, a 60cm gap between glazing contains active blinds which are controlled by sunshine sensors.

Behind the building is Plantation Lane. Here, British artist Simon Patterson has created a magical space called *Time and Tide*, with a 43m-long wall which changes colour, and shows the lunar surface. Historical texts are inscribed in the stone ground.

Willis Building, EC3
51 Lime Street

Tube Bank, Monument
Height 125m 26 storeys
Construction 2004–06
Architect Foster & Partners

In 1975, insurance brokers Willis Faber and Dumas moved into an extraordinary new HQ in Ipswich. The building was completely enclosed in three storeys of curving sheet glass; inside, escalators linked huge open floors. It was the revolutionary project that established the Foster practice on the architectural map. Twenty-nine years later, the same insurance group signed up for another extraordinary Foster-designed HQ...

Moor House, EC2
119 *London Wall*

Tube Moorgate
Height 84m, 18 storeys
Construction 2002–05
Architect Foster & Partners

Foster is very keen on curves, and at Moor House, the partnership ha produced a sexy curved shape that no-one seems to have thought of before. Basically, this 29,000m^2 office development is a quarter slice of a cylinder, but with a roof that sweeps down to the second floor, across the surface of another imaginary cylinder laid perpendicular to the first. It's a very elegant exercise in 3-D circular geometry.

This shape is a solution to how to use a rather small site that was occupied by the 1961 tower of the same name (see *London Wall*), which became moribund and was bought for redevelopment in 1995.

The Willis Building is a development by British Land and Stanhope plc. In 2001, they acquired 51 Lime Street, a previous Lloyd's building, designed by Terence Heysham and opened in 1958 to accommodate the overspill from their 1928 building on the current *Lloyd's* site across the street. This building had some huge thirties-style windows in curved façades. Its replacement would be a new Foster skyscraper, granted planning permission in 2002. In 2004, the Willis Group announced they would take the whole building, and 51 Lime Street became the Willis Building. Willis wanted some changes. They didn't need such huge trading floors in the single building covering the whole site, which allowed Foster to split the building in two, opening a north-south passage. The floor space was trimmed to about 30,000m² and the tower slimmed and increased in height by just 10cm.

This is a dramatic design. The building rises in three great steps facing Lloyd's with sweeping concave façades. This liberates public realm on Lime Street, and creates arc-shaped terraces on the seventeenth and twenty-second floors; the lower terrace is earmarked for staff dining, and the higher one for the board's use.

With Lloyd's, Swiss Re in *30 St Mary Axe* and Aviva in the *Aviva Tower* all grouped together, the area was already the world's insurance centre. The Willis Building brings yet another global insurance giant here, and with it, a little of insurance's raison d'etre – some sweeping drama.

Broadgate Tower, EC2
Primrose Street

Tube Liverpool St
Height 164m, 36 storeys
Construction 2005–08
Architect SOM

In May 2002, Ken Livingstone mused that the area west of Bishopsgate Goods Yard would be 'a great site for a sixty-or sixty-five-storey tower'. British Land always intended to extend its wildly successful Broadgate scheme further north, and in line with the SOM-designed Beaux Art-style offices along upper Bishopsgate they had more twelve-storey offices in mind. A concrete raft over the railway cutting out of Liverpool Street and City planning permission had been long in place for them. Livingstone, however, insisted on a tall element to the scheme. In July 2004, he got his wish – SOM's Chicago office had evolved the design to include a thirty-six storey tower. It was approved in 2005 and construction began in December.

SOM's debut on the London cityscape had been Broadgate, and one of the highlights was Exchange House, a big medium-rise block suspended over a plaza on a giant load-bearing parabolic steel arc. This will now face the new scheme, which contains about 75,000m² of office split between two buildings. 201 Bishopsgate will continue the twelve-storey line, but on the eastern half of the site is Broadgate Tower. Between them will be a galleria, full of retail and spanned by a sloping glass cover. The resulting passage extends the pedestrian route from Liverpool Street to the very borders of Shoreditch. With confidence rising with the property cycle, the scheme is being built speculatively, and Broadgate Tower is aimed at the multiple-tenancy market.

The angular tower itself will be a parallelogram in plan, glazed in blue, with massive white cross-bracing. It has been compared to the SOM's Chicago John Hancock Center, but in appearance it's more like one of Hong Kong's great towers, the 319m-high Bank of China by IM Pei (1989). British Land's most ambitious tower plan, the Rogers-designed *Leadenhall Building*, also has massive cross-bracing. In visualisations, Broadgate Tower has the texture of something that's come out of a huge dust-free facility, like silicon wafers or satellites.

Broadgate Tower stands quite separately to the City's cluster to the south. If it's just another step in the advance of the City Fringes business zone, that's bad news for the buzzing cultural quarter of Shoreditch to the north. If, on the other hand, it stands like a gateway marker to the City to the south, that galleria becomes a brilliant entrance to the financial centre. Either way, the Broadgate Tower will be a sharp American addition to the skyline.

Heron Tower, EC3
Bishopsgate

Tube/Rail Liverpool Street
Height 202m, 46 storeys (242m with spire)
Designed 1999–2005
Construction expected 2007–10
Architect KPF

More even than *30 St Mary Axe*, this was the skyscraper that decided the future of the City's skyline, because it saw off the opposition in an £11m public inquiry. It finally got approved, not just because the City understood the need to build high, but because of world-class design. The Heron Tower brings American skyscraper masters KPF to the Square Mile, and is now the centrepiece of a wider development, Heron Plaza.

As in the 1960s, there is a colourful developer behind this landmark. Gerald Ronson has a formidable reputation and is fond of cigars. He had already built up the Heron Corporation into a huge international property and leisure empire in the 1980s, but the property crash hit Heron badly, particularly in the US. In 1992 Heron owed £1.4bn, and Ronson himself probably lost £600m. IT billionaires Bill Gates and Larry Ellison helped Heron refinance, and, under his renewed chairmanship, Heron in the nineties bounced back – big time. The Heron Tower became a very personal mission for Ronson.

Swiftly following the Gherkin's go-ahead, it was approved by the City in February 2001, but got ensnared by English Heritage's objections about strategic views of St Paul's. The public enquiry that followed in the autumn crystallised the battle between the pro- and anti-skyscraper lobbies, which would decide whether new London skyscrapers were possible outside Canary Wharf. Mayor Ken Livingstone spent £67,000 making his case, with Will Alsop and Richard Rogers as star witnesses. English Heritage was represented by Philip Davies, who made an unexpected attack on KPF's design – a bad move

considering its transparent exterior, intelligent form and technical innovations. The main argument was based on sightlines from Waterloo Bridge, which, it became clear, were actually obscured by trees. The inquiry revealed another strange thing – a majority on English Heritage's London Advisory committee at one stage actually thought that planning refusal was unwarranted. English Heritage lost, and John Prescott approved the Heron Tower in July 2002.

A Tower of Villages Expands
Essentially, KPF had come up with a refreshing new take on Hi-Tech, in the form of a rectilinear glass tower for the multi-occupancy market. This was a Millennial skyscraper, complete with strong green credentials.

The Heron Tower at 110 Bishopsgate places its service core on the south side, thus simultaneously reducing the solar gain and also harvesting solar energy with photovoltaic cladding. Double-decker lifts make the service tower kinetic, as in Richard Rogers structures such as the *Lloyd's Building*. The service tower was designed to rise 183m, with a restaurant near its top, and, above plant floors, a 39m-high spire. As proposed, the main block contained thirty-three storeys of offices in a cross-braced glass box, starting above a 12m-high arcade of shops and cafés, a public space that draws people into the building. On the original construction schedule, the American-style cross-bracing would have been a first in London. Triple-glazing contributes to the energy-efficiency. The interesting thing about the offices is the way they are organised into three-storey office 'villages'. Each village is a module that is basically grounded in a rectangle of open office space, but the two floors above are separated by a gap, creating an atrium. KPF tried this idea with great success in 1998 at Thames Court, a bright, airy development on the City's riverside at Queenhithe. In the Heron Tower, eleven villages would be stacked on top of each other.

At the time, KPF's Lee Polisano said that the then forty-two-storey tower, including five plant storeys, was 'designed to be seen in the round'. There's a cool transparency to it, rather like KPF's *10 Upper Bank Street*, while, because the tower is split and stepped, its verticality is quite different to *30 St Mary Axe* and *Tower 42*. These towers would stand like three tall friends from different schools.

Ken Livingstone maintained from the start that he wanted this tower to be higher. Nothing seemed to happen with it for ages, and the City meanwhile abandoned the idea of limiting towers to 180m, and approved *The Leadenhall Building* and Minerva Tower, both breaking the 200m mark. But Ronson had not been sitting around waiting for tenancies on his site to expire. On the adjoining site, Heron had acquired leases, and in 2004 gained planning consent for a junior tower next door, twenty-two storeys and 98m high. In January 2006, the go-ahead came to boost the original Heron Tower with another office village and an expansion of the roof restaurant, bringing it up to forty-six storeys. The whole development now packs in around a million square feet. Demolition at the site finally began in 2006.

Past Charm, Future Zing

The site was once one of the entrances through the Roman wall, known in mediaeval times as 'Bisshoppes Gate'. An early City high-rise called Kempson House was here, a six-sided 14-storey, 47m-high tower by architects C Lovett Gill completed in 1961. Despite being six-sided, it was not particularly exciting. On Bishopsgate, a later block called Bishop's House looked just plain awful.

To the north was a conservation area. Handsome 1920s buildings faced what was a traffic gyratory system. The new scheme pedestrianises Houndsditch between the new towers. Here, part of the listed Stone House Court is actually relocated, while the Portland stone façades of Stone House on the corner of Bishopsgate, by architects Richards & Gill, will be retained. The old Staple Hall will be lost to the lower skyscraper, now called One Heron Plaza. North of these lies one of the City's unexpected treasures – the narrow, villagey Devonshire Row, busy with old cafés and shops. Its shop fronts will be restored. Alarm bells ring when redevelopment strikes in a conservation area, but in this case, much of the classic structures are given new life.

Heron Tower

The site of the Heron Plaza

Heron Plaza model (before height increase)

If the Heron Tower had been built just after its go-ahead, KPF would have been the first American architects with a City skyscraper. This will now be *Broadgate Tower*, by SOM. Both practices have global portfolios, but set up offices in London, and their City towers are certainly not like some of Canary Wharf's 'New Bland' designs by practices like Pelli, detached geographically from the location. The expanded Heron Plaza scheme tackles a tight, old urban fabric that is very European. Only when it is finished will we see if KPF's incorporation of bits of the past works in their generous new public realm. The City is getting busier and the buzz of people through the scheme is what should give it life on the ground. As for the Heron Tower itself, its busy office villages and moving lifts will give it vertical life as well. Ronson's landmark will prove to be a metallically cool yet zingy addition to the City cluster.

The Leadenhall Building, EC3
Leadenhall Street

Tube Bank
Height 224.5m, 48 storeys
Architect RRP
Designed 2002–04

This great Hi-Tech tower is simultaneously classic Richard Rogers and exhilaratingly the future. A triangular-sided prism tapering to a linear peak is planned for the heart of the City's cluster.

This is not the first Richard Rogers design with this sort of shape. *Montevetro* resembles a fin on a giant sundial, but more similar was a 2000 competition entry for new headquarters for the *New York Times*. There, Rogers proposed a tower defined by a steeply sloping façade opposite a vertical one. Renzo Piano (see *The Shard*) won that competition, but the brilliant concept was not abandoned. When in 2001 British Land held a competition to replace the 13-storey P&O Building (1969), designed with the *Aviva Tower* by GMW, Richard Rogers analysed the site. Two factors made an upstanding wedge the right shape – the south-facing inclined façade leans away from protected views of St Paul's from the west, and it would not loom as overbearingly as would a vertical façade along Leadenhall Street, opposite Rogers' *Lloyd's Building*.

British Land publicly unveiled plans for 122 Leadenhall in February 2004. A massive battle was expected with conservationists, and the *Evening Standard* even printed that the tower 'draws fire from conservationists', but after their public inquiry defeats over the *Heron Tower* and *The Shard*, English Heritage had re-assessed their position and came out in favour. When approved in October, it was the tallest tower with consent in the City.

And what an exciting tower it is! The building is essentially in three parts. The vertical north façade is actually on the service tower, which will stand remarkably close to the *Aviva Tower*. Here lifts, service risers and lavatories are separated from the main building. Escalators scoop people up from the ground to the first floor. The lifts are in three banks, servicing different height regions, with sky lobbies on the tenth and twenty-fourth floors. These lifts will be visible through the service tower's single glazing, and with the classic Rogers tools of colour and light, a trademark Rogers kinetic façade is created.

This leaves the office floors free to be open rectangles, clear but for fire escapes in the corners. They are grouped in six double-glazed seven-storey sections, which on every seventh floor connect to the braced 'tube' perimeter. This huge external megaframe is single-glazed and

exposes its cross-bracing, creating diamond-patterned façades. Essentially, it's a diagrid not dissimilar to that of *30 St Mary Axe*, but bigger, and – crucially – load bearing. The structural engineers are again Arup. Because the ladder frame of the southern side is sloped, the floors get smaller in area with height, but the lowest office floor is actually the seventh, where a sloping glass screen protrudes along Leadenhall, deflecting the wind at street level. This brings us to the building's third part – a vast open space beneath the offices, where mature trees will grow. This contains three storeys of public realm, with lifts to a bar and restaurant above ground level.

With 55,870m² of office space, it's big, but only just over half the size of the biggest rectilinear towers of Canary Wharf, where Rogers was later commissioned to design the Riverside South project. Rogers himself said of Leadenhall that its lightness, clarity and drama will grace London's skyline'. If anything, this is an understatement. Even measured against the Gherkin and *The Shard*, this structure is an inspired design. It may just be the greatest commercial work of a legendary practice.

After planning consent came through, British Land chairman Sir John Ritblat said he was determined to go ahead even without a pre-let. A lot of leases in the P&O Building expire in 2008, so after demolition and foundation work, Leadenhall will probably not be finished this decade. In the meantime, on an adjacent site, DIFA have planned the *Bishopsgate Tower*, which will rise far above it. Despite this new competition for attention, this Rogers masterpiece will positively electrify the City skyline.

Bishopsgate Tower, EC3
Bishopsgate

Tube/Rail/DLR Bank, Monument, Liverpool Street
Height 288m, 60 storeys
Designed 2002–06
Architect KPF with Arup Associattes

Here, as architect Lee Polisano of KPF says, is 'a proposition for a centre to the (City) cluster'. Nearby *Tower42* set out to do the same in the 1970s, but every subsequent new skyscraper detracts from the cluster's focus. The Bishopsgate Tower is an exercise in graceful curvature, designed to rise above all City skyscrapers in an astonishing form like an upended scroll of paper, its edge twirling up in a helical spiral to a pointed peak. It has already been called the 'Helter Skelter'.

Hamburg-based developer DIFA, a property group with funds approaching 15 billion, have long had designs on this site. In January 2000, plans for a sixty-three storey, 220m-high cylindrical tower designed by Chicago's Helmut Jahn practice emerged. It too had a helix twirling to its top, but the massing was heavy and the City had not quite yet decided to re-embrace towers. DIFA bought Crosby Court, the adjoining site, occupied by a 1980s building that curiously seems to be mostly atrium. This gave them not just more space, but would enable them to shift any tower a little to the north, where it would impact less on views of St Paul's. In 2005, the new design emerged…

Bishopsgate model

The outer skin, co-designed by Arup, is quite different from other Millennial skyscrapers. Uniform, flat planes of glass are mounted on the round steel bars of the megaframe, but each overlaps its side neighbour and overhangs those below, almost like roof slates. KPF liken it to snakeskin. Photovoltaics cover the top. (Getting the most out of good ideas, KPF have since then recycled the spiralling peak in a design for AXA in a clustered tower that could become the tallest in La Défense, Paris' Canary Wharf-like satellite business district.) The skin fans out into undulating curtains of glass around its base, where its lower edge will rise into an 18m-high gap on Bishopsgate, as if curtains were being opened. This will lure pedestrians into the three-storey public realm below it, and create an east-west passage. KPF have designed other wind-deflecting skirts that fan out around towers, and this is similar to their 2002 designs for the unbuilt Parkhaven tower in Rotterdam.

The Bishopsgate Tower's six storeys of trading floors are suspended above the public area. Three cores take lifts through the tower, one of them starting from the ninth floor. Near the top of the building, a projected restaurant should become the City's highest publicly accessible vantage point. The tower was planned to be 307m and twenty-four storeys high, but this was reduced by four storeys to 288m because of objections from the CAA. Approval came in April 2006. The 'edge' turning around the tower's axis is orientated so that, viewed from Waterloo Bridge, it would create 'shoulders' against the elevation at 180m and 220m, just at the levels of *Tower42* and *The Leadenhall Building*. If built, it would add yet more thrill to new 'strategic view' of the City's cluster that encapsulates the verve of the world's financial hub.

The Bishopsgate Tower at the centre of the city cluster (Towers left to right Heron tower (behind), One Angel Court (below), Tower 42, Stock Exchange Building, Bishopsgate Tower, Aviva Tower, Leadenhall Building, 6-8 Bishopsgate (below). Lloyds, Willis Building, 54 Lombard Street.

Chapter 8:
The Future

If all the ice in Antarctica and the Arctic were to melt, the sea level would rise by over 60m. A survivor with a boat, however, would still be able to recognise London. In the waters between the island-hills to the north and south, the vast dome of St Paul's would still be above the water, and around it, a peppering of church spires. But, most startlingly, London's skyscrapers would stand like rock outcrops in the sea, water lapping against the far-flung tower blocks, and the great clusters of the City and Canary Wharf rising up like bizarre citadels of a lost civilisation.

This fantastic scenario may render awesome views of London's skyscrapers, but clearly it's not the best way to get to appreciate them. If global warming raises the Earth's temperature by 5°C this century, the sea-level rise will be more like a metre, with consequences for humanity that will almost certainly be devastating. Theoretically, London could hold the sea back, as Holland does. The Thames Barrier (1983) protects perhaps £80bn of property, but it may only provide cover till 2030. Already there is talk of a new barrier across the estuary at Shoeburyness. The Earth seems to be racing towards a tipping-point, though, and no barrier would hold back the potential runaway sea-level rise. There are 10 trillion tonnes of methane hydrates lying on the ocean floor. When the temperature rises enough, greenhouse gases will start bubbling up and make all our CO_2 emissions seem like froth in a tidal wave of global catastrophe.

This extreme scenario does raise two questions – what can skyscraper architects do about global warming, and what should be the heritage of London's skyline for future generations?

L Me If You Can, I'm Feeling Drowned

Skyscrapers are inherently better for the environment than lower-rise buildings, because they concentrate human activity on a small footprint,

taking less land from nature. But that is not enough.

We have already seen how vented façades have cut back the energy consumption of Millennial skyscrapers like *30 St Mary Axe*, and BREEAM ratings have encouraged other CO_2-tackling measures, such as promoting the use of public transport. Architects now are incorporating further sustainable technologies, such as biomass and photovoltaics (as at *22 Marsh Wall*) and wind turbines, along with using the London Aquifer to regulate seasonal temperature (e.g. *Vauxhall Tower*). CPH systems eliminate power loss due to transmission, and can cut CO_2 emissions by up to a half compared to conventional boiler heat and electricity supply – these are also now being designed in.

Almost half of the UK's CO_2 emissions are related to buildings. As part of its commitment to the Kyoto Protocol, the UK government aims to cut CO_2 building emissions by sixty per cent by 2050. In 2006, RIBA went further, outlining plans to make the cut seventy per cent. A crucial government tool to achieve this is a building regulation, Part L, which addresses energy conservation and power. The revisions to Part L coming into effect in 2006 are demanding, and a big challenge to glazed buildings. New techniques constantly emerge, such as filling the gap in double glazing with argon or krypton gas, or a vacuum, while electrochromatic glass can change colour when electrically charged, but applying these technologies to whole building envelopes is expensive.

In early 2005, Make's Ken Shuttleworth issued a rallying call in *Building Design* magazine: 'Wake up all you architectural glass junkies, it's time for a change!' Shuttleworth argues that Part L means glazed buildings will be consigned to history, and that big atria don't help either. Windows in brick walls with a fifty per cent glazing ratio are as energy efficient as the fanciest multiple-glazed façades with ventilation slots. As we have seen, others are thinking on similar lines, such as Jean Nouvel in his Torre Agbar design in Barcelona. What that means for the next generation of skyscrapers could be a return to masonry-heavy buildings, such as *Senate House* or classical American skyscrapers. Make favours metals such as stainless steel, aluminium or zinc. Their latest designs for skyscrapers, such as the twenty-eight-storey Kite project for Leeds, make solid exteriors scintillating.

There is a problem with metals, though – embodied energy. A high-performance material will produce no CO_2 when in place in a structure, but how much energy went into producing it? Australian research suggested that all the embodied energy in the buildings there amounted to a decade of national energy consumption. Wood has low embodied energy, concrete about five times more, glass fourteen times more, and steel a massive twenty-four times more. Recycled materials save embodied energy that would have been thrown away. Architects will now have to factor embodied energy in.

There are new materials with great insulation and other properties. Make are looking at nanogel, a translucent, water-repellent material that is actually 95 per cent air. It has already been used in panels and skylights in the US. Translucent concrete, embedded with glass fibres, promises whole buildings that are solid and full of light as well. In Japan, the architect Kengo Kuma has used surprising materials to make translucent walls, such as bamboo shoots and glass cloth. In Germany, Werner Stock conceived a 300m-high Skin Tower clad in textiles.

There's nothing greener than a plant. As we have seen, Foster's Commerzbank has skygardens, and the practice continues to design them in, for example in the proposed Ellerman House development in the City. In 2000, Ken Yeang designed a forty-storey tower for Elephant & Castle that was brimming on every floor with vegetation. But put plants on big roofs, and the benefits could go further. Green roofs are potentially like magic do-it-all environmental machines. They insulate buildings, absorb noise, dust and pollution, provide wildlife refuges, cut rainwater run-off that overloads sewers, and even moderate microwave radiation levels. Chicago, Atlanta and Tokyo have planning directives requiring them in new developments, but, despite positive biodiversity policies, London lags behind. *One Churchill Square* is a rare example where a stony skygarden has already been designed in.

Skyscraper roofs are traditionally the home of plant machinery, but natural ventilation is already changing that. Cooling towers on the top of skyscrapers extend the passive management of heat. The top of *The Shard* will effectively be a huge radiator of pipes shining heat away.

All these measures are pro-active against global warming, but skyscrapers will have to be reactive to climate change as well. In 2005, the Meteorological Office warned that freak storms will come with increased frequency. More steel in load-distributing structures such as cross-bracing and diagrids can strengthen skyscrapers against lateral wind loads, but as wind loads get bigger, architects will also need to think about dampers – structures at the top of a tower that counter wind movement through sheer mass. Every rigid structure vibrates at certain frequencies for which outside forces can create positive feedback loops until the vibration is uncontrollable. Tuned mass dampers act precisely against this, and Richard Rogers' new 87m-high Heathrow Control Tower has one. Passive dampers don't act but just sit there. By making them with bodies of liquid, the kinetic energy of the fluid's movement could be harnessed as an energy source.

Part L should force the pace of green high-rise

design in the UK, so what sort of skyscrapers will result? 'Smart' office buildings are getting as complex to control as spacecraft, but passive measures in their climate control and materials will probably make them simpler again. As for how they look, it may be too early to write off glazing, but

Kite, Leeds

colour, shape and even texture will change. As we shall see, there is a new generation of London-based architects that are not short of ideas.

Ideally, new buildings should have zero emissions. This may sound impossible, but Arup are already involved in developing a zero-emission 'eco-city' for Shanghai at Dongtan, which is scheduled to come to life by 2010. Making skyscrapers zero-emission is a very different challenge to the conventionally scaled buildings there, but who knows what new ideas will come out of projects like Dongtan? Of course, China is also where most of the current skyscraper action is…

Polycentric

In 2005, there were already twenty-five skyscrapers in the world taller than *The Shard* will be. Of these, eleven are in Chinese cities. These are exploding with skyscrapers in the same way that New York and Chicago were in the 1920s; indeed, from Dubai to the Far East, a building a mere 100m high would be lost in the clattering, raw emerging skylines.

Does London want to be like this? Of course not. But fewer and fewer would prefer a London with no high-rise – a museum city living on Shakespeare-to-Sex Pistols history, but increasingly irrelevant to the global economy. Even the most beautiful old European cities that live by commerce, as well as culture, build high-rise: Amsterdam has its own new quarter of dazzling Millennial towers, while Paris is agonising about whether to allow them back into the sacred cityscape within its Boulevard Periphérique.

London's 2012 Olympic Games will focus developers and, by then, many of the projects we have seen will be joined by as yet unannounced skyscrapers. With the planning process taking around two years and construction about two or three, skyscrapers typically have a lead time of at least five years. That means that anything built by 2012 should enter the pipeline by 2007. If funding is ever sorted out for Crossrail, that too will be an incentive for skyscrapers.

Where will they be?

Vauxhall and the South Bank are already developing skyscraper clusters. When the market is ready, Canary Wharf will extend eastwards to Wood Wharf, where Ballymore and CWG already plan a £2bn development, masterplanned by Richard Rogers. Office towers of thirty-five-storeys have been envisaged. A Rogers masterplan has already been approved for Convoys Wharf across the river in Lewisham, with three residential towers of twenty-six to forty storeys, but the site's ownership has changed since then, and plans may change. London is polycentric, and more clusters will develop. After the Olympic Games, Stratford may be on Crossrail, as well as an international stop on the Channel Tunnel Rail Link, and some see it as another satellite business cluster in the next decade, like Croydon in the sixties or Canary Wharf in the nineties. Nearer the centre – in fact, at London's geographical centre – Elephant & Castle is already being masterplanned by Make, and Southwark Council has 2014 earmarked as the date when a new civic square is ready, overlooked by tall towers.

And London is brimming with architectural talent that may yet make a mark on the skyline. Some of these are foreign-born. Most celebrated is Iraqi-born Pritzker prizewinner Zaha Hadid, a sort of a deconstructional Brutalist. At last she has commissions in London, including the Olympic swimming pool complex. When she gave a lecture in London in 2005, her phrases were exactly like her work: 'Superimposition and juxtaposition of buildings over existing ones. . . cellular organization. . . multiple morphings and distortions. . . fluid interior organization. . . toptonic topography. . . rooms in a space which becomes pixellated'. Imagine such thoughts applied to a skyscraper! She's designed a 185m-high twisting tower for Milan and visualised a replacement for the World Trade Center towers.

Tanzanian-born David Adjaye has not yet designed any skyscrapers, but has an international track record for contemplative cultural buildings, including the Ideas Store library in Bow. In 2006, he's been re-

Foreign Office Architects: Bunch Tower proposal

assessing the tower block for the BBC. Another London practice is the Foreign Office, based on the partnership of Spanish Alejandro Zaera-Polo and Iranian-born Farshid Moussavi, whose buildings in locations such as Yokohama and the Netherlands seem to have no common design ethos except that they are very different from anything else at all. They designed competition proposals to replace the Twin Towers – like Zaha Hadid's designs, theirs had sinuous tubes that touched at different points – and in 2005, their skyscraper design for Elizabeth House, Waterloo, was in the last four.

Practices such as these, wherever they originate, are at the cutting edge of London's artistic reputation for architecture. The commercial developers who will commission the next wave of high-rise are less keen on experimenting than cultural clients, but they know that imagination in design sells offices and flats. In time, we will see a new generation of London skyscraper architects as good as any in the world.

New futures in an old town

London tortures itself about skyscrapers. The question of how London could evolve through this century in harmony with them is crucial. No-one should build high in, say, the Georgian cityscapes of Shoreditch or Fitzrovia, or slap towers down at world-famous sites such as Piccadilly Circus or Westminster, although of course in the sixties, planners and developers wanted to do exactly that, and sometimes did. The real issue is how to mix high- and low-rise, as well as old and new, to make London even more exciting, diverse and sometimes stunningly beautiful than it already is.

London's edge lies in design, clustering and context. The Millennial designs so far have mainly come from architects with global names, whose skyscrapers are often amongst the best in other skylines (for example, Foster in Frankfurt, Piano in New York, or KPF in Shanghai). Their towers promise to cluster into giant sculpture gardens. In the City, the skyline should become a coherent collection of soaring, graceful shapes from a dream of a future urban Utopia. The effect would be breathtaking. Yet all this will be in a context of some remarkable high-rise from decades earlier, some of the world's greatest buildings from centuries before them, and a rich European urban fabric at its base. New skyscrapers can relate to St Paul's rather than oppose it, making the composition better than if either the skyscrapers or Wren's dome and steeples were not there. No other city can do that.

Piers Gough of CZWG once said of skyscrapers: 'the more you build, the better they get, and the bum ones disappear'. But the idea of a bum skyscraper changes with time, just as it does with other buildings. The skyscrapers of Richard Seifert were once dismissed as symptomatic of the malaise of post-war architecture, but gradually they are being seen as exactly the opposite – the most imaginative application of design and engineering of their times. Glass boxes were hated, but GMW's *Aviva Tower* is now respected as the best example of the New York-inspired sixties tower-and-plaza genre. With tower blocks, Goldfinger's *Trellick Tower* was condemned as the ugliest building in the world, but now it's a global icon. London's skyline contains rich strata of different periods, from pre-war semi-classical, through the International Style and Brutalism, then Post-Modernism, to the glass Millennial towers of this decade. Like the centuries of urban fabric below them, the heritage of all these skyscraper periods should have a place in the future.

Columbus Tower, E14
Hertsmere Road

Tube, DLR Canary Wharf
Height 237m, 61 storeys
Construction planned 2007–12
Architect DMWR

This unexpected tower has had to negotiate its way through the challenge of, all things, trains and planes. Sited by the Canary Wharf cluster, it aims to be taller than *One Canada Square* and challenge the area's ubiquitous 'New Bland' box architecture with curves and a lyrical roofline.

When the Columbus Tower was first announced in October 2002, no-one anticipated such a bold plan at the very edge of the Canary Wharf estate. CWG were masters of the manor, and here was a tower quite unlike any of theirs. Initially announced as 226m high, by the time it was ready for the planning process a year later, the £220m, 93,423m^2 project was now the tallest in Docklands at 237m. Its plot ratio is an astounding 24:1, about which CWG, of all people, expressed reservations. Like *One West India Quay* on the same quayside, it's a mixed-use tower. Above a three-storey public winter garden are twenty-two floors of office below twenty-six floors of hotel (including 192 rooms and seventy suites), and two floors of fitness facilities sandwiched in-between, including a 20-metre swimming pool on the twenty-fourth floor! Below ground, just seventy-seven cars will find parking spaces. The very top floors offer a fourth use – a restaurant.

The big thrill is the shape. In plan, the tower is a sliver made by the intersection of two circular façades , while the roof rises up into horned pinnacles at each end. The effect is something like a boat, a homage to the area's maritime past, something Docklands towers have not done since *Cascades*. This dramatic form is exactly the stuff of world-class architecture that distinguishes London's Millennial skyscrapers by literally 'thinking outside the box'. At the Tower Hamlets Planning Committee meeting in March 2004, architect Mark Weintraub talked about how different this was to the 'dominance of North American architecture' in Canary Wharf. It sounded good, coming from an American. The Committee approved it in a vote of three to one, subject to settling an objection from the Civil Aviation Authority.

It seems strange that the CAA should have been so bothered about height with the existing Canary Wharf cluster next door, but because the Columbus Tower is to the north of it, the flight-path envelope for planes approaching City Airport would have been just 105m further north and 90m above the tower. The CAA wanted twenty storeys taken off the building. Collision risk assessments actually reckoned the risk was easily below accepted levels, but the matter rumbled on for over a year before being settled.

Trains rather than planes were a more complex challenge. Crossrail should run under the waters of West India Quay, and the Columbus Tower sits directly above it. This would mean some complex engineering – the tower needs foundations using 'cantilevered pile

Columbus cuts a new profile

Columbus winter garden

Beetham Tower London, SE1
10 Blackfriars Road

Tube Southwark, Blackfriars
Height 225m, 70 storeys
Designed 2005–06
Architect Ian Simpson Architects

On the corner where Blackfriars Bridge crosses to the South Bank, a quite amazing tower is journeying through the planning process. Hopefully, it will be the debut on the London skyline of architects whose designs match those of the global titans of architecture, and yet are virtually unknown in the capital – the Manchester-based Ian Simpson practice.

This is not the first skyscraper proposed for the site, previously the headquarters of J Sainsbury. In 2001, Foster designed an unusual 80m-high building where a curved twelve-storey block stood on a column above a five-storey podium, looking like a rock outcrop eroded by wind. With planning consent, J Sainsbury's cleared the site in 2004, then sold it to a developer with an extraordinary track record…

The North comes to the South Bank
The Liverpool-based Beetham Organization seems to have taken on England's other urban skylines almost single-handedly. So far, sleek Beetham Towers, mixing apartments and hotels, are the tallest in three cities. Two are Simpson designs. The Manchester Beetham Tower, a slipped-slab glass tower forty-seven storeys and 157m high (plus a further 14m of glass blade), became the UK's highest residential building in 2006. The Birmingham tower is 122m tall, and has a convex curving façade like that of *One West India Quay*. In Leeds, for a different developer, Simpson has cantilevered prisms of offices for Criterion Place, one rising 158m. Until Beetham bought the South Bank site, there was no Simpson spectacular planned for London.

In July 2005, Beetham submitted plans for a mind-blowing Simpson design. Like Foster's, it too looks as if it has been sculpted by natural forces, but in this case the soaring, streamlined form is in glass. It has already been dubbed 'The Boomerang'. This £500m tower would house a 395-room luxury hotel to the twenty-seventh floor, and from the thirtieth to sixty-sixth floors, 220 apartments. Sandwiched between hotel and flats would be two storeys of restaurant, and, just like the Columbus Tower, a health spa with swimming pool. Express lifts should whisk the public up to a Sky Deck on the sixty-eighth and sixty-ninth floors, where balconies will be mounted beneath a three-storey sloping window facing north. Coloured panels on the structure within the glazed envelope add warmth to the shimmer of glass. The green credentials are immaculate, and include drawing on the London Aquifer and using CPH. A stacked modular system distributes plant through the structure.

Beetham consulted widely in 2005, including with English Heritage. However, it was Westminster Council who brought up the views issue – in this case, those from

draught' in place before tunnelling can start underneath. That puts a time limit on the work, because the Crossrail plans (as at 2006) aim to start a cofferdam there in 2007, with tunnelling two years later, locking out the site. Allowing five years from breaking ground to finishing construction, it means that the Columbus Tower would be ready in 2012.

The existing 1970s building on the site, Hertsmere House, contains a branch of Barclays and Morgan Stanley offices, so leases need to be bought out. The Abu Dhabi royal family, purchasers of *33 Cavendish Square*, has since sold out of the scheme, and the new owners are Commercial Estates Group. In 2006, they are reviewing the existing planning permission. Any change in the mix of uses will require new planning permission, but the height and shape of the form of Columbus Tower will not change.

Those who watch the ever-changing Dockland's skyline will have waited a long time for Columbus Tower, but this fabulous, slender tower with its graceful roofline will be worth the wait.

the bridge in St James's Park, where the tower would rise over Whitehall's classical buildings. It's an odd objection, as the *Shell Centre* and the London Eye already do so. CABE were critical about the affordable housing, which overhangs Stamford Street at the back of the site, but gave a thumbs-up to the 'dynamic sculptural form and elegant proportions of the tower'.

The outstanding issues are being addressed in 2006, and it's unlikely that Ken Livingstone will fail to push the tower through if necessary. Comparisons will inevitably be made with *The Shard*, with which it shares many features. The Beetham Tower, though, does not challenge *The Shard*'s height, but places another transparent, yet quite different, sublime form on the skyline. It is possible it could be completed before the decade's end. In the meantime, Beetham's billboard at the site on the corner of Blackfriars Bridge gets it right with its copyline: 'Imagine. . .'

Beetham Tower London

The Shard, London Bridge, SE1
St Thomas Street

Tube/Rail London Bridge
Height 310m, 72 storeys
Designed 2000–05
Construction planned 2007–10
Architect RPBW

This is The Shard of Glass, an astonishing crystal spire designed by the legendary Renzo Piano that is set to be London's tallest building. As with the *Heron Tower*, there is a determined developer behind this project, and his consortium had to battle through a key public enquiry against English Heritage.

In April 2000, an incredible plan dropped out of the blue. Irvine Sellar, an entrepreneur who made his first fortune in the fashion trade in the sixties and seventies, produced a design for a 365m-high, eighty-seven-storey skyscraper on the site of *Southwark Towers*. This was a glazed cylinder that above the fifty-fifth floor would be cut by a graceful spiral slope, between the axis and the circumference (a helter-skelter shape similar to Helmut Jahn's sixty-three-storey Bishopsgate design that surfaced shortly after). A radio mast at the top would reach a height of 420m. The architects were Broadway Malyan, who would go on to design *Vauxhall Tower*. The design was inspired, but it was too much. Unsurprisingly, the *Evening Standard*'s high-rise sceptic Rowan Moore declared war on it immediately. But, tellingly, Irvine Sellar told the paper that 'we are willing to commit a lot of money, time and effort to get this tower built'.

Piano Composition
He was serious. He realised that it would need a proven signature architect that sneering critics would find it harder to dismiss. American titans such as SOM or KPF, or British names like Rogers or Foster may have fitted the bill, but Irvine Sellar made a more subtle choice, an architect considered by some to be the best in the world. In 2000, he met Renzo Piano in a café in Potsdamer Platz, the new heart of Berlin that Piano had just masterminded. There and then, Piano sketched out a vision exactly suitable for London, a city he saw as one of church spires and ships' masts. On the back of a menu, he drew a sharp, angular shape – like a spire.

As we have seen, Renzo Piano was Richard Rogers' partner in the Pompidou Centre that electrified European architecture with a Post-Modernism that also happened to thrill the public. Initially, the great spire revealed publicly for London was not dissimilar in shape to San Francisco's iconic skyscraper, the 260m-high pyramid spike of William Perreira's TransAmerica Building (1972), but Piano's pyramid had the transparency of crystal. It would have 130,000m^2 of space, a little less than *One Canada Square* which it would at last displace in London's height ranking. At its base, Piano realised that the space must draw the flow of people, and he created a vast piazza serving the tower and tackling the awkward access to London Bridge station. Bringing the public realm into new structures is now a common feature of Millennial towers – here, Piano raised the bar for such ambitions.

The design was very much a case of evolution. In November 2000, the spire had been extruded into a mast reaching over 400m. Up there, the crow's-nests of tall shipping were evoked, linking the structure to the heritage of the Thames. At one stage, the form was straight up on one side, like a wedge, but thinner than *The Leadenhall Building*. Piano's sketches grouped vertical lines that sometimes broke off from the façades below, and created dense compositions not unlike the unfeasibly thin sculptures of the Swiss Alberto Giacometti. After the height had settled around 300m, the square-plan pyramid became more complex, and the façades became articulated by shards of different shapes to create shadows and gaps. These shards do not actually join at an apex, but reach towards it, ending at different heights, like sheets of thrusting ice broken and frozen.

This is the plan: the tower floats above a huge three-storey public space with retail and restaurants. The lower parts of the building are offices. Starting at 122m are three storeys of public mid-level internal piazza; above that, a 195-room hotel occupies the floors from thrity-three to fifty-two. Above this level are apartments, and observation decks start at 224m. As Piano said, it was 'a vertical town for about seven thousand people and for hundreds of thousands to visit'. The stratification of use meant that the heat rising from the offices below could be stored to heat the residential part, and the excess radiated away from pipes in the building's top. Look at a normal office block, and energy-intensive fans spin excess heat away that in cold weather condenses, making them literally like steaming pots left on a slow flame. The top 60m of The Shard's structure performs this role quite passively, and that open apex will stream with condensation driven merely by natural flow. In all, the energy saved is a third.

Boreholes to the London Aquifer will further regulate the internal climate. With the use of materials variously sourced locally, recycled or with low embodied energy, the design is immaculately green. And there will be just forty-seven car parking spaces!

Clarity at the Inquiry
Irvine Sellar admitted in early 2003 that construction costs would be over half a billion. He wasn't worried. In terms of future cash-flow, he said 'ours is a multi-use building, so there's greater flexibility'. Southwark could be getting 10,000 jobs and find itself on the world stage, so the Council approved it, and its leader Nick Stanton reported at a press conference that he had not received a single local objection. Even the *Evening Standard*'s Moore had come out in favour. But, as we have seen, English Heritage brought it to a public inquiry, on the basis of the views of St Paul's from Hampstead.

They were on sticky ground – Piano had lived in Hampstead, and knew he had to defer to Wren's stone masterpiece, which is precisely why he chose a particular-ly low-iron glass for the tower. The public inquiry was in

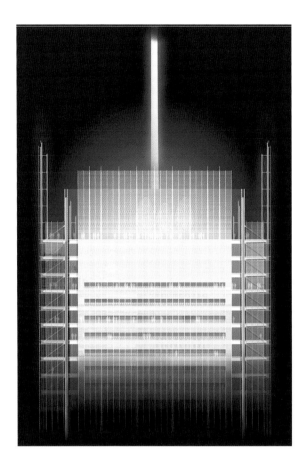

The top of the New York Times Tower

The Shard Apex

April 2003, and as Piano testified in the style of a paternal schoolmaster, Richard Rogers dropped in and gave an encouraging wink to his old friend across the room. Piano said: 'The idea of making the tallest building in Europe doesn't make sense to me. If it happens, it probably happens for a few months'. He went on to tackle English Heritage's main contention: 'St Paul's is talking the language of stone, the other the language of glass'. English Heritage's counsel, Neil King QC, struggled to retain his credibility in the face of such charm and clarity, and his case became increasingly obscure and pompous. It withered entirely when King attacked the 'backpacks' then on the building's lower parts – Piano was steadfast and indignant as he talked of mutilating himself rather than compromising the integrity of the design. Later, Rogers told the inquiry that the tower 'has the potential to become the greatest piece of modern architecture in London'. It was approved in November 2003.

Piano's choice of particularly clear glazing marks the trend that this century's Millennial tower projects increasingly adopt. Interestingly, Piano's simultaneous skyscraper design for the 220m-high New York Times Building in Midtown Manhattan is also set to regenerate a depressed area around a central transport hub. It, too, uses special glass, in order, as he says, 'to allow the building to adapt to the colours of the atmosphere. Blueish after a shower, shimmering red after a sunset.' Both towers will have a tendency to disappear magically into the sky…

The Shard from St Thomas Street

Tha plaza

The Shard is Go

After the inquiry, little seemed to happen. In fact, the hard work of pushing the project forward day-by-day was being inexorably led by Irvine's son James, the MD of Sellar Property Group. He lacks the public profile of his father but has proved he has exactly the same determination. Both Sellars work like men possessed, but in a quiet way. In late 2004, Irvine Sellar said he'd given PriceCoopersWaterhouse a year to quit *Southwark Towers*, and The Shard should be ready by 2009.

There were rumours of a nearby 210m-high KPF-designed tower. The Shard was also challenged in height by KPF's *Bishopsgate Tower* proposal, but the CAA deemed that its height limit of 1000ft (305m) above sea level could not be breached. How The Shard gets around this lies somewhere in continuous Sellar-CAA consultations.

In early 2005, the first 'anchor tenant' was announced, and confidence surged back. Hong Kong-based Shangri-la Hotels had been looking for twelve years for a flagship location to open in Europe, and they signed a thirty year lease. With China rising as a world power, this was a sharp move – many Chinese visitors set to flood European cities will have fulfilled Deng Xiaoping's declaration: 'to be rich is glorious'. Shangri-La Hotels are a five-star chain: along with 195 rooms, they will install two restaurants, conference facilities, and twenty-five suites, each with its own winter garden. The Chinese have had an orgy of building super-tall towers, and this hotel in the sky will be a natural choice for their elite.

In late 2005, another Piano building was announced to replace the undervalued *New London Bridge House*. As with The Shard, the Sellar Property Group is the developer. The Shard itself had already generated imitators. In 2006, Foster announced plans for a Moscow City Tower, twice as high as The Shard. Although it is three-sided in plan, it looks suspiciously similar, right up the broken apex.

The current schedule looks like this: Demolition should begin in 2007, and take nine months. Construction of The Shard will take three years. That means the tower should be ready by 2010. And Piano is committed to see the whole project through.

London Bridge Tower has now been fully rebranded as The Shard, which is significant. It's literally a sharp name to market with, but it also endorses the public view, because it is they who made the name stick. However exclusive it may be in parts, The Shard is incredibly open with its sky piazzas and its huge spaces below – a building for the people. There are many breathtaking towers coming in London, but none are like the Shard. In form it will be the greatest of London spires, an icon as tall as the Chrysler, yet oddly unobtrusive because of its transparency. Close up, its strange broken façades will be fascinating, organically complex yet crystalline, like vast abstract artworks. And inside, all of it will be a shangri-la of light and space. . .

Abbreviations & Technical Words

Art Deco
A style characterised by symmetry, steamlining and stylised elements such as zigzags and sunbursts. It defined many 1920s American skyscrapers.

ASBO
Anti-social behaviour order, a sentence limiting specific actions by offenders.

Backpack
Part of a skyscraper that does not conform to the tower's basic shape, boosting floorspace.

Barrel-vaulted
The result of topping a building element with a semi-circle, usually applied to rooflines or skylights.

Beaux-Art
An architectural style in Post-Modernism that emulates classical forms (often Greek) and ornamentation (often Baroque).

Brise-Soleils
Louvres or thin, flat surfaces placed horizontally to reduce solar gain.

BREEAM
A set of environmental benchmarks for new buildings set out by the Foundation for the Built Environment.

Brownfield
Derelict land previously built on, often abandoned by industry.

Brutalism
An architectural style characterised by extensive use of exposed concrete, that re-surfaced in English architecture of the 1960s and 1970s.

CAA
Civil Aviation Authority

CABE
Commission for Architecture and the Built Environment, a body advising the government on new projects.

Cantilever
A structure that extends out from a building over air.

Chamfer
A diagonal cut across an angled edge of a building.

CHP
Combined heat and power, also known as 'cogeneration', where a single integrated system generates electricity and heat.

Cladding
Exterior finish of a building made by attaching, for example, granite or concrete panels.

Cofferdam
Waterproof walls defining a hole in the ground, to enable the construction of building foundations. Cofferdams are frequently used in London skyscraper construction because of the water-bearing nature of London clay.

Corbusian
In a style following from the ideas of Le Corbusier, i.e. using concrete and regular grids in structures often incorporating piloti.

Core
The internal structure, usually of concrete, that supports the vertical load of a building, and usually carries lifts, stairs and other services.

Corporation of London
The body governing the borough of the City of London, which it is also known as. Other official names include 'The Barons of London'.

Cornice
A linear structure along the roofline of a building.

Crossrail
A proposed underground railway, linking Heathrow and Maidehead with Canary Wharf and Essex via Paddington and the City.

CWG
Canary Wharf Group, owners of the Canary Wharf Estate, now owned by Songbird plc.

Diagrid
An external steel frame made of crossing diagonals that can resist lateral wind load and take vertical load.

Envelope
The outer shape defining a building.

EPR
London-based architects Elsom Pack & Roberts.

Floorplate
The usable floor area between and around support structures.

GLA
Greater London Authority, London's authority from 1999.

GLC
Greater London Council, London's authority 1965-1986.

GMW
London-based architects Gollins, Melvin & Ward.

Groundscraper
A medium-rise building longer than it is high, with large floorplates.

Hammered concrete
A rough-surfaced concrete with embedded angular granite aggregate. Bush-hammering exposes aggregates by bashing the surface with a machine tool, while pick-hammering uses a pick by hand.

Hi-Tech
A Post-Modernist style characterised by service structure on the outside.

International Style
The predominant style of sixties commercial architecture, characterized by curtain-walled rectilinear blocks with flat roofs.

KPF
Kohn, Pedersen Fox Associates, American architects now operating a London office.

LCC
London County Council, London's authority until 1965.

Load

The force exerted on a building. Vertical load is from the weight of the structure and lateral load is due to wind pressure.

London Aquifer

The geological strata beneath the London clay in which the water table lies.

m²

Square metre

m³

Cubic metre

Maisonette

A flat on two or more levels.

Microclimate

A local climate, which in the context of buildings can be controlled for energy efficiency, as first envisioned by Buckminster Fuller.

Miesian

In the style of Mies van der Rohe, i.e. curtain-walled rectilinear glass and steel block.

Millennial

The author's generic term for high-profile, green, heavily-glazed buildings designed from the late 1990s on.

Mullion

Vertical section holding window glass.

ODP

Office Development Permit, required in the 1960s for major schemes.

ODPM

Office of the Deputy Prime Minister. Following public enquiries, the final decision on controversial building proposals is issued from here.

Part L

A UK building regulation that specifies measures promoting energy efficiency.

Piles

Columns driven below the ground to stabilise and support buildings above.

Piloti

Columns that raise a building off the ground. Piloti were favoured by Le Corbusier and revived by van der Rohe. Seifert's piloti are often fashioned as 'dinosaur legs'.

Plot Ratio

The proportion of floorspace in a building to the area of its site.

Podium

A block of conventional height from which a tower rises.

Point Block

Slim tower block of public housing, built around a central shaft lift and stairs.

Punched windows

Windows mounted in spaces cut into solid façades.

Raft

A flat concrete structure below ground on which a tower is built.

RFAC

Royal Fine Arts Commission, who officially advised on new buildings until CABE took over the role.

RIBA

Royal Institute of British Architects

Service riser

A structure vertically carrying pipes, electricals etc to plant machinery.

Service Tower

A structure housing lifts, stairs and other services, separated from the building containing usable floors.

RPBW

Genoa-based architects Renzo Piano Building Workshop.

RRP

London-based architects Richard Rogers Partnership.

Sky lobby

Lobby where people change between lifts to access different floors.

Spandrel

An exterior panel below a window.

Solar Gain

The gain in energy and hence heat a building experiences exposed to sunlight.

SOM

Skidmore, Owings and Merril, an American architectural practice founded in 1936 now operating a London office.

Terracotta

Brown or orange-coloured earthy ceramic clay-based material, similar to brick, used in cladding.

Third Schedule

A provision of the Town & Country Planning Act 1947 which enabled developers to increase the volume of buildings by ten per cent.

Vented façade

The exterior of a micro-climate controlled building, involving triple glazing in which outside air can flow through openable devices such as slits.

Further Reading

Books consulted include:

Allison, Ken *London's Contemporary Architecture* (Architectural Press 3rd ed. 2003)

Booker, Christopher & Lycett Green, Candida *Goodbye London* (Fontana 1973)

Byron, Arthur *London Statues* (Constable 1981)

Dalzell, WR *Shell Guide to the History of London* (Michael Joseph 1981)

Elwall, Robert *Ernö Goldfinger* (RIBA 1962)

Frampton, Kenneth *Modern Architecture, a Critical History* (Thames & Hudson 3rd ed 1992)

Glendinning, Miles & Muthesius, Stefan *Tower Block* (Yale 1994)

Höweller, Eric *Skyscraper* (Thames & Hudson 2003)

Larson & Pridmore *Chicago Architecture and Design* (Abrams 1993)

Laurie, Peter *Beneath The City Streets* (Allen Lane 1970)

Marriott, Oliver *The Property Boom* (Hamish Hamilton 1967)

Pevsner, Sir Nikolaus, and Bridget Cherry *The Buildings of England* (London volumes) (Penguin, Harmondsworth, 1973-2001)

Yarwood, Doreen *Architecture of England* (BT Batsford 2nd ed 1967)

Reports and academic publications consulted include those of:

Al Naib, SK *London Canary Wharf & Docklands* (University of East London, 1992)

Ali, Professor MM *Evolution of Concrete Skyscrapers: from Ingalls to Jin Mao* (from Electronic Journal of Structural Engineering, Vol. 1, No.1 2001)

British Council for Offices *Tall Office Buildings in London, The Economic Realities* (2002)

Church, Chris & Gale, Toby *Streets In The Sky* (report for National Sustainable Tower Blocks Initiative 2000)

London Research Centre *London Skylines* (1987)

Marmot , AMF *'How High Should They Live?'* Dissertation for University of California, Berkeley (1984)

Simpson, R *Classicism & Modernity The University of London's Senate House* (Institute of Classical Sudies, University of London 1999)

The following websites are recommended and frequently updated:
www.skyscrapernews.com
www.emporis.com

Acknowledgements

This book would not be possible without the input of many people. In particular the author is indebted to:

Terry Brown, for his gracious introduction as well as his wisdom and support.
Brian Seifert and Mrs Josephine Seifert
Michael Barrymore-Dunn
Conor McNicholas
Eva-Maria Eigenstiller
Kristen Leep
Finally, thanks go to Leticia Dalli-Wright for continuous faith in this enterprise.

Photography Credits

All other photography other than that listed below is by the author © Herbert Wright

Classical Jazz: p22 Queen Anne's Mansions (© Westminster City Archives) **p26** London 2026 AD 'This Is All In The Air' by Montague B Black, 1926 (© Transport for London) **p27** Charles Holden (RIBA Library Photographs Collection) **Glass Box: p36** Glass Boxes come to the City (courtesy of BP Photographic Services) **p38** Mies van der Rohe (RIBA Library Photographs Collection) **p39** 860 Lake Shore Drive, Chicago (© Josh Kotin) **p40** Gollins, Melvin and Ward (courtesy of GMW Architects) **p43** Felix Fenston (courtesy of Mrs Josephine Seifert) **p44** Richard Seifert (courtesy of Mrs Josephine Seifert) **p45** Harry Hyams (© Topfoto) **p46** Cook County Administrative Building, Chicago (© Josh Kotin) **p49** Thorn House in the eighties (courtesy of RHWL) **p51** Fosterwheeler House (courtesy of Mrs Josephine Seifert) **p52** Empress State Building, 1963 (© Aerofilms) Remodelling (courtesy of Wilkinson Eyre) **p56** Hötorget, Stockholm (picture by Alette of Oslo) **p57** London Wall, 1962 (Hulton Archive © Getty Images) **p62/3** The Pirelli Building, Milano (credit CGIL Milano) **p66** New London Bridge House (courtesy of Mrs Josephine Seifert) **p70** Museum Tower proposal (courtesy of BT Archives) **p71** GPO Tower under construction (courtesy of BT Archives) **p74** Original Scheme (RIBA Library Photographs Collection)
The Rise and Fall of the Tower Block: p76 Le Corbusier (RIBA Library Photographs Collection) **p80** Goldfinger (RIBA Library Photographs Collection) **p82** The collapse of Ronan Point (RIBA Library Photographs Collection) **Conctrete Jungle: p106** Richard Seifert (courtesy of Mrs Josephine Seifert) **p110** Limebank House, Fenchurch Street (courtesy of Barclays) **p133** The Make-over (© Make Architects)
Post-Modernism: p141 Richard Rogers (© Antonio Almos) **p142** John Hancock Center, Chicago (© Josh Kotin) Archigram's Capsule Tower (© Archigram Archives) **p143** Reclining in a Capsule (© Archigram Archives) **p144** Hongkong & Shanghai Banking Corporation, Hong Kong (courtesy of HSBC) **p145** Humana Building (courtesy Michael Graves & Associates) **Water Beds: p168** Pan Peninsula lifestyle (photograph by Lee Powers) **p170** Beetham Tower, Manchester (courtesy of Ian Simpson Architects) Vauxhall Cross proposal (courtesy of Squire & Partners) **p171** The Skyhouse (© Marks Barfield Architects) **p175** Century House before (courtesy of Assael Architecture) **p182** Pan Peninsula (photograph by Lee Powers) **p184** 261 City Road (courtesy of Squire & Partners) **p185** 22 Marsh Wall (courtesy of Squire & Partners and Redwell Investments) **p186** Doon Street Tower (© Coin Street Community Builders and Lifschutz Davidson Sandilands) **p187** Vauxhall Tower (courtesy Broadway Malyan) **Millenium Offices: p189** Commerzbank, Frankfurt (courtesy of Commerzbank) **p195** Vortex (© Make Architects) **p196/7** Allies & Morrison's Three Sisters proposal (courtesy of P&O Estates Ltd) **p198** Britannic Tower (courtesy of BP Photographic Serves) **p202** The History Wall (photo © Stephen Speller) **p208** Torre Agbar (© Jeff Davy) **p211** Willis Building (courtesy British Land) **p212** Broadgate Tower and 201 Bishopsgate (courtesy of British Land) **p213** Heron Tower (Image by Hayes Davidson) **p214** The Leadenhall Building (courtesy British Land) **Page 216/7** City cluster (courtesy of DIFA) **The Future: p218** Ken Shuttleworth of Make (photo by Will Pryce) **p219** Kite, Leeds (© Make Architects) **p221** Foreign Office Architects: Bunch Tower proposal (courtesy of FOA) **p222** Colombus cuts a new profile (DHWR Architects) **p223** Colombus winter gardens (DHWR Architects) **p224** Beetham Tower London (© Ian Simpson Architects) **p225** The top of the New York Times tower and The Shard Apex (courtesy of RPBW) **p226** The Shard from St Thomas Street (Courtesy of Sellar Property Group) **p226/7** The Plaza (Courtesy of Sellar Property Group)

London's Tallest Skyscrapers

Building	Height	Completed	Architect
Completed to 1965			
1. Post Office Tower (now Telecom Tower)	177m	1965	Ministry of Public Building & Works
2. Centre Point	121m	1965	Seifert
3. Vickers Tower (now Millbank Tower)	118m	1963	Ward
4. Shell Centre	107m	1962	Robertson
5. Portland House	102m	1963	Fairbairn
6. Hilton Park Lane	101m	1963	Lewis Soloman Kaye
7. Empress State Building	100m	1961	Stone Toms
8. Tolworth Tower	81m	1964	Seifert
9. Wembley Point (now The Point)	80m	1965	Covell, Matthews
10. St Georges's House	79m	1964	Ward
Completed 1966–1980			
1. NatWest Tower (Tower 42)	183m	1980	Seifert
2. Guy's Tower	144m	1973	committee
3. Barbican towers	128, 126m	1976, 74, 73	Chamberlain Powell & Bon
4. Euston Tower	124m	1970	Kaye & Firmin
5. Britannic House (now CityPoint)	122m	1967	Milton Cashmore and Nelson
6. Commercial Union Building (Aviva Tower)	118m	1969	GMW
7. Kings Reach Tower	111m	1978	Seifert
8. Drapers' Garden	99m	1967	Seifert and Norman Jones
9. Southwark Towers	99m	1976	Bennet
10. Stock Exchange Tower	99m	1972	various
Completed 1990–2004			
1. One Canada Square	235m	1990	Pelli
2. 8 Canada Square (HSBC Building)	200m	2002	Foster
3. 25 Canada Square (Citigroup Tower)	200m	2002	Pelli
4. 30 St Mary Axe	180m	2004	Foster
5. One Churchill Place	156m	2004	HOK
6. 25 Bank Street	153m	2003	Pelli
7. 40 Bank Street	153m	2003	Pelli
8. 10 Upper Bank Street	151m	2003	KPF
9. CityPoint (formerly Britannic Tower)	127m	2000	Sheppard Robson
10. One West India Quay	111m	2004	HOK

Index

The names of buildings covered individually in the text are styled in *italics*.
Page numbers in *italics* refer to illustrations.